Thom.

Cross-Cultural Leadership

Thomas Grisham

Cross-Cultural Leadership

(XLQ)

VDM Verlag Dr. Müller

Impressum/Imprint (nur für Deutschland/ only for Germany)
Bibliografische Information der Deutschen Nationalbibliothek: Die Deutsche Nationalbibliothek
verzeichnet diese Publikation in der Deutschen Nationalbibliografie; detaillierte bibliografische
Daten sind im Internet über http://dnb.d-nb.de abrufbar.
Alle in diesem Buch genannten Marken und Produktnamen unterliegen warenzeichen-, marken-
oder patentrechtlichem Schutz bzw. sind Warenzeichen oder eingetragene Warenzeichen der
jeweiligen Inhaber. Die Wiedergabe von Marken, Produktnamen, Gebrauchsnamen,
Handelsnamen, Warenbezeichnungen u.s.w. in diesem Werk berechtigt auch ohne besondere
Kennzeichnung nicht zu der Annahme, dass solche Namen im Sinne der Warenzeichen- und
Markenschutzgesetzgebung als frei zu betrachten wären und daher von jedermann benutzt
werden dürften.

Coverbild: www.purestockx.com

Verlag: VDM Verlag Dr. Müller Aktiengesellschaft & Co. KG
Dudweiler Landstr. 99, 66123 Saarbrücken, Deutschland
Telefon +49 681 9100-698, Telefax +49 681 9100-988, Email: info@vdm-verlag.de
Zugl.: Melbourne, RMIT University, Dissertation 2006

Herstellung in Deutschland:
Schaltungsdienst Lange o.H.G., Berlin
Books on Demand GmbH, Norderstedt
Reha GmbH, Saarbrücken
Amazon Distribution GmbH, Leipzig
ISBN: 978-3-639-06868-9

Imprint (only for USA, GB)
Bibliographic information published by the Deutsche Nationalbibliothek: The Deutsche
Nationalbibliothek lists this publication in the Deutsche Nationalbibliografie; detailed
bibliographic data are available in the Internet at http://dnb.d-nb.de.
Any brand names and product names mentioned in this book are subject to trademark, brand or
patent protection and are trademarks or registered trademarks of their respective holders. The use
of brand names, product names, common names, trade names, product descriptions etc. even
without a particular marking in this works is in no way to be construed to mean that such names
may be regarded as unrestricted in respect of trademark and brand protection legislation and
could thus be used by anyone.

Cover image: www.purestockx.com

Publisher:
VDM Verlag Dr. Müller Aktiengesellschaft & Co. KG
Dudweiler Landstr. 99, 66123 Saarbrücken, Germany
Phone +49 681 9100-698, Fax +49 681 9100-988, Email: info@vdm-publishing.com
Melbourne, RMIT University, Dissertation 2006

Printed in the U.S.A.
Printed in the U.K. by (see last page)
ISBN: 978-3-639-06868-9

Acknowledgements

I would like to acknowledge the following people without whom this work could not have been completed.

Clyde Gray
for teaching me about leadership

Rory Baxter
for teaching me about compassion, and for opening the international doorway

Dr. Derek Walker
for being my mentor, coach, and guide throughout the doctorate program

Belinda Grisham
for being my confidant, sounding board, and anchor
and, for giving me the freedom to spend long hours away

Table of Contents

Table of Figures

Table of Tables

Appendices

1. Work Introduction

1.1 Chapter Introduction

This chapter introduces the research, and provides an overview of the work. It begins with a description of the Doctorate of Project Management Program (DPM), and a brief summary of my personal background. That is followed by an overview of the Project Management Body of Knowledge (PMBOK) relating to leadership and management in the profession, which leads into the research context and an introduction to my hypothesis. The technique utilized to perform the research and test the hypothesis follows, and then the structure of the work is provided to guide the reader. This Chapter closes with a discussion on the implications that this research has for the Project Management profession, and a summary.

1.2 The DPM Program

The Doctorate of Project Management (DPM) program at RMIT University, led by Dr. Derek Walker, was designed to take advantage of the personal expertise of each of the candidates. The program requires research into four mayor topic areas for Project Management in my view: leadership, knowledge management, ethics and procurement, and one elective. The research is augmented by interaction with Project Management peers in the program for sharing thoughts, ideas, and insights.

The structure of the DPM program is shown in Figure 1. Taking the PM Leadership course as an example, the core research, and the interaction with peers provided the foundation for the topic. That work was followed by a reflective learning module that provided time for reflection upon the core work, and upon personal experience. In providing this iterative approach, context for the explicit information is established, and this enables the transfer of tacit knowledge (Glossary - understanding). The follow on work builds upon this knowledge and provides the opportunity to expand and polish the research in the Research Preparation modules.

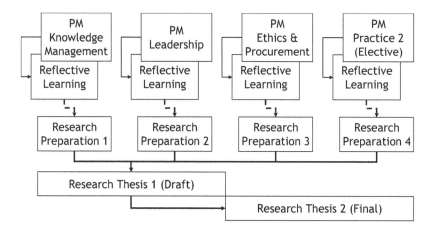

Figure 1 - Walker (DPM course document)

Each module then in turn builds to the overall Research Work. The design of the program facilitates the discipline that is necessary for performing doctoral level research, but at the same time takes advantage of the years of practical of experience available between the peers. For example, my twelve peers and I possessed well over 150 years of Project Management experience. Equally important is the fact that the DPM program nurtured the synergies and creativity that are essential in transforming information and experience into knowledge and creativity – new systems and approaches. Figure 2 provides a graphical representation of the process where I began with a Q1, *as is* condition, moved through a Q3 study and reflective learning process to a Q4 new approach to cross-cultural leadership for Project Management from the general management, psychological, and sociological perspectives.

The DPM program doctoral standards provide a level of expectation for each candidate. Those standards and the effort undertaken for this work are as follows:

- Reviewing the literature relevant to the project – as will be discussed the relevant industry knowledge is quite limited on the topic. The literature from the industry suggests the need for research that borrows from other disciplines. Accordingly this work includes psychological, sociological, anthropological, managerial, business, and cultural disciplines.

- Designing an investigation, and gathering and analyzing information – for this work the initial gathering of information was done through analysis of topics provided as the framework of the DPM. This structure enabled the progressive exploration and evaluation of the research.

2

- Presenting information in a manner consistent with publication, exhibition or public presentation in the relevant discipline – during the term of the DPM, I have published a number of papers ((Grisham 2006); (Hudson, Grisham et al. 2005); (Grisham and Walker 2005)), have presented a number of papers, and was one keynote speaker at the 2005 PMI Conference in Port-of-Spain Trinidad. In addition, I teach Project Management for St. Petersburg College, DeVry University, the International Institute for Learning, and in the masters program at the University of South Florida. For a complete listing see Appendix 9 - Papers.
- Critical appraisal of his/her own work relative to that of others – the results of the testing of this work, and the comparison to existing research is an integral part of my research. In addition, I have offered the hypothesis to hundreds of peers in my seminars and teaching endeavors, and the feedback has been included.
- A significant and original contribution to knowledge of fact and/or theory – as will be described in this work, there is a paucity of work on the issues of leadership and culture. This work is an attempt to open an area of knowledge that has been largely neglected.
- Independent and critical thought – I have interwoven the research with my own practical experience, and have attempted to offer all of the arguments on both sides of the issues investigated as they were discovered.
- The capacity to work independently of supervision – the nature of the DPM program, and one of the reasons it attracted me initially was the desire to work independently.

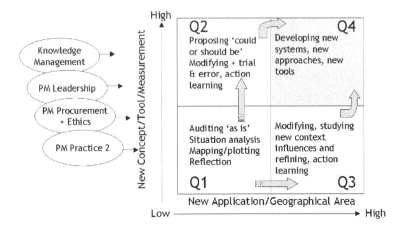

Figure 2 - DPM Course Overview (Walker)

3

1.3   Personal Background

I have over 35 years of international Project Management experience on projects ranging up to $1.5 billion in the power, infrastructure, transportation, education, commercial, communications, manufacturing, and dispute resolution sectors. My experience has been gained in 51 countries, and in numerous business models. I hold a Bachelor of Engineering from Vanderbilt University, and an MBA from Duke University. I have been an adjunct professor on Project Management topics since 1995, and am a Project Management Professional (PMP), a licensed engineer, and an arbitrator and mediator for the American Arbitration Association and the International Center for Dispute Resolution. Additional detail information is available on my webpage at www.thomasgrisham.com.

My experience on international projects has included everything from quick damage-control projects to expatriate assignments where I have acted as a political and social liaison. I have witnessed the work of people who are extremely technically competent, but are completely ineffectual due to their lack of leadership skills. Many such people may be good at managing within their own culture, but are woefully lacking in multi-cultural environments. Some of this is due to a lack of leadership skills, and some is due to an ignorance, or worse insouciance, about other cultures.

It is no longer a world of Anglo expatriates wandering about the planet demonstrating the new technology. Now international projects are headed by expats from many countries. All need the cross-cultural leadership skills to be effective Project Managers, and thus my decision to explore this topic as my work.

1.4   Cross-Cultural Leadership & the PMBOK

In the course of my career, I have learned the importance of so-called people skills for the successful management of projects. When I began working, it was common for an individual to take a theoretical technical degree, and then enter the workplace to learn the application of the technical skills. Academia turned-out trained technicians, with very little or no practical application, and no people skills. The application of the technical skills and the acquisition of people skills were accomplished in the workplace. Most people learned through practice and the guidance of mentors and coaches. Once a firm felt that a person had an adequate technical background, they were promoted to the position of project manager. It was an ad hoc way of creating project managers.

4

The Project Management Institute (PMI) began promoting Project Management as a profession in 1969 (celebrating its 35 year of service) with approximately 100 members. In its 2004 yearly report, the PMI indicated that the membership had grown to over 160,000 in almost 150 countries. In a recent edition of the PMI newspaper, the membership was poised to exceed the 250,000 members mark. More information is available at www.pmi.org. The momentum for rapid increases in membership however took off when the IT profession became a dominant force in the marketplace, and the benefit for Project Management process skills became clear.

The third and most current edition of the Project Management Body of Knowledge (PMBOK 2004) was issued 35 years after PMI began their work. The PMBOK is 390 pages long, and while there are oblique references to leadership and management skills throughout, there are only four pages devoted to the people skills. In the index, there is no reference to leadership or culture, and the only description of culture is related to corporate culture. The *tools and techniques* in the people skills section are listed as: 1) observation and conversation, 2) performance appraisals, and 3) conflict management. The 1996 edition of the PMBOK had a larger percentage of its pages devoted to management, so in 10 years the bible for project managers has not yet escalated leadership to a central skill for the profession. Most of the focus is still on process.

Cecmil and Hodgson (2005) challenge the Project Management profession to undertake a richer and broader approach to research, and a re-assessment of the foundations for project management. They point out that since the 1960's project management has utilized a systems or functionalists approach to project management, with attempts only to improve the processes. The authors say that they took up the challenge (Flyvbjerg 2001) to conduct research (Pg. 12): "that contributes to society's capacity for value-rational deliberation and action," or as the authors say to make social science matter in the context of project management.

Despite the lack of emphasis on leadership and culture, PMI does publish a yearly magazine for its members titled *Leadership in Project Management* that is devoted to this single topic. This magazine has only been published for the past few years, and it is a clear indication of the growing importance that PMI places on leadership in the profession.

Unfortunately, the cross-cultural aspects of managing projects are only not addressed in passing in Section 1.5.3 of the PMBOK where it indicates that (Pg. 14): "The Project team should consider the project in its cultural, social, international, political, and physical contexts." In the literature, the topic of cross-cultural leadership is addressed in books and articles on international Project Management. A search at Amazon.com for *International Project Management* yielded eleven books (only three on the subject), whereas a search for *Project Management* yielded over 2,600 books. One of the three books on international Project Management by Lientz and Rea (2003) devotes over 70 pages of a 277 page book to the issues of leadership and culture.

The PMI and the International Project Management Association (IPMA) both publish theoretical journals for topics related to Project Management. To view the discussion above into another context, a search of the PMI Journal of Project Management, and the IMPA International Journal of Project Management articles were performed for the period of 1995 through 2005. The search utilized the EBSCO and Science direct database *default* function (searches the title, abstract, and keywords). The results are shown in Table 1. Over the 10 year period less than 10% of the articles dealt with the issues of culture and/or leadership, and none with cross-cultural leadership. These are all of the articles that mention the terms culture or leadership. If the search is amended to seek the author-supplied keyword leadership, for example, the total falls from 11 articles as shown in the table, to four. Suffice to say that there is not a surfeit of research or publication on cross-cultural leadership targeted to the Project Management profession.

This paucity of literature, coupled with my understanding of the importance of cross-cultural leadership skills in delivering successful projects are the driving forces behind this work. The implications on the profession of Project Management will be discussed in a separate section, but first I will discuss the context for the research that was performed.

Table 1 - Project Management Articles

Year	Project Management Journal (EBSCO Default Fields)			International Journal of Project Management (Science Direct)		
	Leadership Citations	Culture Citations	Total Citations	Leadership Citations	Culture Citations	Total Citations
2005	1	2		5	9	
2004	3	2		4	4	
2003		1		3	2	
2002				2	4	
2001	2	1		2	1	
2000	1			3	3	
1999	3				5	
1998	1				2	
1997				3		
1996				1	3	
1995				1	3	
Subtotals	11	6	332	24	36	841

Total Citations	1,173
Total Leadership and Culture Citations	77
Total Cross-Cultural Leadership Citations	0

1.5 Research Context

Outside the Project Management profession, there is no shortage of theory and research on leadership and culture. Both topics have been discussed and studied for over 2,000 years. However, in the 20th century there was a great increase in the contributions to the body of knowledge from psychology, sociology, anthropology, religion, philosophy, management, business, and more. Leadership and culture are by their nature broad topics with an infinite number of potentials for research. Using the metaphor of a Quibla compass,[1] this work will suggest that *etic* (universal) (Pike 1967) patterns exist in the knowledge base that point toward Cross-Cultural Leadership Intelligence (XLQ) dimensions that are effective globally. Describing these dimensions is the focus of this research. By introducing this theory from outside the Project Management radar screen, the goal is to improve performance on international projects, as shown in Figure 2.

Smith (2001) discusses the work of Schon (1987) who was one of the most influential theorists on reflective learning. Smith quotes Schon as saying (Pg. 2): "reflection entails diagnosis, testing, and belief in personal causation. Diagnosis is the ability to frame or make sense of a problem through use of professional knowledge, past experience, the uniqueness of the setting and people involved, and expectations held by others."

---

[1] Moslems pray facing Mecca. To do this, they must know the direction of Mecca, which they call the Qibla.

After more than 35 years of practical experience, I decided to reflect upon the lessons learned in my career, to explore the literature, and to attempt to test my experience and ideas by undertaking the DPM program. My experience pointed toward threads of commonality in cross-cultural leadership practice, and I wanted to pursue them to a natural conclusion through the published research. The scarcity of academic consideration in the profession forced me to turn my focus to other disciplines like sociology, psychology, anthropology, business, philosophy, etc. In these disciplines, I found a great richness of thought and research, but generally conducted within a specific discipline, and often very narrowly focused. The challenge thus became to consider the aspects of the literature that could be applied to the profession of Project Management.

My experience on international projects motivated me to search for a cross-cultural leadership model, or Quibla compass, that could be utilized for Project Management, for I found that many were using a grass roots or ad hoc type of approach on international ventures. As a result, this research was undertaken to search for a compass for leadership dimensions than could be utilized in different cultures (social and corporate) for projects with multi-cultural teams (virtual and co-located).

In a global economy, leadership skills are critically important. Lean business models that manage change and knowledge effectively, and efficiently are essential today. Firms need individuals that are qualified to lead, and follow, and to embrace change effectively and gracefully. As firms move from regional to transglobal enterprise models, leadership must provide the bridge between cultural diversity and repeatable business processes in a very competitive economic environment. With the pace of business, the ability of a leader to manage change effectively is a critical issue in the international environment.

As competitive pressure and the knowledge economy accelerate, firms must become leaner. As firms trim their workforce, it is more critical that the core people retained are multi-faceted, capable of doing many different tasks, creative and innovative, have the ability to work with multiple cultures in a virtual or co-located environment, and have the ability to lead successfully. The workforce today is becoming younger, with few mentors and coaches remaining, and they have little time to devote to such activities. One of the key aspects of Knowledge Management and the formation of communities of practice (COP's) (see (Lave and Wenger 1991); (Drucker 1988); (Hildreth, Kimble et al. 2000); (Brown and Estee 1995)) is that a firm must find time for people to interact if they are to share more than explicit information.

The speed of business today and the continual connectedness (BlackBerry's, Treo's, cell phones, wireless, etc.) reduces the time people have to reflect, consider, and think. This means that there is less time for communication, and more room for misunderstanding. Most scholars agree that leadership skills can be learned, and certainly cultural intelligence (CQ) can be acquired through study. The issue is, are people given the time, mentors or coaches, and the experience they need before they have to react.

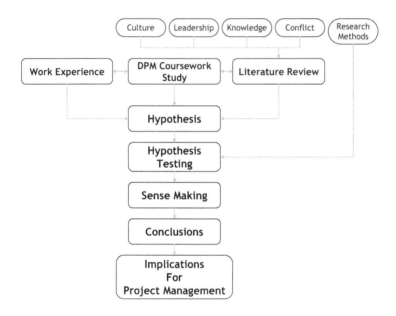

Figure 3 - Work Map

Figure 3 provides a graphical overview of the work, and maps the process undertaken in completing the work. It is founded on a combination of practical experience, the RMIT Doctorate of Project Management (DPM) coursework, and a three-year review of the literature. While I had an outline of what experience showed to be critical dimensions for XLQ, the hypothesis evolved from this rich research material, and the DPM study. I chose a Delphi Panel testing technique to test the hypothesis, and both the hypothesis itself and the testing are described in the following two sections.

After the testing was completed, the results were considered in the perspective of my practical experience to provide a litmus test or sense making check to correlate the findings back to real-world experience. The conclusions and the implications for international Project Management section provide a summary view of the work.

In the international business world, what I think of as a Formula-1 racetrack, it is obvious to me that a model is desperately needed so that professional Project Managers can acquire the skills that they need to lead cross-cultural teams successfully in a dynamic environment of rapid change. This work is an attempt to merge experience with published research in the creation and testing of such a model. The model, like the Quibla compass, is intended to be a directional indicator for Cross-Cultural Leadership Intelligence (XLQ).

1.6 Defining the Hypothesis

I have found that there is significant diversity in the international markets, with many of my projects included teams working in four or more countries, with teams consisting of individuals from a dozen or more cultures. Despite this fact I have found that there are cross-cultural leadership dimensions that are recognized globally (*etic* (Pike 1967)) trust, empathy, power, and communication skills. As I progressed through the coursework and research, and reflected back on my experience, I began to see the added dimension of transformation emerge. As will be described in detail, the research found significant support for all of these attributes.

From my experience, there are three aspects to leadership interaction – the leader, the follower, and the situation. The characteristics (personality, intelligence, education, will power, experience, etc.) of the leader are the foundation to the transaction, for the leader must (to use a metaphor) hold the mirror for the followers and situation. Or, said another way, the characteristics of the leader have no context without the followers and situation. Therefore, this work considers the validation of trust, empathy, transformation, power, and communication to be the domain of the follower and the transaction.

Trust, Empathy, Transformation, Power, & Communications

Figure 4 – XLQ Leadership Dimensions (Grisham)

10

Each of the five dimensions subsumes numerous other attributes and considerations. As mentioned above, this research also bores down into communication by undertaking a more detailed review of conflict management, and of cultural intelligence. The five dimensions require that leaders understand the people that follow them, and that they have the ability to communicate gracefully and effectively. Managing conflict and having cultural knowledge are as basic as is email in today's marketplace, thus the reason for a more thorough review of these two aspects of XLQ.

For the purposes of this work, culture is considered personal, business, or societal. The reason is that each layer of culture modifies the others and depends upon the intelligence, experience, and genetic make-up of each person. A Chinese-American individual could have predominately Chinese or American personal values and ideas, or a mixture. A Chinese-American working for Cisco systems or for General Electric could have a significantly different corporate cultural perspective. A Chinese-American working in Sao Paulo or in Berlin would have a different societal perspective on business values and norms. The hypothesis is that trust, empathy, transformation, power, and communication are *etic*, or global, dimensions of cross-cultural leadership regardless of the culture(s).

One of the first things uncovered by the research was that there are almost an infinite number of definitions of leadership. Leadership has been discussed since language was first developed, and there are many who have ventured definitions. The definition that I have created is based upon the work of others that are referenced later in this work. The definition gives due regard to cross-cultural considerations, and due regard to the notion that followers and context validate leadership. The definition of Leadership utilized in this work is:

> The ability to inspire the desire to follow,
> and to inspire achievement beyond expectations

Figure 5 – Leadership Definition (Grisham)

Beyond expectations means those of the leader, the follower, and third parties. One major issue that had to be overcome was the method to be used in performing and codifying the research. That is the subject of the next section.

1.7 Research Approach – Exegetical Method

The published literature on culture and leadership is long, rich, and diverse. As I began reading through books and articles it became clear why more had not published in the Project Management literature – the information is diffuse. At the beginning of the research, I had considered following a disciplinary structure for the work. As the issues of leadership and culture are themselves not well defined, I also found that many of the authors moved between disciplines in an effort to connect the prevailing theories to their particular areas of interest. The techniques and methods utilized in management research are significantly different that those utilized in psychological or anthropological research. As I attempted to organize the literature in this manner, I found that the threads of the theories and hypothesis were being lost.

I then attempted to arrange the research by XLQ dimension. As with the disciplinary approach, much of the research addressed multiple dimensions within a single study. In separating the works by dimension, either the flow of the authors work was jeopardized, or the repetition of an author's work was excessive. This then left me with the only viable option, which was to organize the research in chronological order. One subsidiary benefit of this approach was that the evolution of the thinking could be considered as the theories developed. One disadvantage was that works referred to in a publication were kept with the date of the publication for context, not with their individual publication dates. Also in the case of Hofstede, his initial work is not readily available, but later revisions of his initial work are. Others (Mayo and Nohria 2005) have utilized this approach to take advantage of a historical view of a topic. In this work, the publication date is the one used for consistency.

This chronological approach provided the basic structure, and then the decision was on how to connect the research and the hypothesis. After three years of discussions and method research, my coach suggested that I consider returning to a method utilized for centuries - an exegetical approach.

According to www.wikipedia.com: "Exegesis (from the Greek ἐξηγεἓηγι 'to lead out') involves an extensive and critical interpretation of a text, especially of a holy scripture, such as of the Old and New Testaments of the Bible, the Talmud, the Midrash, the Qur'an, etc. An exegete is a practitioner of this science, and the adjectival form is exegetic. The word exegesis means *to draw the meaning out of* a given text. Traditional exegesis requires the following: analysis of significant words in the text in regard to translation; examination of the general

12

historical and cultural context, confirmation of the limits of the passage, and lastly, examination of the context within the text."

Also according to www.wikipedia.com: "Hermeneutics may be described as the theory of interpretation and understanding of a text through empirical means. It should not be confused with the concrete practice of interpretation called exegesis. Exegesis extracts the meaning of a passage of text and enlarges upon it and explicates it with explanatory glosses; hermeneutics addresses the ways in which a reader may come to the broadest understanding of the creator of text and his relation to his audiences, both local and over time, within the constraints of culture and history."

The research was performed by maintaining the author's use of their terminology, the context of their discipline, and the cultural context of their studies. Once the research was complete, an analysis was performed to draw the meaning out of the text, and connect it to the XLQ dimensions. The first step was to list the synonyms utilized by the authors, and to search for their relationship back to the GLOBE study and others. The GLOBE study is a broad recent study of culture and leadership that is discussed in detail in Chapter 2, Section 2.6. The reason for this first step was an attempt to tie my research back to a thorough, broad, and recent global study of culture and leadership. More is provided on this important work later in this work.

The second step was to design groupings to consolidate the terminology from the various authors into common themes. In this step, consideration was given to the original author's terminology, the GLOBE terminology, and my own experience. The third step was to group these themes into the XLQ dimensions, and the last step to build a correlation matrix. Appendix 1 provides an example of this process in matrix format.

Each of the synonyms shown in this Appendix is for trust. In this work, the words in bold describe the XLQ dimensions for cross-cultural leadership that are correlated back to the author's terminology. This provides the connection between the work of each author studied, and the hypothesis of this work. There has been no attempt to redefine the terminology provided by other authors, but rather to interpret it, and give it meaning in the context of this work, to the best of my ability and experience.

The next section provides a map of the work, a description of its organization, and the topics that are included.

1.8 Hypothesis Testing – Delphi Technique

Another challenge that had to be addressed for this work was the method(s) to be utilized to prove or disprove the hypothesis. Hofstede was fortunate to have a captive audience when he did his pioneering global survey of IBM personnel. The GLOBE survey had significant grants and funding, and the support of a wide range of researchers located around the globe. My ability to attack a topic of this complexity was of course limited to a single lifetime and a finite budget. However, more importantly, the topic is so diverse and complex that a standard survey of managers, subordinates, etc. could not hope to provide a complete and integrated view of the international marketplace in a single survey.

What was needed were a group of trained professionals from academia and practice who understood the issues of culture and leadership. What I needed was a group who could synthesize their wisdom, and apply it to complex issues in a holistic manner. My coach, Dr. Derek Walker, suggested that I should investigate the Delphi technique. I was familiar with the technique from my business and teaching experience, and undertook some research on the method. That information will be provided in Chapter 6.8 of this work.

The big advantage in using this technique was that the people participating in the survey are seasoned professionals in academia and practice, so they bring the best of both worlds to the XLQ hypothesis. I selected people from numerous cultural backgrounds as well so the responses were not just a USA based view of the world. All of the participants had over 20 years of experience, and experience in and across multiple cultures. There were 24 panel members that participated. Two sessions of questions were provided to the panel members, with feedback on the initial session prior to the second session.

In a Chapter 6.8 the theory of the technique, the structural method utilized, the questions asked, and the results are provided.

1.9 Structure of the Work

Before introducing the structure of the work, it is necessary to discuss the relationship between the research, the empirical testing, and my experience. The topic is a broad and diverse one, with literally centuries of published academic though available. The topics are multi-disciplinary and multi-cultural, and therefore are not codified. This work does not attempt to codify the body of literature on the topics, but rather to offer a broad sampling of thought on cross-cultural leadership across disciplinary bounds. The goal being to provide numerous and rich perspectives, that can be organized and analyzed. This work begins by constructing a knowledge foundation based on the work of many different researchers and thinkers.

Building upon this foundation, the empirical work had its formations in experience, in that there were ideas existing but in need of a foundation. As the foundation was being constructed, the empirical side of the work began to take shape from the hypothesis. Thus, there is more emphasis placed upon the review of the literature in this work.

The structure of this work is as shown in Figure 6. After the introduction, the work is divided into the four major area of concentration of cultural theory, leadership theory, cultural knowledge, and conflict management. This is then followed by sections on the hypothesis, testing of the hypothesis, and conclusions reached.

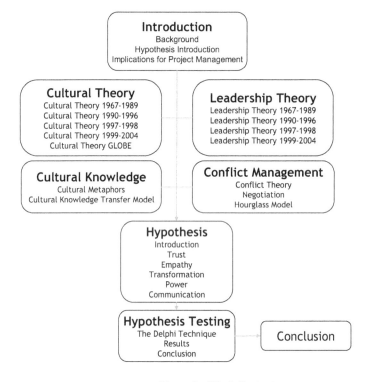

Figure 6 – Work Content

1.10 Implications for Project Management

The need for Project Managers to be effective leaders in cross-cultural environments is critical. A Project Manager's primary goals, according to the PMBOK, are to assure that a specified project scope is completed on time, within budget, and to the quality specified. A Project Manager has implied responsibility, according to the PMBOK, to lead a diverse workforce to succeed in meeting these goals through leadership. Currently the Project Management literature does not provide adequate guidance on what skills are necessary for a Project Manager to accomplish this.

The research performed for this work was undertaken to acknowledge the contributions from the many disciplines that have added value to our understanding of culture and leadership. History teaches that we must learn from our past, and therefore we must take full advantage of the incredibly rich knowledge base that exists on these topics. The challenge is to interpret and structure that knowledge in such a way as to make it useful in promoting skills that are essential to the profession of Project Management.

The results of this work will recommend that there are Cross-Cultural Leadership Intelligence (XLQ) dimensions that Project Managers must learn if they are to be effective in current markets. The XLQ model provides a guide for understanding culture, leadership, conflict, and cultural knowledge acquisition. It also provides benchmarks for the five XLQ dimensions of trust, empathy, transformation, power, and communications.

1.11 Chapter Summary

This chapter introduced the research, and provided an overview of the work. It also described the Doctorate of Project Management Program (DPM), my personal background, an overview of the Project Management Body of Knowledge (PMBOK), the technique utilized to perform the research and test the hypothesis, the structure of the work, and the implications that this research has for the Project Management profession.

The work is organized into Chapters for ease of reference, and a brief description of each is provided here.

Chapter 2 Cultural Theory provides a review of the research on culture from 1967 through 2005.

16

Chapter 3 Cultural Knowledge provides a review of the research on how cultural knowledge is effectively transferred, from 1950 through 2005. It discusses the use of metaphor and provides a suggested knowledge model.

Chapter 4 Leadership Theory provides a review of the research on leadership from 1862 through 2005.

Chapter 5 Conflict Management provides a review of the research on conflict from 1973 through 2005. It discusses the use cross-cultural conflict and provides a suggested model for conflict management.

Chapter 6 Cross-Cultural Leadership Hypothesis discusses the Cross-Cultural Leadership hypothesis of this work.

Chapter 7 Research Design for Hypothesis Testing discusses the Delphi technique, methods and findings.

Chapter 8 Results provides a discussion and analysis of the results of the Delphi survey.

Chapter 9 Conclusion provides the conclusions reached by this work, and the implications for the Project Management profession.

Chapter 10 References

Chapter 11 Glossary

Chapter 12 Appendices

2. Cultural Theory

2.1 Chapter Introduction

Cultural theory has predominately been the domain of sociologists, psychologists, and anthropologists. Project Management has paid little attention to the topic in the last ten years as discussed in Chapter 1.4. As noted in the introduction, cultural intelligence is a critical attribute for leaders. Cultural Intelligence influences, and is influenced by, each of the five leadership dimensions of trust, empathy, transformation, power and communications. In this section, the research will focus on the cultural aspects of Cross-Cultural Leadership Intelligence (XLQ). For consistency, any references to other authors in a citation are kept with the citation to provide continuity of context throughout this work.

This chapter has been divided into periods to give a sense of the progression of the research, and theory. In addition, a separate section discusses the GLOBE survey specifically as it serves a central role in this research.

As many of the following authors address both leadership and culture, I have made efforts to separate their writings where possible into culture, this chapter, and leadership that are discussed in Chapter 4. The one exception is the GLOBE survey where the citations have been kept together.

2.2 Cultural Theory 1955 thru 1989

Margaret Mead (1955) was a well known anthropologists, and contributed significantly to the United Nations. When working with UNESCO (United Nations Educational, Scientific, and Cultural Organization) she undertook to edit a book that addressed the effects of technological change on indigenous peoples, from a long-term mental health perspective. She introduced the topic by making a clear connection between the habits and practices of parents and children, and the systematic application of those principles and practices in the employer/employee relationship, the speaker/audience relationship, the teacher/pupil relationship, etc.

I find that Mead's definition of culture is best suited to the discussion of universal leadership as it provides the versatility required to address intra/inter cultures, organizations, or groups. She said (Pg. 12) culture was: "...a body of learned behavior which a group of people who share the same tradition transmit entire to their children, and, in part, to adult immigrants who become members of the society. It covers not only the arts and sciences, religions and philosophies...but also the system of technology, the political practices, the small intimate habits of daily life...as well as the method of electing a prime minister." Darlington (1996) author quotes a definition of culture by Margaret Mead (1955)[2] as (Pg. 33): "a body of learned behavior, a collection of beliefs, habits and traditions, shared by a group of people and successively learned by people who enter the society." This definition is the one used in this work for culture. It not only covers the conventional societal meaning of culture, but it also covers the use of culture in a corporate sense. Section 6.1 of this paper restates Mead's definition.

The starting place for a review of culture is naturally with Hofstede (2001) who performed his original study in 1968 and a subsequent study in 1972. The version of the text referenced thus incorporates his original work. Hofstede begins by defining culture as (Pg. 1): "the collective programming of the mind; it manifest itself not only in values, but in more superficial ways: in symbols (metaphors), heroes, and rituals." Hofstede uses culture from the national cultural perspective thought he does discuss the organizational cultures in one chapter. The author says that values and culture are the key constructs for the work. He points to Kluckhohn's (1967) anthropological definition of value (Pg. 5): "a value is a conception, explicit or implicit, distinctive of an individual or characteristic of a group, of the desirable which influenced the selection from available models, means and ends of action." Hofstede also points to the work of Schwartz (1992) who found that values clustered into the categories of **power**, achievement, hedonism, stimulation (**transformation**), self-direction, universalism, benevolence, tradition (**empathy**), conformity, and security (**trust**).

Hofstede emphasizes that there is an important distinction between *desired* (what people want) and *desirable* (what people should want) values. In the GLOBE study described later in this work, the researchers actually measured this in the questionnaires that were utilized. Hofstede believes that culture cannot be understood without the study of history. This will be discussed later Section 3 of this work.

Hofstede's validated conclusions are described in the following five well-known dimensions:
- Power Distance – the extent to which the less powerful members of organizations and institutions accept and expect power is distributed unequally. The degree of inequality (**power**). Hofstede provides a Power Distance Index (PDI) that describes examples of

---

[2] Note – The Darlington reference was from the 1951 version of the 1955 reference from Mead.

the differences between countries with high and low PDI's:

> In the family – Low PDI parents treat children as equals; High PDI parents teach children obedience.
>
> In the work organization – Low PDI decentralized authority, flatter organizations; High PDI centralized authority, more vertical structure.

- Uncertainty Avoidance - the extent to which a culture programs its members to feel either uncomfortable or comfortable in unstructured situations. The degree to which people try to control the uncontrollable, and their resistance to change (**trust**). Hofstede provides a Uncertainty Avoidance Index (UAI) that describes examples of the differences between countries with high and low UAI's:

> For trust – Low UAI most people can be trusted, less resistance to change. High is the opposite.
>
> Stress - Low UAI low anxiety, emotions controlled. High is the opposite.

- Individualism or Collectivism – the degree to which individuals are supposed to look after themselves or remain integrated into groups, usually around the family (**empathy, power**). Hofstede provides a Individualism Index (IDV) that describes examples of the differences between countries with high and low IDV's:

> In the family – Low IDV strong family ties, no one alone; High IDV is the opposite.
>
> Personality and behavior – Low IDV avoid confrontation, other directed behavior; High IDV is the opposite.

- Masculinity-Femininity – the distribution of emotional roles between the genders - tough masculine to tender feminine. Hofstede provides a Masculinity Index (MAS) that describes examples of the differences between countries with high and low MAS's:

> In the family – Low MAS weak gender differentiation, positive feelings about home and family; High IDV is the opposite.

- Long-Short Term Orientation – extent to which a culture programs its members to accept delayed gratification of their material, social, and emotional needs (**transformation, empathy**). Hofstede provides a Long Term Orientation Index (LTO) that describes examples of the differences between countries with high and low LTO's:

> In the family – Low LTO children learn tolerance and respect for others, less

satisfied with daily human relations; High LTO children should learn the truth, and daily human relations are rewarding.

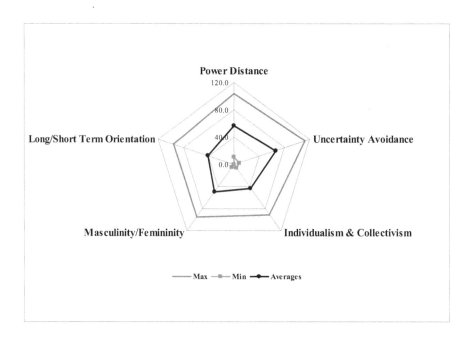

Figure 7 – Cultural Dimensions (Hofstede modified)

Figure 7 displays the information from the Hofstede IBM survey in a different format from that provided by the author. As shown, there are significant ranges on each of the dimensions with average scores of over 50 on Uncertainty/Avoidance and Power Distance. On the other dimensions, the average scores were 43.43 for Individualism & Collectivism, 48.84 for Masculinity/Femininity, and 40.50 for Long/Short Term Orientation. On the high end of the scale, all of the dimensions are at or above 100.

One interesting survey by Cottle (1967)[3] explored the concept of long term orientation studied by Hofstede. Cottle asked people to draw their concept of time using circles for past, present and future. People were instructed to draw the size of the circles proportionate to the importance of past, present and future. People were also asked to draw the circles in such a

---

[3] For copy of graphs see Trompenaars, A. and C. Hampden-Turner (1998). <u>Riding the Waves of Culture:</u>
<u>Understanding Cultural Diversity in Global Business</u>. New York, McGraw-Hill.
   (Pg 130)

21

way as to show the overlap, if any, between the past, present and future. Figure 8 shows the results, and the marked differences between how different cultures envision time. Note the difference between Japan and Venezuela.

Hall (1983) writes about intercultural relations from the perspective of time, and its explicit and tacit aspects. He points out that within cultures the ability to display polychronic and monochronic attitudes exist. He uses the example of the French who are monochromic intellectually but polychromic in behavior. Hall notes that in cultures that keep the past alive (Asian for example) there is less stress because their concept of time is slower (due to the influence of history), and therefore there are less at odds with the chronometers used in the West.

Hall discusses time and the rhythm of life by saying that the more perfect the rhythm, the easier it is for another person to perceive our intentions. As part of his studies, a student filmed children at play during recess. In carefully studying the film, they could see that a single girl skipped and danced around the schoolyard, and all of the other children seemed to find themselves in rhythm, sycophancy, with this girl. They also found that the rhythm were following was exactly the same beat as a current popular song.

In this work, rhythm is considered a part of **empathy,** for it requires a party to find a common understanding of, in this case, a musical beat. The musical beat being a commonly understood vibration, rather than a commonly understood idea. Similar to the idea proposed by Schein that follows.

Schein (1985) provides a view of cultures, that begins with assumptions and progresses to the actual artifacts of the culture.

Ronen and Kraut (1977) reviewed several empirical studies using attitudinal data to cluster countries as a field of inquiry on comparative management: (Haire, Ghiselli et al. 1966); (Sirota and Greenwood 1971); (Ronen and Kraut 1977); (Hofstede 2001)(1976 version); (Badawy 1979); (Griffeth, Hom et al. 1980); and (Hofstede 1980). Their discussion includes country clusters and their underlying dimensions, purpose and implications of clustering, and critiques of the cluster approach. Ronen and Shenkar grouped the clusters into Nordic, Latin Europe, Latin America, Far East, Arabic, and Independents. These grouping are very similar to those used in the GLOBE survey – see Appendix 3. The authors point to the lack of studies in Africa and the ex-soviet union, and the scarcity of results in the Middle and Far East.

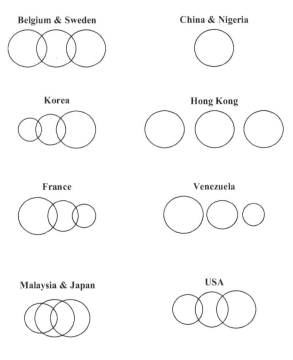

Figure 8 – Perceptions of Past Present & Future (Cottle - modified)

2.3   Cultural Theory 1990 thru 1996

Hall and Hall (1990) describe yet another way to understand cultures through effective communications. They describe the key concepts as:

- Culture is **Communication** – comprised of words, material things, and behavior. The authors say that the essence of cross-cultural communications has more to do with releasing the right responses than with sending the right messages.
- Fast and Slow Messages – consideration of the medium like written, TV, spoken, etc.) (**communication**).
- High and Low Context – high context cultures like the Japanese that rely heavily upon relationships, compared with Americans who rely upon contracts (high = rich) (**communication**).

23

- Space – territorial, personal, and multi-sensory give *tone* to communications.
- Time as **Communication** – monochronic one thing at a time (America), and polychromic many things at one time (Arabic). The authors also include the concepts of past, present, and future in this consideration. They also address the issues of being in *rhythm* with the culture and the issues of appointments and proper timing for **communications**.
- Information Flow – fast or slow, and where does it go or the breadth and speed of **communications**.
- Action Chains – the chain of individuals and actions that are required to achieve a goal. The authors suggest that monochromic/low-context cultures are sensitive to interruptions and are more vulnerable to breaking action chains.
- Interfacing – the greater the context, complexity, cultural distance, and number of levels in the system, the greater the interface problems and need for human talent.
- Releasing the Right Responses – knowing the degree of information required, and using the right cultural interpreter.

Arrien (1993) quotes *Zen Lessons* (1989) as saying that the body of leadership has four limbs: enlightenment and virtue (**inspire**), speech and action (**communicate**), humaneness and justice (**empathy** and **trust**), etiquette and law (**empathy** and **trust**). The author indicates that there are three types of **power**: the power of presence or charisma (**transformation** -mental, emotional, spiritual, and physical), the **power** of communication, and the power of position.

Arrien suggests that the person who embodies all three types of power would have big medicine, or be a so-called great man. Arrien provides a few quotations that are illustrative of the principles (Feldman and Voelke 1992): never spend time with people who don't respect you – Maori proverb; every head is a world – Cuban proverb; if you are not good for yourself, how can you be good for others – Spanish proverb; truth may walk through the world unarmed – Bedouin proverb; with a stout heart a mouse can lift an elephant – Tibetan proverb.

Arrien also studied shamanic traditions of indigenous peoples, and concluded that virtually all draw on the **power** of the:
- Warrior – choose to be present
- Healer – pay attention to what has art and meaning
- Visionary – tell the truth without blame or judgment
- Teacher – be open to outcome not attached to outcome.

- Egalitarianism (human) – recognition of people as moral equals.
- Harmony (human) – Fitting in harmoniously with the environment.
- Embedded ness (human) – People are part of a collective.
- Hierarchy – Unequal distribution of power.
- Mastery – Exploitation of the natural or social environment.
- Affective autonomy – Pursuit of positive experiences.
- Intellectual autonomy – Independent pursuit of ones ideas.

Enshassi and Burgess (1990) wrote an article in the International Journal of Project Management that discusses training for construction site managers involved with multicultural teams for projects in the Middle East. The authors begin with a brief discussion of cultural theory, and conclude that it is difficult to conclude which variables have the greatest effect on managerial behavior. The authors argue that general cultural training, is essential to imbue the learning habits in managers required to understand other cultures. They argue for cultural training in religion, values and attitudes, tradition, and language. They conclude that construction organizations should provide cultural training if they are to be successful. Enhassi and Burgess do not address the use of metaphors to transfer the knowledge (how to do it), but rather that the knowledge must be communicated (what to do).

Goleman (1995) describes the concept of Emotional Intelligence (EQ) which addresses issues that relate to the non-IQ aspects of personalities. Goleman points to the work of Peter Salovey and John Mayer who originally introduced the term EQ. He indicates that EQ includes abilities such as:
- Being able to motivate oneself and persist in the face of frustration.
- Being able to control impulse and delay gratification.
- Be able to regulate one's moods and keep distress from swamping the ability to think.
- Being able to **empathize** and to hope.

Since his work was published, there has been a spate of books on the subject (the tenth edition of Goleman's Emotional Intelligence was published in September 2005). EQ is an important aspect of XLQ for a number of reasons, the first being the ability to empathize. From a cultural perspective, it is important that a leader understands his or her EQ, and emotional tendencies. A bombastic or effusive style will not serve a leader well in all societies, especially those that value emotional control in public.

Arruda and Hickson (1996) address the features of management and organization are most affected by culture. The authors cite the work of Tayeb (1994) as the approach that they mimicked. They found that interpersonal and philosophical issues are the most susceptible to cultural variation. Interpersonal issues are the societal norms, patterns, and processes that are unique to each culture. The philosophic issues, or values, are sometimes more challenging as they depend heavily upon the individuals perspective and moral fiber. In practice, both of these form the basis of cultural intelligence (CQ) which will be discussed later in this work. Darlington provides a comparison of the methodology that different authors have used to study culture in the period of 1961 to 1994 as shown in Table 2. This table illustrates the variety of approaches taken to the study of culture.

Darlington (1996) indicates that there are over 160 definitions of culture (Kroeber and Kluckhohn 1985). The author states that various writers have largely validated the work of Hofstede especially the Power Distance and Individualism indices. Darlington also points out that Hofstede's work has also been validated by Hoppe's (1990) work.

Note, the references for Table 3 are as follows: (Kluckhohn and Strodtbeck 1961), (Hall 1960), (Hall 1966), (Hall and Hall 1987), (Hofstede 1984) through (Hofstede 1991), (Trompenaars 1984) through (Trompenaars 1993; Trompenaars and Hampden-Turner 1998), and (Maznevski 1994).

Darlington also provides a matrix that compares various authors across cultural aspects that were defined by Darlington (e.g. human nature) - Table 3. Most of the authors displayed concur on the aspects of time, but have different opinions regarding issues like human nature (Darlington's category). The author also points to a paper by Bonthous (1993) that describes four other dimensions of culture from studies in five different countries. The work provides a good summary of previous studies and methodologies.

Tung (1996) explores the East Asian concept of *guanxi* (connections)[4]. The author states that according to King (1991) *guanxi* is a key building block of Confucian societies. Tung also goes on to say that under Confucianism, governance by ethics (*li zhi*) has been preferred over governance by law (*fa zhi*). Hofstede's dimension of long-short term orientation is based in part on this same concept. Tung also addresses the issue of face by pointing out that there is *lian* (decency, integrity) or moral character and *mianzi* or status/reputation that must be

---

[4] Reference the Three Kingdoms by Lo Kuan-chung, and the Book of Five Rings by Musashi

considered in interpersonal transactions. A loss of *lian* is devastating while a loss of *mianzi* may be tolerated. This issue of social versus personal value or stature is a consistent theme, both in the cultural and leadership literature. It connects the dimensions of trust and empathy.

Table 2 – Cultural Researcher Matrix (Darlington Table 3.1 modified)

Researchers	Perspective	Methodology	Implications
(Adler 1991)	Trends in OB/HRM publishing	Literature Review	Shift to Cross-Cultural interaction. Recognition of Culture's importance. Leadership of Academic/ Professional Community of Discourse
(Bonthous 1994)	Types of intelligence system	Comparative analysis of preferred styles	Need to develop a balance of all styles to avoid an organizational learning disability
(DiStefano 1992)	Differences in Value Orientation	Case Studies Literatiure Review	Profile of effective global executives
(Hampden-Turner and Trompenaars 1993)		Dilemmatics	Seven Cultures of Capitalism- different sustainability
(Heller and Wilpert 1981)	Participation in Decision Making	IPC Questionnaire	Five methods of Decision Making and Power Displacement Effect
Hofstede (1982), (1991), (2001) (1991 edition noted)	Differences in behaviour	Work related value survey	Distinct national cultures
(Laurent 1983)	Managers' implicit theories on management	Questionaire survey	Country clusters of implicit theory, e.g. organizations as authority systems
(Lessem and Neubauer 1994)	Multiple levels of difference based on philosophies	Comparative surveys of art, religion, literature, philosophy and societal constructs	Four diverse management systems form a basis for European unity
(Maznevski 1994)	Differences in Value Orientation	Value OrientationsTraining Intervention with Performance Assessment	Proposed Model of Synergistic Integration
(Said (1991), (1994)	National literaturetextual style and content	Comparative analysis	Appreciate the differences and recognize we make culture as part of self-organization process
(Tayeb (1988), (1994)	National and Corporate attitude surveys	Literature, cultural and work	Proposed causal model ofculture
(Trompenaars 1984)	Differences in behaviour	Value Orientations	Distinct national cultures e.g.

Table 3 – Comparison of Cultural Dimensions (Darlington Table 3.2 modified)

	Kluckhohrn, Strodbeck (1961)	Hall (1960, 66, 73), Hall & Hall (1987)	Hofstede (1984...1991)	Trompenaars (1984...1993)	Trompenaars and Hampten-Turner(1994)	Maznevski (1994)
Human Nature	Good, Evil, Neutral, Mixed: Changeable, unchangeable	Agreements	Uncertainty Avoidance Index	Universalism & Particularism	Universalism & Particularism	Good/evil: Chageable
Relation to Nature	Subjugation, Harmony, Mastery		Uncertainty Avoidance Index	Internal: External Orientation	Inner: Outer Directed	Subjugation, Harmony, Mastery
Activity Orientation	Doing, Being, Being in becoming	Monochronic,Polychronic (interacts within ividualism)	Masculinity index	Achievement: Ascription	Masculinity index, Ascription: Analysing: Integrating	Doing, Being,Containi ng and Controlling (Thinking)
Human Relationships	Individual, Collective, Hierarchical	Amount of space, Possessions, Friendship, Communicatio n	Power Distance index, Individualism index Affective: Neutral	Equality: Hierarchy. Individualism: Collectivism.	Equality: Hierarchy. Individualism: Communitarian ism.	Individual, collective, Hierarchical
Relation to Time	Past, Present, Future	Past, Future Orientation	Long-term	Sequential: Synchronic. Past, Present, Future	Sequential: Synchronic	
Space Orientation	Public, Private, Mixed	Public, Private				

Hui and Graen (1997) also explore the Chinese relational system called *guanxi* and its potentially compromising effect upon western leadership. Leaders who attend to the issues of face (self and others) are effective in most cultures. Leaders who understand this are patient and have a long-term view of business, relationships, and success.

Hampden-Turner and Trompenaars (1996) provided a view of South Asia that they described as ships that pass in the night to describe the differences, and similarities, between Western and Asian managers. The idea that they describe is that cultures have built-in benchmarks that they utilize in culturally automatic ways. In effect a caution about the pitfalls of stereotyping.

Hofstede (1996) describes a term habitus as a system of permanent and transferable dispositions (Bourdieu 1980). In this particular work Hofstede uses the work of Hoppe (1990) relating to Europeans to support his five cultural dimensions. Hofstede indicates that most Europeans cannot understand the daily fight for survival in Eastern Europe. He quotes the Hungarian political philosopher Bibo (1986) as saying (Pg. 161): "one of the most characteristic features of the soul that has been tortured by fear and feelings of insecurity in major historical trauma and injuries is…in this state of mind the individual loses his sense of

28

moral obligations and responsibilities to the community." Here Hofstede points to one of the major cultural considerations, the potential for suspension of values during times of trauma. For leaders this is an important consideration during times of change and turmoil. Hofstede also adds the fifth dimension, long-short term orientation, to his cultural model.

Leeds (1996) points to the work of Hofstede (1991), and to the work of Lessem and Neubauer (1994). Lessem and Neubauer's work was based on the work of Carl Jung and Myers Briggs who found that the four core values people identified were pragmatism, rationalism, wholism, and humanism in their surveys of European management styles.

Luthans and Hodgetts (1996) emphasized the fact that the work of Hofstede was based upon the western model. They point to the Chinese Culture Connection (1987) which designed a questionnaire based upon traditional Chinese sayings, which was then translated into different languages and given in 22 countries. The findings affirmed the power distance, individualism-collectivism, and masculinity-femininity dimensions proposed by Hofstede. The findings did not affirm the uncertainty avoidance dimension. The surveys also identified the added dimension of Confucian work dynamism. The meaning of the term is a combination of deference, thrift, loyalty, and long-term commitment. Luthans and Hodgetts also point out that subcultures are an important consideration.

Indeed subcultures are an important consideration. Within countries such as Russia, China, and India there are numerous languages, religions, value systems and social customs. If one thinks of an international company, it is not difficult to see the parallels of having numerous societal, political, and religious cultures. One example from experience was a quest to find a listing of Indian holidays. My friends in Mumbai, Delhi, Calcutta, and Chennai told me that such a thing is not possible for there are too many regional holidays. Some speculated that most every day could be a holiday somewhere in India.

2.4 Cultural Theory 1997 thru 1998

Earley and Erez (1997) edited a book that explores global leadership issues from the psychological perspective. The book has a wealth of detailed psychological perspectives on culture, motivation, power, and cross-cultural theory.

Erez (1997) describes four major types of motivational practices that managers utilize across cultures:

- Reward allocation – guided by equity, equality, and the principle of need, to each according to need (**empathy**)
- Participation in goal setting and decision making (**power, transformation**)
- Job and organizational design (**power, transformation**)
- Quality improvement (**communication**)

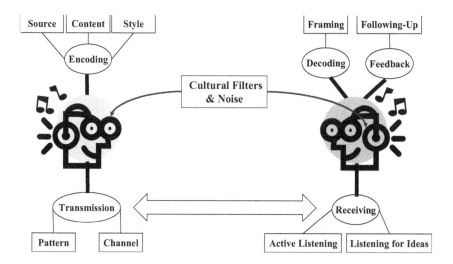

Figure 9 - Gibson (modified)

Gibson (1997) discusses issues surrounding **communications** across cultures. She begins by separating the process into five steps as shown in Figure 10. The author contends that intercultural differences in communications occur due to differences in cognitive styles (methods), and cultural values (particularly Hofstede's masculinity-femininity, individualism-collectivism, and power distance dimensions). Gibson describes the processes and features as follows, and defines her hypothesis as described:

Encoding

- Source – internal or external. Individualistic cultures will tend to rely on internal, collectivistic cultures external.
- Content – emotional or rational. Collectivistic cultures emotional, individualistic cultures rational.

30

- Style – Implicit or explicit.   Collectivistic cultures use implicit, individualistic use explicit.

Transmission
- Pattern – high context or low context. High context tend to use multiple patterns and methods.
- Channel – formal or informal. High Power distance cultures use formal channels.

Receiving
- Active listening – Listening without judgment, and without filters.
- Listening for Ideas – Help overcome collectivistic/individualistic or high context/low context hurdles for example.

Decoding
- Framing – the ability to **empathize** with the sender.

Feedback
- Following-up – Rapidly repeating the sender's message.

House, Wright et al. (1997) provided a thorough and lengthy review of the cross-cultural leadership studies performed since 1989. The authors quote Hofstede and Bond (1988) as saying (Pg. 574): "both **power** distance and individualism (**transformation**) affect the type of leadership likely to be effective in a country. The ideal leader in a culture in which **power** distances are small would be a resourceful democrat; on the other hand, the ideal leader in a culture in which power distances are large is a benevolent autocrat (or "good father"). In collectivist cultures, leadership should respect and encourage employees' group loyalties; incentives should be given collectively, and their distribution should be left up to the group."

House, Wright, et al. state that there are some near universal propositions for leadership. One example they cite is Bass (1997) who argues that the three components of **transformational** leadership (charisma, intellectual stimulation of followers, and individualized consideration toward followers) are more effective than contingent reward.

The authors also suggest triangulation when sampling to avoid bias. They suggest a technique called *unobtrusive measures* to help in reducing bias. In this type of technique, questions are asked of people who may not be able to sense the underlying meaning – for example if intolerance of uncertainty were the aspect to be studies, and then ask the mean age of the executive officers.

In an extremely large political science study Ingelhart (1997) describes the results of the World Values Survey that was conducted in 43 countries that represented 70% of the world's population. The design of the surveys considered the theory of intergenerational value change. Inglehart argues that economic development, cultural change, and political change go together in somewhat predictable patterns or the Marxian view. Compared to the Weberian view that culture shapes economic and political life. In a very condensed summary, the post modernization era that the authors explore is described as an era of diminished materialism and increased social issue consciousness.

The massive data was plotted in a number of unique ways showing traditional versus secular-rational authority, survival versus well being, and showing rich and poor country extremes. The plots also show the changes in the variables between 1981 and 1990 for a number of countries, thus indicating that cultures fluctuate over time, economically. Inglehart also groups the countries into clusters (e.g. Catholic Europe) that imply historical connections that have not changed markedly like conditions in East Germany, whereas there has been a movement away from traditional authority in West Germany.

Cusher and Brislin (1997) edited an excellent manual for cross-cultural training. They argue that training requires four stages: 1) awareness (of another culture), 2) knowledge (knowledge of the culture), 3) challenge to peoples emotions (getting over discomfort), and 4) skill development.

Trompenaars and Hampden-Turner (1998) presented the findings from their cross-cultural training programs, and from research in 50 countries with 30 different companies and 75% of the participants being managers. Their database as of 1998 included 30,000 participants. The authors view culture as an onion with implicit basic assumptions as the core, then norms and values of the culture, and lastly artifacts and products (business). As with Schein (1985), noted earlier, they also view culture as consisting of three levels: 1) artifacts and products, 2) norms and values, and 3) basic assumptions (this theme is similar to the green belt, black belt, and master black belt approach described later in Section 3.6). Their research describes cultural differences in the following dimensions:

- Universalism versus Particularism (rules versus relationships) – universal rights compared to the particular requirements of individual relationships. Particularist groups seek gratification through relationships, and tend to develop their own local identities in global firms. The authors utilize a situational hypothetical of a person breaking the speed limit, and by not telling the truth a friend can escape punishment. The authors state that they find that the universalistic response is that as the seriousness of the accident increases, the obligation to the friend decreases. They also argue that the Particularist cultures may put enough pressure on people not to break the speed limit in the first place. Of the 31 countries reported on all but four had a percentage greater than 50% responding that the truth needed to be told. The values of either extreme go to the issues of **trust** and **empathy** described in the hypothesis of this work.

- Communitarism versus Individualism (group versus the individual) – self-interest compared to the community interests. The authors point out that this follows a Protestant-Catholic divide as well. They also point out that unaccompanied people (no entourage) assume a lack of status in some societies. Communitarian societies will refrain from voting on decisions to show respect for those in the minority. The values of either extreme go to the issues of **power** and **empathy** described in the hypothesis of this work.

- Neutral versus Emotional (the range of feelings expressed) – being objective and detached compared to being effusive and expressive. The authors describe considerations starting with time and tone of voice in communications. The concept of waiting for a person to finish talking before one begins talking for example. They tell the story of a colleague who was raised in Curaçao and Surinam. In Curaçao, his grandmother would slap him in the face for not looking at her when he talked, and his grandmother in Surinam would slap him in the face for making eye contact. Of the 49 countries reported on all but 10 had a percentage less than 50% responding that they would not show emotions at work. The values of either extreme go to the issues of the ability to **communicate** described in the hypothesis of this work.

- Diffuse versus Specific (the range of involvement) – contractual approach compared with relationship approach, or low context versus high context. The authors point to the work of Lewin (1936). The so-called U-type (American) and the G-type (German) illustrate the concept of what is the size of public and private spaces. One example used is that of a U-type person visiting the home of a G-Type person and wandering around their home uninvited. The U-type sees as public a person's kitchen for example - visiting a person's kitchen or wandering about the house without a guide. Whereas the G-type person sees such areas of a home as very personal. A U-Type person has a small personal space and a G-Type person a very large personal space. The authors describe the work of Parsons (1951) and the dimensions of neutral, affective, diffuse, and specific for considering regional cultural differences. All of these dimensions go to the leadership dimensions of **communication**, **trust**, and have **empathy** described in the hypothesis of this work.

* Achievement versus Ascription (how status is accorded) – individual performance compared to position. This dimension differentiates cultures that hold authority to be more important than individual performance. The values of either extreme go to the issues of the leadership dimensions of **power** and **trust.**

Trompenaars and Hampden-Turner point to the work of Kluckhohn and Strodtbeck (1961) who identified three types of cultures: 1) present oriented, 2) past oriented, and 3) future oriented. The concept is similar to that in the previous example of Figure 8. The authors also consider national cultures, and the corporate cultures that are more compatible with them. Trompenaars and Hampden-Turner describe four dimensions of corporate images using the metaphors of incubator (self-expression and fulfillment and emotions top-left quadrant), family (**power** oriented with leader as father bottom-left quadrant), Eiffel tower (bureaucratic, broad at the base and narrow at the top bottom-right quadrant), and guided missile (egalitarian and goal focused top-right quadrant). Figure 10 presents the results of their research for selected countries. The authors go on to point out that, the importance of transnationals is that they balance the centralization and de-centralization of corporate cultures by using portions of both and by adjusting. They point to the work of Goold (1990) and state that the only strategic system for a genuinely international company is the strategic control model that Goold described.

Trompenaars and Hampden-Turner see culture as having a normal distribution, which is to say that there are overlaps in the normal distributions across cultures, where some values and beliefs are common. Said another way, there are variations within cultures that can share portions of values and beliefs with people in other cultures. The authors warn against stereotyping for this reason and state (Pg. 46): "transcultural effectiveness is not measured only by the degree to which you grasp the opposite value (another cultures' differences). It is measured by your competence in reconciling the dilemmas."

The authors also point to the work of Hall (1960) who described polychronic (synchronous) time and societies who put value on doing activities in parallel. The example used is for Japanese negotiators (polychromic) to make their major concessions after the American partners were confirmed on return flights (Americans unwilling to change plans - monochronic). Many authors have addressed this concept and the ways that different cultures consider time. The answer to the question *what time is the 9:00AM meeting* is often, it depends on the country, and it depends if you are the buyer or the seller of a service

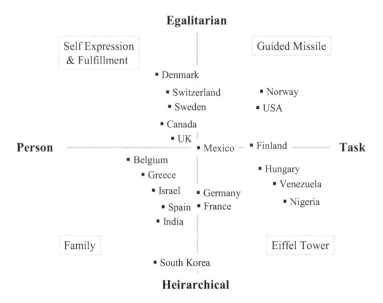

Egalitarian

| Self Expression & Fulfillment | Guided Missile |

- Denmark
  - Switzerland   - Norway
  - Sweden   - USA
- Canada
- UK

Person ———————————— • Mexico − • Finland ———— **Task**

- Belgium
  - Greece   - Hungary
    - Israel   • Germany   - Venezuela
      - Spain • France   - Nigeria
    - India

| Family | Eiffel Tower |

- South Korea

Heirarchical

Figure 10 – Cultural Aspects (Trompenaars & Hampden-Turner modified Pg. 184)

2.5   Cultural Theory 1999 thru 2005

Den Hartog, House et al. (1999) have performed some of the most comprehensive work on cross-cultural leadership. In the reference article, the authors stated (no page numbers HTML format), "attributes associated with charismatic/**transformational** leadership will be universally endorsed as contributing to outstanding leadership, and the findings were that the combined results of the major GLOBE (Global Leadership and Organizational Behavior Effectiveness) study and the follow-up study demonstrate that several attributes reflecting charismatic/transformational leadership are universally endorsed as contributing to outstanding leadership." The authors went on to say that "these include motive arouser, foresight, encouraging, communicative, trustworthy, dynamic, positive, confidence builder, and motivational. Several other charismatic attributes are perceived as culturally contingent. These include enthusiastic, risk taking, ambitious, self-effacing, unique, self-sacrificial, sincere, sensitive, compassionate, and willful. None of the items universally perceived as impediments

35

to outstanding leadership describe transformational/charismatic leadership" (**trust, empathy, transformation, power,** and **communication**).

Rosen, Digh et al. (2000) completed a study of 75 CEO's and 1,058 respondents in 18 countries. They present a view of culture with leadership at the core, followed by business, nation, and world – see Figure 11. Implied in this design is that the proximity and frequency of interaction determine the layer of culture. At the center lie leadership, and the various aspects of how people perceive leadership. At this level, the relationships are more intimate and immediate. At the business level, the culture impinges upon the individual from 40 to 60 hours each week. The diagram also suggests that the components are not separable, meaning that without the national view, the lower layers are without context. The adage of *think globally and act locally* is another way to look at the diagram.

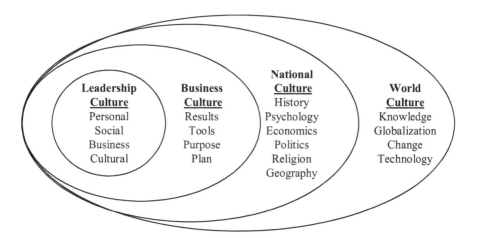

Figure 11 - Cultures of the twenty-first century business (Rosen, Digh et al. modified)

From the interviews and surveys, Rosen, Digh et al. developed a different view of cultural intelligence (CQ), what they call global literacy[5]:

- Personal literacy – understanding and valuing yourself. Leadership mastery of key behaviors of aggressive insight, confident humility (**power**), authentic flexibility, reflective decisiveness (**communicate**), and realistic optimism (**transformation**).
- Social literacy – engaging and challenging others. Leadership behaviors include pragmatic **trust**, urgent listening (**communicate**), constructive impatience, connective

[5] Website - www.healthycompanies.com

teaching, and collaborative individualism.

- Business literacy – focusing and mobilizing your organization. Leader skills include chaos navigator (**transformation**), business geographer, historical futurist, leadership liberator (**power**), and economic integrator.
- Cultural literacy – valuing and leveraging cultural differences. Leadership roles include proud ancestor, inquisitive nationalist, respectful modernizer (**empathy**), cultural *bridger*, and global capitalist.

Sagiv and Schwartz (2000) found the three universal needs of people to be: 1) humane requirements, 2) the preservation of society, and 3) the relationship of people to their natural environment. In the survey that examined 57 cultures, there were seven fundamental value dimensions identified: harmony, embedded ness, hierarchy, mastery, affective autonomy, intellectual autonomy, and egalitarianism. These dimensions can be found in the work of other authors like Hofstede's power distance and individualism-collectivism, and the GLOBE research program egalitarianism as some examples. The issue of the relationship of people to their natural environment is a concept that is not often addressed in the literature on culture.

Pheng and Leong (2000) explore lessons learned on the construction of a hotel in China. They describe the characteristics of the Chinese construction industry, including those relating to relationships and high/low context communications. Pheng and Leong point to the characteristics being trust and respect, family business structure, use of concise simple contracts, focus on profits not financial matters, and the unfortunate reality of bribery and bureaucracy being alive and well. The authors conclude that building such a project requires not only an understanding of cross-cultural management, but also of Project Management, and of human resources management.

Gannon (2001) takes an approach of starting from Hofstede's work and enriching the information with in depth studies of individual cultures. He does this to establish cultural metaphors that take account of history, philosophy, politics, religion, customs, art, economics (Fiske 1991), humor, holidays and ceremonies, education, food, technological change, music and more ((Kashima and Callan 1994); (Lakoff and Johnson 1980); (Gelfand and McHusker 2002); (Geertz 1973)). Gannon uses the framework developed by Triandis and Gelfand (1998) that divides cultures into four types: horizontal collectivism (community sharing), vertical collectivism (hierarchical ranking), horizontal individualism (equality matching), and vertical individualism (market pricing). Gannon points toward the work of other psychologists and anthropologists for the construction of cultural metaphors, including:

(Kluckhohn and Strodtbeck 1961)

- Does the society consider people good or bad?
- Does the society believe people should live in harmony with nature?
- Does the society assume individualism or collectivism for relationships?
- What is the primary mode of activity (go with the flow, doing something, setting goals)?
- What is the perception of space?
- What is the society's temporal perception (past, present, future)?

(Hall and Hall 1990)

- Context (high or low) – amount of explicit information in communication (Japanese high context society aphorism: "he who knows does not speak; he who speaks does not know").
- Space
- Time
- Information flow (fast or slow)

(Hofstede 2001)

- Power distance
- Uncertainty avoidance
- Individualism
- Masculinity
- Time horizon

Gannon also uses Huntington's (1996) concepts of *torn* cultures (torn from its cultural roots like Russia) and *cleft* cultures (diverse cultures that are difficult to integrate) to divide his book. For example, Russia was severed from its social, economical, and cultural roots four times, by the Tartars, by Peter the Great, by communism, and then by the falling of the *iron curtain*. He then sets forth a four-stage model for cross-cultural understanding.

Stage 1 is the foundation considerations in the development of knowledge of a culture. In Stage 2 Gannon refers to Fiske (1991) who relates dimensions to statistical scales: nominal (community sharing), ordinal (authority ranking), interval (equality matching), and ratio (market pricing). Stage 3 incorporates other *etic* or culture-general dimensions such as

38

motivation (Osland and Bird 2000), uncertainty avoidance, time horizon, masculinity (Hofstede), and rules (Triandis and Gelfand 1998). In Stage 4, one then employs cultural metaphors for understanding cultures. Osland and Bird introduce the concept of cultural trumping (certain values take precedence in certain situations).

Gannon states that there are times that culture is less important or indeed not important at all. Some examples cited are occupational similarities, such as communities of practice (CoP's - e.g. doctors), social class similarities (e.g. middle-class), exclusionary powerful groups (e.g. apartheid), and partnerships. He also states that when **trust** is present, culture decreases in importance (Jarvenpaa, Knoll et al. 1998), and that in the case of the internet that it has led to more differentiation than integration. Gannon believes that cultural matters most when there is a scarcity of resources, opportunities, and feelings of inequity. From this point Gannon devotes attention to the development of metaphors for the cultures addressed. Gannon's work is covered in more detail in Section 3.5 of this work.

Jarvenpaa, Knoll et al. (referenced by Gannon above) approach the antecedents of **trust** in a global virtual team setting by studying seventy-five teams in different countries. The authors state that from the rational perspective the existence of **trust** enables people to take risks, and from the social perspective trust centers on moral duty or values (Kramer and Tyler 1996). The authors note that there are four perspectives taken in researching trust: 1) individual personality differences (Frost, Simpson et al. 1978), 2) institutional phenomenon ((Lewis and Weigert 1985); (Sitkin and Roth 1993)), 3) cross-cultural issues (Farris, Senner et al. 1973), and 4) interpersonal relations ((Deutsch 1958; Cummings and Bromiley 1996);(Mayer, Davis et al. 1995); (McAllister 1995)).

Jarvenpaa, Knoll et al. quote the Mayer, Davis et al. definition of **trust** as being (Pg. 31): "the willingness of a party to be vulnerable to the actions of another party based on the expectation that the other will perform a particular action important to the trustor, irrespective of the ability to monitor that other party." The authors refer to the work of Scott (1980) whose research showed that **trust** varied more on the basis of the trustee's attributes rather than the trustor' propensity to trust. The authors also hypothesized that integrity and ability (technical, interpersonal, etc.) predicted trust better than benevolence, which is often acquired through team building exercises.

39

Brake (2002) suggests some simple but important advice for cross-cultural leadership. Leaders should study respected leaders in other cultures, and then be prepared to adjust one's style to be resonating with the local perception of leadership.

Earley and Ang (2003) point to the work of Lee and Templer (2003) who set forth a theory of Cultural Intelligence (CQ). The theory is that as with emotional intelligence (EQ), and intellectual intelligence (IQ), CQ is a pre-requisite for the effective leadership and management of diverse cross-cultural groups. In the introduction the authors say that (Pg. 2): "people having a high social or emotional intelligence are thought to the relatively more able to **empathize**, work with, direct, and interact with other people...social intelligence is an important factor in understanding a leader's capacity to shape and respond to the needs and reactions of followers."

Earley and Ang state that the essence of a charismatic leader is the ability to generate congruence between the followers and the leader's concerns for solving a problem (one enemy). The authors define CQ as (Pg. 9): "a person's capability for successful adaptation to new cultural settings, that is, for unfamiliar settings attributable to cultural context." Earley and Ang describe the three fundamental components of CQ, and the four levels of intelligence as shown in Table 4.

Earley and Ang point to the issue of values as well by referencing the work of Wilson (1993) who proposed that there were four universal morals: sympathy (**empathy**), fairness (**trust**), self-control (**communication**), and duty (**trust**).

Earley and Ang also address the issues of social and emotional intelligence (EQ). The authors point to the work of Riggio, Maessamer et al. (1991) and their model for social intelligence based on three skills:

- Expressivity – skill in encoding messages and engaging others (**communicate**).
- Sensitivity – skill in decoding messages and understanding social norms and roles (**communicate, empathy**).
- Control – skill in personal control or roles and emotion (**trust, inspire**).

Table 4 – CQ Components (Earley and Ang compiled from book)

Cognitive	Motivational	Behavior	Levels
The ability to develop patterns from cultural clues, and to transfer knowledge from one culture to another	A person's desire to engage with others.	A person's capability to appropriately enact selected behavior.	Metacognitive – thinking about thinking
Declarative (what we know about something)	Efficacy (pursue goals)	Repertoire	Universal – knowledge of the universal concept of humanity
Procedural	Persistence	Practices and Rituals	Mediate – culture-specific knowledge
Analogical	Goals	Habits	Proximate – knowledge tied specifically to context, people, and events
Pattern Recognition	Enhancement/Face	Newly learned	
External Scanning	Value Questioning and Integration		
Self Awareness			

Earley and Ang describe the work of Wagner and Sternberg (1985) relating to Practical Intelligence – the ability to solve practical rather than intellectual problems. Earley and Ang point to this use of tacit knowledge as an indicator of a person's ability to shape the environment. A scarcity of research has been performed on this topic, but clearly, there is a connection between this and the concept of Black Belt training described Section 3.6.3 of this work.

Lee and Templer (2003) provide a review of the measurement techniques and tests available for measuring CQ. One of those tests, the Overseas Assignment Inventory (OAI) that considered a wide sampling of subject was conducted by Tucker (1999)[6] and it covered all of the dimensions described in the Earley and Ang book.

Thomas and Inkson (2004) describe the concept of Cultural Intelligence (CQ) as having the components of mindfulness, behavioral skills, and knowledge. Knowledge means knowledge of culture and the principles of cross-cultural interactions. Mindfulness means to pay attention to the cues in cross-cultural situations. Behavior skills mean using appropriate skills developed from a repertoire of cross-cultural skills. The authors note that social learning research confirms that the repetitive sequence of knowledge-mindfulness-behavioral skills leads to the development of CQ. Earley and Ang's three components of cognitive (knowledge),

---

[6] Website www.tuckerintl.com

motivational (mindfulness in a way), and behavior are very similar in concept to those discussed by Thomas and Inkson.

Shore and Cross (2005) explore the role of national culture on international science projects. They begin by saying that (Pg. 55): "national culture and its influence on the Project Management process have received little emphasis in the literature." One issue that Shore and Cross address is the issue of pay inequity on multicultural international projects. While this topic is beyond the scope of this work, suffice to say that trans-nationals and other international firms must establish policies to address this issue head-on. The authors pose a number of questions that they answer in the conclusion to the paper. As these perspectives specifically address Project Management, they warrant paraphrasing here:

- Is the study of culture relevant to the Project Management process? Yes.
- Which cultural dimensions are likely to affect the management process? The authors point to Hofstede and the GLOBE survey: power distance, uncertainty avoidance, individualism, future orientation, performance orientation, and humane treatment.
- Which management issues are linked to the influence of culture? The authors found that management structure, geographic work distribution, budgetary commitment, family and education, and pay equity are linked to the cultural dimensions noted just above.
- Does culture affect project outcomes? Yes, but how it does is unclear.
- How can knowledge of these issues be useful to project managers? One more piece of the jigsaw puzzle.

In another recent article by Henrie and Souza-Poza (2005) the authors did a thorough review of the Project Management literature from 1993 through 2003 that addressed the issue of culture. They reviewed 770 Project Management journal articles (Project Management Journal and the International Journal of Project Management) and 93 books. Their findings confirm those that are shown in Table 1 in this work.

Their conclusions were that (Pg. 5): "the lack of leading Project Management culture literature provides challenges for the Project Management researcher and busy project manager. As the Project Management literature indicates, researchers will need to incorporate theories and concepts, developed in other disciplines, to build Project Management-specific culture based theories and research methods. Is the Project Management profession including culture as part of its research agenda? The answer is yes, to a very limited degree. Earlier literature reviews and this review show a consistently low level of culture-specific literature within the leading Project Management journals. For the busy project manager, the implication is that he or she must look outside Project Management literature for information and guidance on culture and the implications it has toward project team success. To overcome the lack of available culture information within the areas surveyed, the project manager must expand his or her reading and learning to other culture-based discipline areas."

This work addresses this gap in the knowledge base, and gives Project Managers a long needed tool to help them improve their chances of success in this multi-cultural world.

2.6 The GLOBE Survey

In one of the broadest and most thorough studies of leadership and culture, House and Javidan (2004) reported on the Global Leadership and Organizational Behavior Effectiveness Research Program (GLOBE) that surveyed 17,300 mid-level managers representing 951 organizations (financial services, food processing, and telecommunications) in 62 cultures. The research addressed how organizational practices are influenced by societal forces, and it cross referenced the work with that of Hofstede (2001), and Schwartz (1994). The editors found that leadership is culturally contingent upon the culture in which the leader functions.

Javidan and Hauser (2004), as part of the GLOBE study, point to other cultural databases that bear upon the issues of how and why cultures are different. They point to the UN Development Program *Human Development Report*, the *World Value Surveys* by Inglehart, and the World Economic Forum's *Executive Opinion Survey* as databases utilized to consider the economic, development, and quality of life in different cultures.

The GLOBE survey (House and Javidan 2004) definition of leadership is (Pg. 15): "the ability of an individual to influence, motivate, and enable others to contribute toward the effectiveness and success of the organizations of which they are members." The GLOBE definition of culture is (Pg. 15): "shared motives, values, beliefs, identities, and interpretations or meanings of significant events that result from common experiences of members of collectives that are transmitted across generations."

Specifically, the GLOBE's survey objectives were to answer the following questions (quoted from the text):

- Are there leader behaviors, attributes, and organizational practices that are universally accepted and effective across cultures?
- Are there leader behaviors, attributes, and organizational practices that are accepted and effective in only some cultures?
- How attributes of societal and organizational cultures influence specific leader behaviors, and if they will be accepted and effective?
- How do attributes of societal and organizational cultures affect selected organizational practices?
- How do attributes of societal cultures affect the economic, physical and psychological welfare of members of the societies studied?
- What is the relationship between societal cultural variables and international competitiveness of the societies studied?

The results of the GLOBE survey identified nine independent variables or *cultural dimensions*, measured by questions that asked how things were in their organization (*practices*), and how things should be (*values*) in their organizations. Appendix 7 provides a cross reference to other selected authors assembled from data in different sections of the GLOBE survey. Some of these authors were used by the GLOBE survey used as benchmarks for their background research. Appendix 3 and Appendix 4 provide the values for the nine cultural dimensions. A description of the nine dimensions follows:

- Uncertainty Avoidance – extent that people strive to avoid uncertainty by relying upon social norms, rituals, and bureaucratic practices. Origin (Hofstede 2001) for all items noted as Hofstede (**trust**).
- Power Distance – degree that people expect and agree that power would be stratified and concentrated at high levels of organizations. Origin was Hofstede (**power**).
- Institutional Collectivism – degree to which society and organizations encourage and reward collective distribution of resources. Origin was Hofstede, as a single dimension, modified resulting from the work of Triandis (1995) (**trust, empathy**).
- Group Collectivism – degree to which individuals express pride, loyalty and cohesiveness in their organizations and families. Origin Hofstede, as a single dimension, modified resulting from the work of Triandis (1995) (**trust, empathy, communication**).
- Gender Egalitarianism – degree to which societies and organizations promote gender equality. Origin Hofstede, as a single dimension of *masculinity* (**power**).
- Assertiveness – degree that an individual expresses assertive, confrontational or

aggressive behavior in organizations and society. Origin Hofstede, as a single dimension of *masculinity* **transformation, power**).

- Future Orientation – degree to which individuals engage in future activities such as planning and postponing collective gratification. Origin Kluckhohn and Strodtbeck (1961), and generally similar to Hofstede's *Confucian Work Dimension* (**empathy, transformation, communication**).
- Performance Orientation – degree to which society or organization rewards performance and excellence. Origin McClelland (1961)(**power, transformation, communication**).
- Humane Orientation – degree that societies and organizations reward fair, altruistic, friendly, generous, and caring for others. Origin Kluckhohn and Strodtbeck (1961) (**empathy, transformation**).

On the leadership aspect of cross-cultural leadership, the results of the GLOBE survey identified six dependent leadership variables or *global leadership dimensions* from culturally endorsed implicit leadership theory (called CLT by the authors). They identified 21 universally effective leadership behaviors, eight that were considered impediments, and 35 that were considered impediments in some cultures but benefits in others. The six *global leadership* characteristics are listed below and the values obtained from the survey are shown in Appendix 5:

- Charismatic/Value Based Leadership – the ability to inspire and motivate. It includes subcategories of visionary, inspirational, self-sacrifice, integrity, decisiveness, and performance orientation.
- Team-Oriented Leadership – ability to build common purpose. It includes the subcategories of collaborative team orientation, team integrator, diplomatic, malevolent, and administratively competent.
- Participative Leadership – degree to which others are involved in decisions. Includes the subcategories of non-participative and autocratic.
- Humane-Oriented Leadership – includes compassion and generosity. Includes the subcategories of modesty and humane orientation.
- Autonomous Leadership – individualistic, independent attributes.
- Self-Protective Leadership – ensure safety and security of self and group. Includes the subcategories of self-centered, status consciousness, conflict inducer, face-saver, and procedural.

Dorfman, Hanges et al. (2004) described the theory and methodology behind the leadership scales utilized in the GLOBE study. They begin by noting the potential problems with empirically developed scales (construct developed from statistics), and with theory-driven scales (construct written and tested). The authors decided to utilize the theory-driven approach similar to that of Smith and Schwartz (1997).

Hanges and Dickson (2004) contend that culture and culturally endorsed implicit leadership theory (CLT) are *convergent-emergent* constructs (Kozlowski and Klein 2000). The authors explain convergent and emergent by stating that (Pg. 124): "convergent because the responses from people within organizations or societies are believed to center about a single value usually represented by scale means...emergent because even though the origin of these constructs are a function of cognition, affect, and personality of the survey respondents, the properties of these constructs are actually manifested at the aggregate or group level of analysis."

Some of the theories that guided the GLOBE study are as listed below:
- Implicit Leadership Theory (Lord and Maher 1991)- individuals have implicit beliefs, convictions, and assumptions regarding attributes that differentiate leaders from followers.
- Value-Belief Theory (Hofstede 1980); (Triandis 1995) – the values and beliefs of a culture influence the actions and acceptability of actions.
- Implicit Motivation Theory (McClelland 1961) – conscious and non-conscious motives of achievement, affiliation, and power drive behavior.
- Structural Contingency Theory – not used in the study.
- Integrated Theory – that attributes of a culture will predict organizational behavior and leadership attributes.

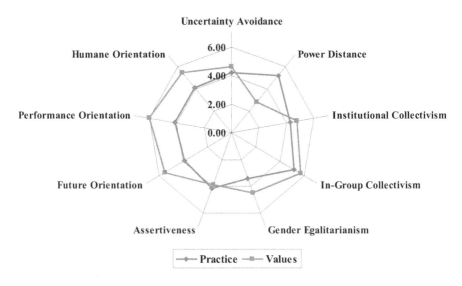

Figure 12 – GLOBE Cultural Dimensions (House & Javidan complied from)

Figure 12 was compiled from data presented in the GLOBE study from House and Javidan (2004). It shows the average overall responses to the survey on each of the cultural dimensions (the scale is from 1 to 7). Differences between the practice (as is conditions), and the values (should be beliefs) were both measured by the GLOBE survey, and are displayed in red and green respectively. The GLOBE survey explored the differences between how people see actual practice in the workplace versus what values that believe should be in the workplace. For example, notice the difference on the Hofstede dimension of Power Distance. This provides an interesting view of the data originally collected by Hofstede.

Hanges and Dickson (2004)constructed what they called *quartets* of questions to separate the social cultural opinions from the organizational cultural opinions by asking respondents to respond to the same questions for how things are, *as-is*, and how things *should-be*. The scale they established for this examination ranged from individual interests as a one, to collective interests being a seven. For the CLT scale they selected a range of one (this behavior or characteristic greatly inhibits a person from being an outstanding leader), to seven (this behavior or characteristic contributes greatly to a person being an outstanding leader). They then conducted two pilot studies to test the psychometric efficacy and the robustness of the questions in a number of countries. They then compared their findings to those of Hofstede, Schwartz, and the World Value Survey.

Appendix 7 provides a comparison of the GLOBE data to that of other authors described in this work. It provides a systematic comparison that includes Hanges and Dickson results. The authors work correlated, as predicted, with those of other authors as follows:

- Hofstede - strongly on the dimension of power distance (as-is scale), moderately on the dimension of uncertainty avoidance (should-be scale), and negatively on the dimension of individualism (should-be scale).

- Schwartz – Sagiv and Gupta (2002) found 48 countries in common between Schwartz's survey and that of GLOBE (all compared to the should-be scale). They found good correlation with embedded ness (minimization of disruptions to social order), negative correlation with intellectual autonomy (emphasis of promotion and protection of individual intellectual directions), some correlation with hierarchy, good correlation with egalitarianism, and small correlation with mastery (social endeavors to modify the environment).

- World Values Survey - Inglehart, Basanez et al. (1998) found 39 countries in common but utilized adults rather than business leaders. In general, the findings were well correlated with the GLOBE survey.

As part of the reporting on the GLOBE study, Dorfman and House (2004) provided a review of the literature and theory of the study. They point out that international convergence is difficult to assess, because of the interrelatedness of the global community. They point to the work of Ralston, Gustafson et al. (1992) who found that Hong Kong managers reflected more western values than on Chinese values, and that Chinese managers reflected more on Chinese values than western values. Clearly economic advancement, or globalization, alters perceptions.

The authors note that there is little evidence of fundamental changes in values since Hofstede did his survey between 1967 and 1973 (Hoppe 1993). However, they do point out that since the Bass and Stogdill's (1990) review, leadership theory and research has improved immeasurably pointing to the work of ((Dorfman 2004); (Chemers 1997); (House, Wright et al. 1997); (Peterson and Hunt 1997); (Misumi 1985); (Sinha 1984); (Hagan 1995); (Ali 1990); (Ling and Fang 2003); (Scandura, Von Glinow et al. 2003)).

Dorfman, Hanges et al. (2004) discuss implicit leadership theory (ILT), and culturally endorsed implicit leadership theory (CLT). ILT theory is that people have ideas of what constitutes a leader and that they can recognize these people in business, government, etc. CLT theory is that cultures have ideas of what constitute leaders. In their study, the questionnaires consisted of 112 behavioral attribute descriptors, and there were 17,000 questionnaires.

The results are shown in Figure 13, which is constructed from the data presented in the author's work. In general the authors considered their hypothesis proven if the average scores were greater that 5.0. It is interesting that Charismatic-Value Based, Team Oriented, Participative, and Humane Oriented were all at or above the 5.0 threshold. In the other cases, Self Protective and Autonomous, the numbers were below 4.0.

The Dorfman, Hanges, et al. data is presented in this section of the work to keep it with the other GLOBE survey data albeit it pertains to the leadership aspect of cross-cultural leadership.

There were a number of additional articles that were discovered, but not included in the current research due to the scope limitations of this work including:

- (Peterson and Hunt 1997) who discuss the issues of *emic* and *etic*.
- ((Schwartz 1999); (Sinha and Kanungo 1997) who provide research relating to Indian attitudes relating to the new organizational changes.
- (Dorfman and Howell 1997) who discuss leadership in Asian countries.
- (Nemetz and Christensen 1996) who discuss cultural diversity.
- (Hui and Graen 1997) who discuss Sino cross cultural leadership.
- ((Graen and Hui 1996); (Trice and Beyer 1991)) who discuss cultural leadership.
- (Roth, Prasnikar et al. 1991) who discuss the importance of culture rather than markets.
- ((Adler 1983; Adler and Bartholomew 1992; Adler 2002; Adler and Kwon 2002)) who discuss publishing trends for cross-cultural publications.
- ((Adler and Kwon 2002); (Adler and Graham 1989)) who discuss an increased need for cross cultural interaction research.
- (Tayeb 1994) who discuss organizations and national culture.
- (Tayeb 1987); (Lachman, Nedd et al. 1994); (Triandis 2004); (Triandis 2003) who discuss contingency and culture.
- ((Joynt and Warner 1996); (Child, Boisot et al. 1990); (Connection 1987); (Ronen 1986); (Hoppe 1990); (Maznevski 1994); (Tayeb 1994); (Schwartz 1994); (Smith and Peterson 1994); (Yang 1988)) on a variety of topics.

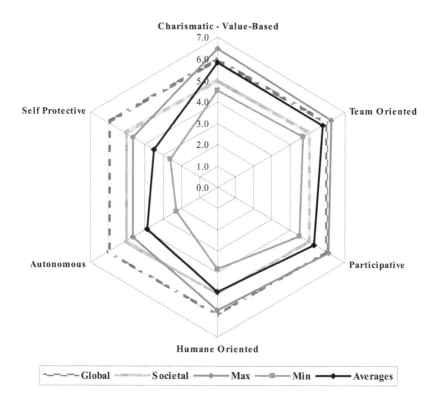

Figure 13 – GLOBE Leadership Dimensions (Dorman, Hanges et al. data complied)

2.7 Chapter Summary

In this chapter, the research on culture was provided from 1967 through 2005, beginning with Hofstede and ending with the GLOBE survey. The differences in cultures were explored, and the studies provide leaders with the tools to calibrate themselves to the differences. As Earley and Ang point out however, the acquisition of knowledge and cultural intelligence (CQ) is a critical component if a leader is to utilize these tools effectively. The next chapter addresses CQ, or cultural knowledge.

3. Cultural Knowledge

3.1 Chapter Introduction

In the global economy, it is important that people develop the ability to empathize with other cultures, rapidly. In an environment that relies heavily on virtual communications with teams spread around the globe, building trust and providing leadership are critical business and Project Management skills. There is a significant body of literature on cross-cultural issues, but often it focuses on a thin band of customs and business practices. While this knowledge is essential, it generally is only durable enough for short business engagements. It is not adequate for extended expatriate assignments, or for extended projects with virtual teams. Another method is needed if one is to learn more quickly about other cultures.

One potential method that has emerged is the use of metaphors to provide a window into other cultures that is rich and informative, not judgmental. The literature on metaphors begins with Aristotle, and has a long history of debate between those who believe metaphors to be a knowledge transferable representation of complex ideas, and those that believe it to be an intellectually lazy way to avoid detailed descriptions of complex ideas. There are also those that have argued that metaphors in the cultural domain are in danger of crossing the line into stereotypes. Metaphors are a way to increase the understanding of other cultures, and thus empathy. Further, the study of metaphors will help those from low context cultures, like the Unites States, to develop sensitivity for communications in high context cultures.

In this Chapter, the research on cultural knowledge and metaphors is explored. The research portion of the chapter begins with a review of the early literature and ends with a review of Gannon's work on cultural metaphors. The last section in the chapter proposes a cultural knowledge model that is based on the literature, and on personal experience on a number of ex-patriate assignments. The acquisition and transfer of cultural knowledge is a critical component of Cross-Cultural Leadership Intelligence (XLQ).

As with Chapter 2, this section is also arranged in chronological order of publication.

3.2 Cultural Metaphor Theory -1950 thru 1997

Knowledge acquisition and transfer of different cultures is critical in developing and nurturing the concepts of empathy, trust, power, transformation, and communications. Since values vary widely, this section will also look at international value systems. Values, ethics, and moral judgment are integral to the five dimensions of leadership proposed in this work, and directly with trust.

Wiener (1950) wrote that information that proceeds backwards, and is able to change the method of performance, can be called learning. Weiner concluded that knowledge could be created only if the explicit information is internalized and used. Chase (1938) points to the work of a Polish mathematician Korsbybski (1933) who suggested that if people wish to understand the world and themselves, it follows that we should use a language whose structure corresponds to physical structure. Korsbybski believed that mathematics was the only well-ordered language. The metaphor used is a map: you cannot drive on a map but it represents essential information if one is to drive from one point to another.

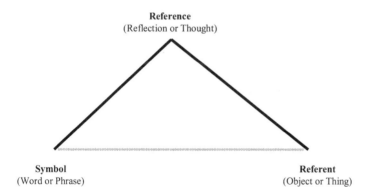

Figure 14 – Understanding (Ogden & Richards Pg. 324 modified)

Wiener also describes the work of Ogden and Richards (1936; 1995) who propose a model that underlies the confusion of words and the things that they are intended to represent – Figure 14. The key is that the triangle has no base (dashed line) and that there is no direct relation between a thing and a word. Ogden and Richards argue that one cannot sit on the word chair for example, but that all three aspects must be present for effective communications, and understanding, to occur.

Turbayne (1962) cautions that one must not confuse literal truth, and metaphor. Turbayne quotes Aristotle as saying (Pg. 11): "metaphor (*meta-phora*) consists of giving the thing a name that belongs to something else; the transference (*epi-phora*) being either from genus to species [general to specific] or from species to species..." Turbayne explains that this definition includes synecdoche (society for high society, cutthroat for assassin, creature for man, or boards for stage), metonymy (lands belonging to the crown), catachresis (blind mouths), and metaphor or analogy (giving a thing that has a name another name). Turbayne cautions that one should not mistake the *mask* (the mask we wear for society) for the *face* (who we really are) in the use of metaphors.

In *The Myth of Metaphor* (Turbayne 1962), Turbayne states that all overt acts may be thought of as a metaphor expressing some inner condition. Among the many citations of literature, art, music, architecture, and poetry, the author cites MacBeth as saying (Pg. 73): "we know a thing when we understand it, and we understand it when we can interpret or tell what it signifies." He also points to Hamlet who said before speaking with his mother (Shakespeare 2005) (Pg. 29): "I will speak daggers to her, but use none." This is a use of language to indicate far more that just the overt interactions between mother and son, and as a larger view of how people pursue the reconciliation of social differences. Turbayne states that the image of the tree as a metaphor for life and immortality is widely used by nearly all peoples.

McLuhan (1964) suggests a variation on Robert Browning's poem (McLuhan's version): a man's reach must exceed his grasp or what's a metaphor. McLuhan says that all media are in fact active metaphors and information provides the power to translate experience into senses rapidly. McLuhan quotes Bertrand Russell as saying that the great discovery of the twentieth century was the technique of suspended judgment – critical to effective communications, and to knowledge transfer. He also tells a story of Tzu-Gung who is passing by a farmer that is irrigating his fields by carrying which he obtains through climbing up a well. Tzu-Gung suggests the use of a lever and rope, but the farmer refused saying that he would then become like the machine. McLuhan also proposes that games are substitutes for stress, and represent models of culture.

Wheelwright (1967) begins a discussion on metaphor by quoting the *Tao Te Ching*: "the Tao that can be spoken is not the real Tao" illustrating the difficulties of communicating deep and complex ideas with language. The author describes the use of epiphor to describe similarity between a thing that is relatively well known and a thing that is more obscurely known. Wheelwright uses the example of Edgar describing maturity and readiness in *King Lear,* as *ripeness is all.* The author describes a diaphor as a juxtaposition of experience and movement, and illustrates a combination of epiphor and diaphor in the *Tao Te Ching*: "we put thirty spokes together and call it a wheel; but it is on the space where there is nothing that the usefulness of the wheel depends." The author also quotes Alan Watts: "myth is to be defined as a complex of stories – some no doubt fact, and some fantasy – which, for various reasons, human beings regard as demonstrations of the inner meaning of the universe and of human life." The idea being that myths reflect the metaphoric constructs of different cultural groups.

Wheelwright also describes the diaphoric myths of the Vedic god of fire, Agni – he lights up the world and therefore is the god of wisdom; he burns and therefore is a stern judge and punisher. The author says that presence, to know someone as a presence instead of as a lump of matter, is to meet him or her with an "open, listening, responsive attitude." A connection to their presence must consider their culture, myths, epiphors and diaphors.

Wheelwright ends her work by stating, "a person of intellectual sensitivity is plagued by the sense of a perpetual Something More beyond anything that is actually known or conceived. A wise beginning for any large inquiry is to entertain the postulate that reality, or a goodly part of it, is not obvious and discoverable by overt public methods of investigation, but is latent, subtle, and shy." This suggests why metaphors are so important in cross-cultural understanding.

Hawkes (1972) describes the forms of transference in speech as figures of speech or tropes (using a word in a sense to which is does not properly belong), and that metaphors are the fundamental figure of speech. The first traditional category is a simile, which proposes the transference by use of *like* or *as if.* Hawkes suggests that a simile involves a more visually inclined description than a metaphor (example like a red-faced farmer).

Next is the synecdoche, in which the transference is something, carried over to stand for another thing (example twenty summers for twenty years). The last method being metonymy, where the transference occurs as the name of a thing takes the place of something else (example the white house for the president of the United States). Hawkes states that all are forms of metaphor. Hawkes believes that all meanings are universally relative, appropriate to and valid in the cultural context in which they occur (Richards 1965), and that language actually causes reality to exist. He also states that the use of metaphors give messages complexity of meaning. Hawkes ends by contrasting the neo-classical view that metaphor is a romantic extension or foreground of language, with the neo-romantic view that metaphors create reality.

Cohen, Wheelwright, and Hawkes point to the important use of metaphors in understanding and communicating complex ideas. Time is scarce for Project Managers, and having tools that facilitate a rapid transfer of knowledge is a valuable commodity. In addition, a nuance rich communication format may elevate the dialogues in other aspects of the interpersonal interactions of a team with a leader.

Cohen (1979) notes that the works of Hobbes and Locke drove the thinking on metaphors as being frivolous and inessential until the twentieth century, and that they do not contain or transmit knowledge, do not connect directly with facts, and do not offer genuine meaning. Cohen points to the work of Max Black (1954-55), and his belief that metaphors hold a cognitive status, not just an emotive one. Cohen suggests that metaphors achieve intimacy (**empathy, trust,** and **communication)** between the speaker and hearer by: 1) the speaker issues a sort of concealed invitation, 2) the hearer expends special effort to accept the invitation, and 3) the transaction constitutes the acknowledgement of a community. Cohen points to Aristotle who said that a good metaphor implies an intuitive perception of the similarity in things that are dissimilar.

Nisan and Kohlberg (1982) performed a moral judgment (**trust**) study in Turkey. According to the authors, moral justifications can be broken down into four modes:

Situation Bound

- Norm following – A justification in terms of existing rules. Example, one should not steal
- Utilitarian – A justification in terms of the material consequences

Interpretative

- Perfectionist – A justification in terms of achieving harmony. Example, avoiding guilt
- Deontological – A justification in terms of justice or equity

Nisan and Kohlberg hypothesized that the situation bound modes were farther from the experiences of the study group than were the interpretative modes. Their test groups were students that lived in villagers and urban environments in Turkey. The results of the study showed that the modes described above were indeed universal as hypothesized when compared to similar surveys conducted in the USA. Not surprisingly, the study found a slower rate of development of moral judgment in the villages in Turkey than in the USA. A leader must imbue the culture of the organization(s) and the team to each member. Components of culture are values and character, and the way that such knowledge is provided to the members must be dependent upon the culture.

Smith and Simmons (1983) argue that organizational psychology should become more attuned with myths (a chief executive's deification for example), and that metaphors must have a context if they are to be understood. The author's points to two metaphors - *the snow blankets the ground* and *the thick smog blankets the city* – as illustrations for the necessity to understand context when considering the metaphorical use of the word blanket (**communications**). Without knowledge of what snow or smog is the metaphor will not take root. The authors also study the transformation of an organization under inspirational leadership in what they call a *rumpelstiltskin* organization. In such an organization, there is the belief that straw can be turned into gold.

Gioia and Poole (1984) address the issue of scripts in organizations. They contend that understanding is frequently accomplished by means of metaphor (Lakoff and Johnson 1980), and that a script is a heuristic device that helps people understand a new issue in terms of an old one (**communications**). They contend that scripts are metaphorical in nature, and go on to propose future research into scripts and their use in organizations.

In one of his many books on myth, Campbell (1986) points to the work of Adolf Bastian and his notion of local and universal myths and metaphors. Of the universal primal compulsions, Campbell points to the voraciousness of life, the sexual generative urge, and the impulse to plunder. He describes the metaphorical voyages in religious belief of examples like Jesus rising from the dead, and suggests that the metaphors become myth when transformed by the fusion with concordant insights.

Campbell said that myths are like dreams, being derived from experience and making use of metaphor. He describes a formula from Immanuel Kant who defines the psychological and metaphysical aspects of myths and metaphors as: "the promotion of the happiness of the children (a) is related to the parents' love (b), so is the welfare of the human race (c) related to that unknown in God (x) which we call God's love (a is to b as c is to x – an imbalanced relationship)."

Campbell closes by describing the reason that human beings rely on myth and metaphor, particularly in religions. He quotes Gothe as saying, "everything transitory is but a metaphor," and Nietzsche as saying, "everything eternal is but a metaphor." This describes the universality of need for cultures to devise myth and metaphor to define and describe religious beliefs, and by extension complex ideas.

Mac Cormac (1990) states that there are three levels of metaphors (**communications**): 1) a linguistic surface level, 2) a deeper linguistic level, and 3) the deepest level of cognitive activity. The author considers metaphor within a knowledge process, and that metaphors construct linguistic bridges from the embodied mind to culture.

Highwater (1994) writes about the artistic use of metaphors to describe the indescribable. The author considers most of the arts in his survey including visual arts, music, written art, and dance. He points to the Balinese *Barong* (mythical character) and *Wayong* (theatre) as metaphors for their culture, and believes that they convey far more than just the movements of physical shapes. Highwater also points to Picasso's Guernica as being the essence of metaphor as it elicits a response from a viewer through allusions (**empathy** and **communications**). As with the authors above, Highwater describes the issue of complexity and subtlety in the communication of knowledge.

In an article about American art and metaphors Sweet (1995) opines that (HTML no page numbers): "A society is as strong as the belief in its metaphors permits, and it lasts as long as that belief continues. In addition, because metaphors are images, images are pictures, pictures can be made of or evoked through words, paint, clay, and sound, then art must be viewed as a fundamental means of sustaining existence and identity. After all, most cultures have assumed the primacy of art from the Cro Magnons of the Lascaux caves, through fifth century BCE Athens, to the Florence of Michelangelo and da Vinci. When a general such as Sophocles wrote plays and popes knew power to be maintained via images, we'll have to assume those fellows were aware that fighting and praying were dependent on the metaphor and not the other way around, as our present culture would have it" (**communications, power,** and **empathy**).

3.3 Cultural Metaphor Theory -1998 thru 2003

Jolley, Zhi et al. (1998) found that there is a progression from color, to subject matter, to metaphor from childhood to adulthood in both Britain and China. Interestingly they found that the Chinese group was more likely to match drawings on visual metaphors than those children in Britain were, and that this may be due to the differences in art education in the two groups. This could also be the due to the fact that in China the language itself is a series of pictographs.

Lennie (1999) begins an article by surveying the warring factions over the use of metaphors in management thinking: those who believe the metaphor is overemphasized (Reed 1990), those who believe it is a critical component (Morgan 1986), and those who believe it has become static and cumbersome (Peters 1992). Lennie points to the work of Ricoeur (1977) who believed that we only know things in relation to other things, and to *metamorphize* is the ability to make these connections between things known and not known. Lennie states (Pg. 49): "all metaphor generates knowledge, but not all metaphor generates relevant knowledge," and that metaphor is experience in the knowledge that is produced, not a disembodied concept.

Lennie argues that metaphoric experience forms chaotic and fragmentary ideas into a whole concept, and therefore is an organizational talent. Lennie uses one example of a performance review where the manager doing the review describes her feelings and impressions, by using metaphors, to organize her own internal feelings and observations – part of a management skill set.

Loosemore and Muslmani (1999) prepared an article for the International Journal of Project Management that focused on inter-cultural communications on construction projects in the Persian gulf. They begin with an overview of the cultural identities in the region, and point to the cultural differences in how information is processed (high context and low context communications), non-verbal considerations like kinesics (body movements) and proxemics (physical proximity), paralanguage (how something is said), and object-language (physical appearance). The authors also point to the considerations of monochronic (structured) and polychronic (non-structured) views of time, and power distance (Hofstede).

Loosemore and Muslmani investigated the degree of sensitivity that UK nationals have towards the Arab cultures, and how to predict potential communication problems. What they found was (Pg. 5) "not very encouraging" due to the insensitivities and lack of cross-cultural training and knowledge. This is not, unfortunately, an uncommon problem in the international marketplace from personal experience. Frequently, cross-cultural training is simply self-inflicted and ad-hoc.

Kociatkiewicz (2000) explores the potential for role playing as a metaphor for organizing. The author states that organizations, and the process of organizing, can be accomplished through myths or stories that are negotiated and told by the participants. As with the definition of leadership utilized in this work (inspiring the desire to follow – Figure 5) the process of empowering this communication and storytelling, the members of an organization invent the organization.

Marquardt and Berger (2000) point to the work of the Caux Roundtable (Curtin 1996; Carlson and Blodgett 1997) which developed what is believed to be the first international code of business ethics in 1994:

- Responsibility of business to look beyond their shareholders and economic growth toward stakeholders by improving lives (**empathy**), sharing wealth, and shaping the future (**transformation**) of the global communities in which they operate.
- Economic and social responsibilities of businesses to contribute to the social advancement, human rights, education, and vitalization of host nations and the world community.
- Need for **trust** and sincerity in business behavior to facilitate business transactions on the global scale.
- Respect for international and domestic rules.
- Protecting and improving the world environment.
- Support for multilateral trade systems worldwide.
- Avoiding participation in and not condoning unethical and illegal business practices.

As indicated above, knowledge of cultural ethics and values are essential for leaders. However, it is essential that a leader provide a benchmark or goal that her followers strive to achieve, part of a team culture.

Gibson and Zellmer-Bruhn (2001) state that metaphors are a (Pg. 276): "key mechanism through which we comprehend abstract concepts and perform abstract reasoning. Furthermore the metaphor is a source of cognitive priming in that it brings forth semantic, behavioral, and affective responses (Blair and Banaji 1996)..." (**communications**). The authors point to the sports metaphors used in America as describing specific roles, limited time, clarity of context, hierarchical recognition, and sense of belonging for the US people. The authors contend that the two cultural values likely to influence teamwork are power distance and individualism (Hofstede 1980), and that in high power distance cultures metaphors with clear roles will be used (**power**). As noted with American metaphors, cultures with high individualism will be less likely to use metaphors that involve broad activity scope – they tend to be well defined. Gibson and Zellmer-Bruhn note that research has demonstrated that organizational cultures and national cultures are not parallel constructs, but they have distinct contents and influences, thus metaphors vary across organizations.

Gibson and Zellmer-Bruhn conclude that their study confirms that teamwork metaphors vary according to culture and organization. They point to the work of Adler who argued that is it legitimate to use stereotypes in cross-cultural contexts if they are (Pg. 297): "descriptive rather than evaluative, substantiated, and subject to change." They also caution that metaphors do not pertain evenly to all subgroups in a culture, but that they highlight cultural frames providing a rich vocabulary for discussion and mutual understanding (**empathy**). They conclude that a given metaphor is likely to convey complex meaning, and that it is best comprehended alongside a rich understanding of the cultural or organizational context.

Cornelissen (2002) addresses organizational identity and the use of live and dead metaphors. According to the author live metaphors as precursors to theory, and dead metaphors are concepts that have become second nature to the organization (**empathy** and **communications**). The author points to the work of Montuschi (1995) and his outline of the four stages of metaphoric transfer:

- Transposition – projection of source domain on a target domain to establish equivalence (speaker, listener, common context).
- Interpretation – further hypothesis and synthesis.
- Correction – is the metaphor apt.
- Spelling out – acceptance of the heuristic.

The knowledge transfer from explicit to tacit follows a similar path. One difference is that in metaphor a concept rather than chains of linguistic information are being projected.

Boers (2003) suggests that Conceptual Metaphor Theory (CMT) is still vying with other theories on how metaphors can best be applied for pedagogical purposes. He states that there are three types of cross-cultural variation in metaphor usage (**empathy** and **communication**):

- Differences in source-target mapping – people with different context
- Differences in value-judgments – people with different values
- Differences in pervasiveness – compared to other metaphorical figures

Boers separates metaphors into primary (image-schema) and complex categories. He argues that the primary type is more a universal metaphor (an example of primary would be *more is up*, *less is down*), and that the complex type is more apt to cultural-specific variations (an example *theories are buildings*).

Deignan (2003) addresses the variability of metaphors across cultures, and their source domains. He begins by stating that there are cross-linguistic differences in metaphors, that some metaphors may not exist in another language, and that some have different details. One example he uses is of *parent company* which in Farsi means one that supplies raw material to a company that uses them in manufacturing (Henderson 1986) (**communications, power, empathy**). Deigman argues that different cultures hold different beliefs about attributes of the source domain, and that the source domain may be less salient in different cultures. The author suggests that there is a widespread tendency to draw on the animal kingdom as a source of similes for human behavior. Deignan concludes by saying that many of the metaphors he found had a historical basis.

Kövecses (2003) studies the usage of metaphors in helping people to learn a foreign language. He concludes that conceptual metaphors are cultural entities just as are cognitive ones.

Maasen and Weingart (2003)[7] provide an overview in their book relating to metaphors (Pg. 2): "As any other unit of knowledge, or even better than others, metaphors indicate a certain promiscuity of knowledge, in general. Metaphors are special only in that they bear the traces of their journeys through diverse areas of knowledge more obviously. Politics, science, art, technology, media, economics, religion …" The authors describe the long and wide debate regarding the importance and dangers of metaphors.

---

[7] For a complete bibliography see Noppen, van, J.P. and Holst, E. (1990) Metaphor II. A Classified Bibliography Publications, 1985–1990, Amsterdam: John Benjamins Publishing Company. And, Noppen, van, J.P, de Knop S. and de Jongen, R. (1985) Metaphor. Bibliography of Post 1970 Publications, Amsterdam: John Benjamins Publishing Company.

On what the authors call the *supradiscursive* approach (top-down), the authors quote from Harrington (1995) who says (Pg. 359): "metaphors do much more than just lend old lexical meanings to new objects: they are literally ways whereby societies 'build' webs of collective meaning; create what we would call cultural cosmologies or meaning-worlds that, once built, for better or worse become the 'homes' in which we reason and act, places that constrain without determining any of our particular conclusions or actions" (**communications** and **empathy**).

On what the authors call the *subdiscursive* approach (bottom-up), Maasen and Weingart point to the work of Lakoff (1995) who says (Pg. 170): "moral action is conceptualized in terms of financial transaction. Just as literal bookkeeping is vital to economic functioning, so moral bookkeeping is vital to social functioning." Lakoff was analyzing the right-to-life discussions in America.

Maasen and Weingart state (Pg. 33), "most fundamentally, in our view, metaphors do not rule discourse 'from below' [bottom-up] in a somewhat mysterious fashion. Rather, metaphors perform their task on the surface of discourses. Here we can observe the discursive selection of certain metaphors, the emphasis of certain aspects of a metaphor (and the suppression of others), and the performance of certain functions (in favor of others)." The authors review the semantic approach where metaphors serve to describe a phenomenon, the pragmatic approach where metaphors serve in a direct **communicative** way (words mean what they mean), and the constructivist approach where the metaphor serves to create a new vocabulary. The authors also view chaos as a metaphor (chaos theory connection).

Özçalişkan (2003) writes about the Turkish metaphorical structure of death, life, sickness, body, and time by using the Conceptual Metaphor Theory (CMT). The author begins his article by saying that the metaphor of life as a journey is included in Turkish thought (Pg. 284): "Dünyaya ilk geldihim anda Yürüdüm aynk zamanda Idki kapklk bir handa Gidiyorum gündüz gece (Veysel 1991: 221) or The first moment I came to the world, I walked at the same time, In a caravanserai with two doors I am going day and night." His conclusion is that there is a high degree of similarity between English and Turkish metaphorical mappings. He speculates that the lack of variation could be because both cultures are western, secular, and literate. He also suggests that Christianity, Judaism, and Islam are western religions and therefore share concepts about birth, death, and after life (**trust, empathy, and communications**).

Renard and Eastwood (2003) use the metaphor of masks in a paper that focuses on sub-cultures. They remind us that masks have been used since early Greek dramas, and that the actor became a part of the metaphor of the prop when wearing the mask. The authors argue that a one-size-fits-all approach to culture will fail when individual characteristics are taken into consideration. Renard and Eastwood argue that one must speak in congruence with the mask or they risk being misunderstood (**communications** and **empathy**), considered as an outsider, or considered disruptive.

Ryan (2003) introduces what he calls a matrix to describe the basis of symbolic western concepts. Ryan describes the matrix as having four pillars on the horizontal axis of justice, beauty, goodness, and truth - justice and beauty being meaning, and goodness and truth being values. On the vertical scale Ryan places the nature concept (humanity), and the God concept (spirit). Ryan argues that this matrix constitutes a metaphoric way of looking at and understanding metaphors, or as the title of the article indicates a Geography of the Symbolic. The author quotes Geertz's statement about humans without culture (Geertz 1973) (Pg. 212) : "They would be unworkable monstrosities with very few useful instincts, fewer recognizable sentiments, and no intellect: mental basket cases. As our central nervous system—and most particularly its crowning curse and glory, the neocortex—grew up in great part in interaction with culture, it is incapable of directing our behavior or organizing our experience without the guidance provided by systems of significant symbols" (**communications, power, trust, empathy, transformation**).

Ryan notes that ritual burial and the creation of symbolic objects can be traced back some 28,000 years, and the ability to speak back 60,000 years. He concludes that (Pg. 213): "The symbolic can be regarded as the administration of all awareness and experience, not 'working upon' already perceived objects and events, but 'working upon' the act of perception. The matrix has a double hold on meaning, constituting both vocabulary and grammar, or form and content, or site and method, or building plan and building material. The symbolic is thus the scheme of things as well as the notion of the 'scheme of things'; it is the horizon that cannot be transcended even as we attempt to reduce it to one of our tools."

Schneider and Barsoux (2003) reference an article that addresses a conceptual model of corporate moral development (Reidenbach and Robin 1990) that includes five stages:

- Stage I – the amoral organization. The get away with all you can stage.

- Stage II – the legalistic organization. Push the technical rules, and use damage control when social problems occur.
- Stage III – the responsive organization. Reactive mentality but a growing balance between profits and ethics.
- Stage IV – the emerging ethical organization. Active concern for ethical outcomes. Ethical perception has focus but lacks organization.
- Stage V – the ethical organization. Ethical analysis is fully integrated. Balance between economics and ethics.

Schneider and Barsoux explore an important aspect of cross-cultural leadership knowledge, that of ethical development. In cross-cultural leadership, a person must understand the ethics and morals of the organization within which the team functions. As shown in Figure 11, the level of organizational culture is important in developing knowledge of the surroundings, and then communicating them to the followers.

Yu (2003) presents a case in which the abstract concept of courage is understood in part via a conceptual metaphor grounded in the body, but shaped by a culture-specific metaphorical understanding of the gallbladder (Pg. 15): "courage (boldness, bravery, daring, pluck, and spunk) is *Qi* in gallbladder" (**transformation** and **power**).

According to Yu (Pg. 14): "the interaction between common bodily experiences and varied cultural experiences determines the extent to which conceptual metaphors are universal, widespread, or culture-specific (see also (Lakoff and Johnson 1999))." Yu also goes on to say that (Pg. 14): "at the same time, the same basic embodied experiences, in which many conceptual metaphors are grounded, may be defined differently by different cultural beliefs and values.[8]" He quotes a Chinese proverb as saying (Pg. 15): "*Wu-dan zhi ren shishi nan -* everything appears difficult to people without gallbladder," and points out that proverbs are generally regarded as repositories of folk wisdom.[9]

The author also provides examples of negative idioms such as (Pg. 21) dan-da bao-shen (gall-big wrap-body) "courage appears to be bigger than body; audacious in the extreme." Yu

---

[8]See also Gibbs, R. (1999). Taking metaphor out of our heads and putting it into the cultural world. In R. Gibbs& G. Steen (Eds.), Metaphor in cognitive linguistics (pp. 145–166). Amsterdam: John Benjamins.
[9] See also White, G. (1987). Proverbs and cultural models: An American psychology of problem solving. In D. Holland & N. Quinn (Eds.), Cultural models in language and thought (pp. 151–172). New York: Cambridge University Press.

provides the following mapping to describe the connections (it should be noted that other authors have used a similar device to illustrate the connections between conceptual ideas (source domains) and how they map onto target domains):

Source domain	Target domain
physical container of courage	→ gallbladder
gaseous energy of qi in the container	→ gal rage
capacity of the container	→ aa al dt a gal rage
degree of internal pressure of the container	→ degree a gal rage

Yu explains that the gallbladder is related to the liver which relies on the gallbladder for wisdom and judgment (**transformation** and **trust**), and to the heart in making just decisions – the gallbladder as prime minister. He contends that the metaphor is in keeping with an ancient Chinese philosophy, which advocates that man is an integral part of nature, and for Taoists that the body is a microcosm of the universe.

Yu (2003) concludes with (Pg. 17): "that is, conceptual metaphors are usually derived from bodily experiences; cultural models, however, filter bodily experiences for specific target domains of conceptual metaphors; and cultural models themselves are very often structured by conceptual metaphors. As indicated by the direction of the arrows, any one element constraining the next one will affect the third one as well. In short, without the body there would be no worldviews. However, the lenses of worldviews are 'culturally colored' and 'metaphorically framed.' It is through such "glasses" that we cognize the world" (**communication**).

Yu states that the central metaphor in English and Indo-European languages is *the mind is a body* ((Lakoff and Johnson 1999); (Jakel 1995); (Radden 1996) and others) with four special cases which occur in Chinese as well as Western cultures:
- Thinking is moving - si-lu [thinking-route/path] 'train of thought; thinking'
- Thinking is perceiving - kan-fa [see-method] 'a way of looking at a thing; perspective; view; opinion'
- Thinking is object manipulation - sixiang baofu [thought bundle] 'load weighing on one's mind'
- Acquiring ideas is eating - hulun tun zao [whole swallow dates] 'swallow a date whole—lapup information without digesting it; read without understanding'

Yu concludes that while there are conceptual similarities between Chinese and Western cultures in the *mind are a body* schema, there are specific differences at the linguistic level (**communication**). Part of this is due to such considerations as the heart and mind being conceived of as the homes of emotion and thought in Western cultures, whereas in Chinese culture both functions reside in the heart. Yu closes by quoting Neumann (2001) saying that cross-linguistic studies of metaphors (Pg. 162): "furnish methodologically sound evidence for the cognitive status of metaphor, as cannot be derived from a monolingual perspective."

3.4 Cultural Metaphor Theory - 2004 thru 2005

Hunter (2004) suggests that the Bible, Koran, Aristotle, and Confucius set forth principles and values such as integrity (**transformation**), respect for human life, self-control, honesty (**trust**), courage (**transformation**), commitment, and self sacrifice as accepted and shared values. He suggests that people can teach and discipline ourselves to do what is not natural until it becomes a habit. Hunter recounts a Zen Buddhist story of a samurai that asked the Zen master to explain the difference between good and evil. The Zen master responded (Pg. 137): "I will not waste my time with such scum as you, where upon the samurai flew into a rage and threatened to cut the Zen master into pieces for the insult. The Zen master responded, that is what evil is like. The samurai understood the wisdom of the statement and responded thank you for your insight, good master. The Zen master then said, that is what goodness is like."

According to Kramer (2004) metaphors in music construct a bridge between the body with the external world (Pg. 11): "where music is concerned, this bridging connects the acoustic reality of music to the full array of its worldly circumstances, be they social, psychological, cultural, political, material, or historical. These spheres are not really separate, but they often seem to be, an illusion we have long been taught to cultivate." He also quotes Wittgenstein[10] as saying (Pg. 14), "Worter sind Taten - Words are deeds," and draws the conclusion that metaphors in music do matter. Kramer goes on to say that (Pg. 18): "metaphysics forms images of **truth** that prove, in the end, to be metaphors; metaphors construct metaphysical fictions that prove themselves, in the end, by their value as truth. Language, we might speculate, has a tendency to slow this process; music accelerates it." The consideration of music in understanding culture and cultural metaphors is one component of cultural intelligence (CQ).

---

[10] See Ludwig Wittgenstein: Culture and value, ed. GH von Wright with Heikld Nyman, trans. Peter Winch (Chicago: University of Chicago Press, 1980), p.46.

Perkins (2004) in a recent book regarding the USA described what he called the *corporatocracy* – the promotion of corporate interests as a foreign policy, without due regard to the future, by using aggressive leadership (what he states became the hallmark for USA business schools). The author uses the examples of Guatemala, Panama, Venezuela, Iraq, and Indonesia to illustrate his contentions. One of the prerequisites for him was always to prepare for work in other countries by learning as much as possible about the culture where he would be working before his departure. Perkins believes that people will warm to you if you open yourself to their culture. The author describes his role as an *Economic Hit Man* (EHM) for US interests. As an EHM, his job was to overstate the long-term economic viability of large expensive projects, obtain development bank loans, create business for large US firms, and to saddle the country with long-term debt and economic dependence on the US. US managers need to understand that many people either know or suspect this about the United States.

Szulanski and Jensen (2004) open their article by saying (Pg. 347): "a central tenet in viewing transfers of knowledge as the replication of organizational routines is the importance of the template. We hypothesize that a template, i.e. a working
example, is essential in replicating knowledge assets effectively." The authors confirmed that templates increase the stickiness (ability of knowledge to be replicated) in the knowledge transfer process. More will be discussed about the usefulness of a routine, largely unwritten as the authors suggest, in Section 3.6.

Kövecses (2005) cites the work of Lakoff and Johnson who claimed that people actually understand the world with metaphors, and he provides test data from other studies to support this assertion. The author contends that linguistic metaphors are expressions of metaphorical concepts in the brain's conceptual system. Kövecses asserts that a metaphor includes linguistic, conceptual, social-cultural, neural and bodily components. The author believes that abstract concepts are largely metaphorical, and that the source and target domains help to explain the universality and particularity of metaphors. For example, in the statement, *love is warmth,* warmth is the physical or source component and love is the target or abstract component.

Kövecses believes that the *correspondence* between source and target domains is what makes a metaphor. He uses Hungarian, English and Chinese to put forward his contention that basic metaphors such as happiness, anger, time, event structure and self are in fact near universal. It is interesting to note that the dimensions of time and self are decidedly different in the work of

Hofstede and others. While the linguistic metaphors themselves are considered to be near universal, Kövecses notes that the *congruent metaphors* are culturally specific and are filled-in from the near universal level. One example he uses is the concept of *hara* in Japanese, meaning anger is in the belly. No other culture uses this adaptation of the near universal anger metaphor. In this way, the Japanese are *congruent* with the near universal level, but are culturally specific.

Kövecses cites the work of Heine who indicated that spatial reference, relating to the body, is of primary importance in the construction of metaphors. Kövecses summarizes that the components of metaphors are:

- Source domain
- Target domain
- Experiential basis
- Neural structures
- Relationships between source and target
- Metaphorical linguistic expressions (**communications**)
- Mappings
- Entailments
- Blends
- Nonlinguistic realizations
- Cultural models (**empathy**)

Kövecses separates the causes of variations in metaphors into differential experiences and differential cognitive preferences. Experiences because our experiences as human beings vary, and cognitive preferences for abstract thought. The author considers both of these as being affected concurrently, and makes connections back to the work of Hofstede. Kövecses considers the following items influence the differentiation of metaphors:

Context
- Physical environment – geography, flora and fauna, dwellings, etc.
- Social – **power** relations, social pressure

Cultural
- Differential Memory - Social History, and Personal History
- Differential Concerns & Interests - Social, Personal
- Experiential Focus – References to personal body

- Viewpoint Preference – choice of different options in a culture
- Prototypes and Framing – Source domains, and context (Berger and Mohr 1982)
- Metaphor versus Metonymy Preference

Kövecses closes by reiterating that the three main components of diversity are embodiment (bodily experience), context (social-cultural experience), and cognitive preferences.

Nicholson and Anderson (2005) address the issues of myth and metaphor in an article focused on entrepreneurs and the linguistics of news reports. They begin by quoting Schramm (cited in (Brassington and Pettit 2000)) as saying that communications is (Pg. 156): "the process of establishing a commonness or oneness of thought between a sender and receiver." The authors observe that news in general is (Pg. 158): "not an inert mirror but rather plays an active role in the creation and manipulation of reality" (**communication**). Thus, the global news information services such as CNN or Al-Jazeera not only report facts, but also create reality through metaphors.

Nicholson and Anderson say that (Pg. 166): "enterprise culture has all of the defining features of a social anthropological belief system or way of seeing" (Berger and Mohr 1982) (**trust** and **empathy**). For example, in 1989 one comment made to describe an entrepreneur was (Pg. 164) "a hero conquering disability or economics, at the end of the political evolutionary scale," contrasted with the vision in 2000 of rarely portrayed as a hero. The authors point out that the media is constructing an image of business in the international markets that connects this notion to the notion of capitalism. Nicholson and Anderson argue that this alters cultural perceptions.

3.5 Cultural Metaphor Theory - Gannon

One of the most significant works on cultural metaphors discovered in this research was that of Gannon (2004). Gannon begins by quoting Lakoff and Johnson (1980) as saying (Pg. xiii): "if we are right in suggesting that our conceptual system is largely metaphorical, then the way we think, what we experience, and what we do every day is very much a matter of metaphor." Gannon then defines cultural metaphors (Pg. xiii): "A cultural metaphor is any activity, phenomenon, or institution with which members of a given culture emotionally and/or cognitively identify. As such, the metaphor represents the underlying values expressive of the culture itself…Culture allows us to fill in the blanks, often unconsciously, when action is required, and cultural metaphors help us to see the values leading to action."

Gannon divides his book into the framework developed by Traindis and Gelfand (1998), Fiske (1991), and Huntington (1996): 1) horizontal collectivism or community sharing, 2) vertical collectivism or hierarchical ranking, 3) horizontal individualism or equality matching, 4) vertical individualism or market pricing, and 5) cleft cultures or cultures torn from its roots with diverse subcultures.

Gannon first points to the work of the anthropologists Kluckhohn and Strodtbeck (1961) and their six dimensions of cultural comparisons (**empathy, power, communications, trust, transformation**):

- Does the society consider people good, or bad?
- Does the society believe people should live in harmony with nature?
- Does the society assume individualism or collectivism for relationships?
- What is the primary mode of activity (go with the flow, doing something, setting goals)?
- What is the perception of space?
- What is the society's temporal perception (past, present, future)?

Gannon also describes the work of Hall and Hall (1990) and the cultural dimensional system that they defined:

- Context – the amount of information that must be explicitly stated if a communication is to be successful.
- Space – the way societies deal with personal space.
- Time – polychromic (multi-tasking) and monochromic (one thing at a time).
- Information flow – the structure and speed of messages (**communications**).
- Gannon then points to the work of Hofstede (2001) who developed, as noted earlier, five dimensions for comparing cultures (**power** and **empathy**).

Gannon explains that his work utilizes all of these concepts. The author then lists the topics that were considered when undertaking the research including:

- Religion
- Aural space and the degree to which society reacts negatively to loud noise
- Holidays and ceremonies

- Humor
- Language, both oral and written
- Non-oral body language communication
- Sports as a reflection of cultural values
- Political structure of the society
- Educational system of the society
- History of the society, but only as it reflects cultural mindsets
- Food and eating behavior
- Rate of technological and cultural changes
- Organization and perspective on the work ethic and the relationship between superior and subordinate

Gannon describes the methodology utilized to frame the analysis of each culture that was studies. The author explains that Stage 1 provides a basic understanding of the culture, and that Stage 2 ((Triandis and Gelfand 1998); (Fiske 1991)) is needed to better specify the differences particularly in the relationship between culture and economics or business practices. Stage 3 includes the remaining *etic* considerations from Hofstede (2001) and Osland and Bird (2000). In Stage 4 Gannon applies the considerations listed above (religion, etc.) to the dimensions of Stages 1 thru 3.

Gannon warns, however, that sometimes culture is not important, and at other times critical. The author points out that an issue like economic status can neutralize cultural backgrounds. On this topic he uses the example of the positive reinforcement for children of middle-class families who enroll their children in music lessons, compared to the potential of negative reinforcement of *blue collar* families on skill development (Kagitcibasi 1990). The author also points to other conditions that produce stereotypes in cultures, like apartheid in South Africa.

Gannon says that (Pg. 15): "when **trust** is present, culture decreases in importance." He points to the work of Jarvenpaa, Knoll et al. (1998) who did a study of virtual teams and found that *quick trust* did in fact diminish the impact of culture.

On the issue of stereotypes, Gannon describes them as shorthand ways to classify multitudes of stimuli. He indicates, correctly, that stereotypes can be either positive or negative, and that the word has become more associated with the negative than with the positive. The author states

71

that social psychologists recognize that there are differences between people, and that the negative connotations relating to stereotypes have led us to deemphasize these differences. The author points to the work of Adler (1997) who argues that it is legitimate to use stereotypes, as long as they are descriptive rather than evaluative. Gannon contends that metaphors are not stereotypes, and the research results are provided to natives from each culture to assure that the findings are in fact descriptive.

To provide an overview of the 28 cultures in Gannon's book, it is best to begin with an overview of the sections. The following is a partial list of the different categories of cultures, and a brief description of some of the metaphors to provide a fuller understanding of the concepts:

Authority Ranking Cultures

* The Japanese Garden – there are wet and dry gardens in Japan. Wet gardens have water flowing and dry gardens are of the Zen Buddhist type with sand as a metaphor for water. Japanese society is fluid and changes without altering its essential character. As Gannon says (Pg. 31): "alone each droplet has a little force yet when combined with many others, enough force is produced to form a waterfall, which cascades into a small pond filled with carp." The garden is a reminder of the centrality of nature in Japanese society, religion (Shinto), and art. Gannon describes Japanese society in the four parts of harmony (*wa or shikata*) or the proper way of doing things, the combination of droplets or energies into group activities, spirit training (*seishen*), and aestetics.

The Japanese borrowed the techniques of rice farming from the Chinese, and the interrelatedness of tasks led to the importance of group activities. Gannon points to the proper way of doing things (*katas*) as a key component of the society. He describes the tendency of Japanese to wait at a cross walk for the permission to cross, even when no traffic is present. Experience indicates that Japanese in Tokyo would point to Japanese from the south as those who would be crossing in the absence of traffic. Having lived in Tokyo, this is a common occurrence and common knowledge for those who live there.

Gannon quotes a Japanese proverb to illustrate the idea of the individual droplets *the protruding nail will be hammered.* The Japanese sense of aesthetics is distinctive and embodied in the Japanese garden through the tranquil effect (*shibui*), and the merging of identity with object or mood (*mono-no-aware*).

India: The Dance of Shiva – there are numerous deities in the Hindu religion that represent manifestations of one supreme being. The Dance of Shiva reflects the cyclical (Brahma the creator, Vishnu the preserver, and Shiva the destroyer) nature of Indian culture, and dancing is considered one of the most important arts. Gannon relates the story of Ganesh as a symbol of the Indian people's recovery from episodes of hardship and occupation – a symbol of good arising from adversity.

Gannon states that in Hindu philosophy, the world is like a dream and the results of God's amusement (*lila*), and this philosophy leads people along a path as the Dance of Shiva leads the cosmos through its cycles. Gannon describes the close relationship between daily life, philosophy, and religion. He also goes on to explain the social fabric that includes the role of men and women, arranged marriages, caste, and families. Gannon quotes one Indian proverb relating to children, as (Pg. 56): "a son should be treated as a prince for 5 years; as a slave for 10 years; but from his 16th birthday as a friend." The author concludes by saying that the key to understanding Indian culture is Hindu philosophy and the journey toward salvation (*moksha*).

Equality Matching Cultures
- The German Symphony

Market Pricing Cultures
- American Football

Cleft National Cultures
- The Malaysian *Balik Kampung*

Torn National Cultures
- The Mexican Fiesta

Same Metaphor, Different Meanings
- China's Great Wall and Cross-Cultural Paradox – Gannon begins by describing the difficulty of assessing such a diverse culture, and points to the work of Ming-Jer Chen (2001) as an excellent reference - Chen indicates that paradox is central to Chinese thinking. Gannon says that the great wall has served the Chinese well throughout their difficult history, and that it has served their culture well. The author also notes that the concept of a long-term plan in China may be 50 to 100 years. The great wall construction was begun by Qin Shi Huang in 221 B.C., and was added to by subsequent emperors through the Ming dynasty in 1368.

As with many of the cultures studied, Gannon first turns to the issues of beliefs:

73

Confucianism and Taoism. Confucianism thought can be encapsulated in five terms: 1) human-heartedness (*jen*), 2) a superior man that is ready to accommodate others as much as possible (*chuntzu*), 3) propriety or the way things should be done (*li*), 4) the **power** by which men should be ruled (*te*), and 5) prominence of the arts (*wen*). Gannon points out that Confucianism is not a religion but a set of social/moral principles.

Taoism was supposedly created by Lao Tzu who was born in 604 B.C. (*Tao Te Ching*). The *Tao* has three overlapping meanings: 1) that it can only be known through mystical insight, 2) that it represents the rhythm of life, and 3) that it represents the way man should order his life in balance with the universe. The wall, which was constructed to both repulse and retain was constructed over a long period and is still the only man-made structure visible from space. Gannon points to the work of Fang (1999) for an in-depth review of negotiating styles between the Chinese and the west. Fang compares the work of Sun Tzu to that of Clausewitz.

Perspectives on Continents

- Australian Outdoor Recreational Activities

Gannon (2002) provides a description of the use of cultural metaphors to provide a direct window into other cultures (**empathy, communications, trust**). He suggests that cultural metaphors can facilitate a quick general understanding or sensitivity. In this article, Gannon describes his use of experiential exercises, video clips, and discussion to educate people about cross-cultural issues.

Gannon provides a metaphor for America to illustrate his idea about metaphors. It clearly demonstrates that the metaphor is an access portal, and not a detailed accounting of a culture. Gannon notes that at the turn of the 20th Century baseball may have represented an effective metaphor because of its link to the USA's agrarian origins. Gannon points to the work of Kaufman (1999) who points out, today many business leaders see their game as more like football. In football, independent players with multiple skills cooperate in a rule-oriented game that moves toward a goal in ten-yard increments.

Gannon suggests that training, at the MBA level, begins with a series of engaging but non-threatening questions like does culture matter, then do a short experiential exercise, and follow with a video clip. The author presents the five dimensions developed by Hofstede (2001) to students and then asks what is missing. When considering the metaphors for different cultures (American and Japanese for example) there is clearly far more to consider than just the dimensions developed by Hofstede.

Gannon points to the work of Fieg (1976) to describe how he came to understand cultural metaphors, and to reconcile the paradoxes in Hofstede's work to Gannon's experiences in Thailand. Fieg notes that in both cultures, there is a love of freedom, a dislike of pomposity. However, Thai's follow a complex group-oriented authority-ranking system of status where the leader is expected to ensure the welfare of subordinates, much like a father or mother. Fieg uses the metaphor of a rubber band to demonstrate the critical differences. In the United States, the rubber band tight most all of the time where in Thailand, the rubber band is loosely held most of the time. Thais feel work should be fun or *sanuk,* but when a superior issue an order compliance tends to be swift Thais want everyone to be happy, and there is the notion of *mai pen rai.* Virtually untranslatable but along the lines of *don't worry about anything.*"

Gannon believes that cross-cultural training should include three topics that are a dimensional perspective, cross-cultural communications (Hall and Hall 1990), and cultural metaphors. He describes one class example that requires teams to develop a marketing/advertising campaign for travel to another country that utilizes all three training topics. The slogan for the advertising campaign, he suggests, should not exceed 50 words.

3.6   Cultural Knowledge Transfer Model

Considering the above research, this work proposes a model for the transfer of cultural intelligence (CQ). When these dimensions are superimposed on cultural dimensions, there is a requirement for Cross-Cultural Leadership Intelligence (XLQ). The model proposed below suggests a process for acquiring this intelligence.

In the international business environment, change occurs quickly, and people must be ready and able to adapt quickly. A new business opportunity or project can well force a business manager or Project Manager into a cultural soup within hours. From experience, it is necessary to develop a quick understanding of basic customs and practices so that mistakes and faux pas are minimized. Then a rich knowledge and understanding of the culture can be achieved through the window of metaphors. A deep cultural understanding takes time to develop, and immersion in the culture is required. This three step process will be defined as basic customs ((Morrison, Conaway et al. 1994); (Harris, Moran et al. 2004)), cultural metaphors (Gannon 2004), and cultural immersion or living with/in the culture (Osland 1995). To borrow terminology from Six Sigma, basic customs would be considered *green belt* level knowledge; metaphors would be considered *black belt* level knowledge, and immersion *master black belt* level knowledge.

The knowledge transfer can be accomplished in a conventional manner: 1) Explicit information would be provided from books, on-line articles, tapes, recordings, lectures, and so forth, 2) Internalization of the information can be accomplished by discussion groups, self-study, exercises, case studies, etc., and by reflection, and 3) Application or externalization would be accomplished via presentations and explanation of the culture to other people. This process should then be utilized for each level in the model. It needs to be emphasized that this approach is intended to be an expedited one at the first levels, and not an exhaustive study of a country or culture. The idea is to provide enough knowledge for a person to work effectively and avoid big mistakes, while acquiring more knowledge.

For the best training, it is recommended that an individual from the culture who is part of the same company participate in the development of the exercises and the sessions. In this way, the culture of the firm may be integrated with the local culture. In a diverse economy, it is often the case that people may come from a lineage of a culture that is different from the one in which they are raised. This will skew the considerations and introduce more variables into the training and knowledge transfer efforts.

3.6.1   Green Belt

At this level, the individual would demonstrate a basic understanding of the culture and its customs along the dimensions listed below. The work of Morrison, Conaway et al. (1994) provides a solid approach to this first level. Their outline follows and is used for each of the sixty countries that they describe. To use a metaphor, this is the recognition that a cultural house exists, and how it differs from the one that is native to the observer:

Regional Background (Harris, Moran et al. 2004)

- Geography
- Trading treaties
- Demographics – basics

Country Background

- Geography (added) – where is the country and who are the neighbors
- History – one paragraph review
- Type of government – democracy, dictatorship, kingdom, etc.
- Language – primary language or languages
- Religion – majority religions
- Demographics – basics
- Time zone(s) (added)

Cultural Orientation

- Cognitive styles – how information is processed
- Negotiation strategies
- Value systems – very brief

Business Practices

- Appointments – the concept of time
- Negotiating - techniques
- Business Entertaining – some basic do's and don'ts

Protocol

- Greetings
- Titles and forms of address
- Gestures
- Dress
- Gifts

The approach taken by Harris, Moran et al. (2004) is based upon a regional perspective, for example Latin America. It covers the same items as are listed above, but from the generalized regional perspective. Thus, note the addition of the Regional Background as the first item.

At the completion of the *green belt* level, the individuals will have an understanding of how the new culture differs from their native culture, and some issues that need to be either addressed or avoided in interpersonal business **communications**. As *quick* ***trust*** is (Jarvenpaa, Knoll et al. 1998) essential for cross-cultural leadership (one hypothesis of this work), and empathy is closely related to developing trust, a *green belt* would be able to demonstrate a sensitivity and general understanding of the culture, and thus start the process of building trust.

3.6.2   Black Belt

At the more advanced level, individuals will need to further develop their understanding of the culture.   As has been described in this work, the use of metaphors will aid in the **communication** and understanding of complex ideas, and the **empathy** of understanding another culture.   Cultural metaphors will provide a means of developing a richer and broader understanding of a culture.   The list that follows is provided by Gannon (2004) as dimensions considered in the development of his cultural metaphors.   Some of the items are also addressed in the *green belt* level of knowledge, but are taken to a deeper level for the *black belt*.   To use a metaphor, this is the recognition that a cultural house exists, and that a metaphorical window permits the inspection of the interior of the house.

- Religion
- Early socialization and family structure
- Small group behavior
- Public behavior
- Leisure pursuits and interests
- Total lifestyle including work, leisure, home, and time allocations to each
- Aural space and the degree to which society reacts negatively to loud noise
- Roles and status of different members of society
- Holidays and ceremonies
- Greeting behavior
- Humor
- Language, both oral and written
- Non-oral body language communication
- Sports as a reflection of cultural values
- Political structure of the society
- Educational system of the society
- Traditions and the degree to which the established order is emphasized
- History of the society, but only as it reflects cultural mindsets
- Food and eating behavior
- Social class structure
- Rate of technological and cultural changes
- Organization and perspective on the work ethic and the relationship between superior and subordinate

At the completion of the *black belt* level, the individuals will have rich understanding of how the new culture differs from their native culture. Individuals will appreciate not only the superficial differences, but also the reasons underlying differences. Metaphorical knowledge will enable people to anticipate actions and reactions in the new culture, and to adapt the knowledge to new circumstances not studied. At the completion of *black belt*, training in the new culture the individual should see **trust** as developing and strong, **empathy** more deep and sustaining, **power** (referent) increasing, and **communication** skills strong and improving.

3.6.3   Master Black Belt

Ideally thought not often, an individual should have completed *green belt* and *black belt* training before becoming an expatriate. Then after living in the culture for at lease six months, an individual will have gained a richer knowledge of the culture by receiving explicit information, questioning, practicing, reflecting, and transforming this information into tacit knowledge. Also, and perhaps most important, an individual would have had the opportunity to employ the knowledge in the business and private arenas. This externalization, and the subsequent reflection and consideration, would broaden the knowledge of the culture. A *master black belt* would be capable of interpreting cultural behavior under circumstances of change. To use a metaphor, this is the recognition that a metaphorical doorway exists, and the individual has entered and explored the interior of the house and its occupants.

The additional training that should accompany the *master black belt* level of knowledge should include a thorough review of *etic* and *emic* cultural considerations described by such authors as: ((Triandis and Gelfand 1998); (Fiske 1991); (Huntington 1996); (Kluckhohn and Strodtbeck 1961); (Hall and Hall 1990); (Hofstede 2001); (House and Javidan 2004)). Experience shows that once the neural pathways have been created by learning a culture at the *master black belt* level, the exploration of other cultures becomes faster, and more nuanced. Thus, a firm can leverage their training costs, and improve their return on investment by training a pool of *master black belts*.

In a marketplace where cost minimization is essential, it is critical to deliver just enough cross-cultural training to fill the needs of the project or company. On some efforts, the basic understanding of other cultures is adequate, for the cost of the failure to act in an acceptable manner or aggravate those in other cultures can be minimized or repaired if necessary. A two-day business meeting in a different country can be accommodated by the *green belt* level training through self-study. On a project that will develop over three years, there is time for the parties to learn one another, and time to provide training at the *black belt* level at reasonable costs. However, short-term projects or endeavors (less than six months) that are complex (large number of partners or subcontractors, and/or technically challenging, and/or subject to rapid changes in the external environment) permit no time for blunders, or worse. The firm must prepare its own calculus relating to the risk/reward of not providing the level of training that is appropriate for the undertaking, and appropriate for the level of risk of failure. Figure 15 provides a graphic representation of the concept described for XLQ.

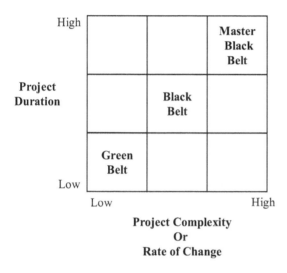

Figure 15 - Cultural Knowledge (Grisham)

3.7 Chapter Summary

This Chapter has provided a review of the literature on metaphors, and on how metaphors help people to communicate complex cultural information. The use of metaphors, storytelling, and poetry is further explored in a separate paper that expands on the use of these tools and techniques in an XLQ context (Grisham 2006). Included in the Chapter was a process model for the acquisition of XLQ. Thus far, culture and metaphor have been explored. In the next Chapter, the aspect of leadership will be examined in the Cross-Cultural Leadership Intelligence (XLQ) context.

4. Leadership Theory

4.1 Chapter Introduction

There are no shortage of leadership theories and studies, and there are numerous overlaps in terminology relating to the differences between leadership and management. This section of the work will focus on published leadership issues, research, and theory. Since some of the published research is related to culture, there are some unavoidable overlaps with the cultural section of this work. In addition, much of the literature is from a Western perspective.

This Chapter focuses on the leadership aspects of cross-cultural leadership intelligence XLQ.

4.2 Leadership Theory -1862 thru 1990

Jomini (1862), a military strategist that is still revered in military thinking, said of leadership that first requirement for a man's success as a leader is that he/she be perfectly brave. Jomini believes that when a general has a truly martial spirit and can communicate it to his soldiers, he can commit faults, but will still gain victories (**transformation, power,** and **communication**). In the *Psychology for the Fighting Man* (Journal 1944) that was prepared by a group of psychologists and used by the US military for training, it says that a good leader knows how to handle his men. The manual says it is not possible to handle men, but rather a leader actually handles him/herself. The soldiers then react to this deportment. A good experienced leader inspires respect, confidence, and loyalty in his subordinates, all of which enable him to get from his men performance far above what a new leader might command (**power, empathy,** and **transformation**).

Watts and Huang (1975) point out that the Chinese language has retained substantially the same form for over 2,500 years, and that anyone speaking it today can better understand Confucius than an English speaker can understand Chaucer. In English, there is a tendency to use management and leadership interchangeably, with the managerial meaning similar to that of *ling dao*. Thus, the literal meaning of leadership will vary with culture. This is perhaps one reason that the Chinese view of time is different that that in the west, the durability of the language presages the longer more patient view of time. Watts and Huang also emphasize the loose and interchangeable usage of management and leadership in English.

Shirer (1979) recounted the concept of *Satyagraha* that was coined by Gandhi to describe the process of civil disobedience and passive resistance. Shirer said of Gandhi that he displayed gentleness without egoism, was without the slightest pretense of trying to impress, had no fear of anything, and had an iron will. According to Shirer, Gandhi understood that the riddle of communications is that it is a two-way phenomenon. Shirer recounted that Gandhi was not a great orator, and that he spoke softly, but that people came to hear him to receive his *darshan* (blessing). According to Shirer Gandhi knew that the British had been weakened by the world war, and would ultimately yield to independence. Gandhi said that those who say that religion has nothing to do with politics do not understand what religion means. Critically sound advice for leadership on both the importance of **communications**, and the consideration for religion.

According to Wofford (1982), there is a Leader Environment Follower Interaction (LEFI), an extension of the Path-Goal Theory, that is present for transactional and **transformational** leaders.

In a study on military personnel Bass (1985) found that the **transformational** leadership dimensions of charisma, individual consideration, and intellectual stimulation were more closely related to perceived effectiveness than were transactional issues. He found that people described charismatic leaders as those that made people enthusiastic about assignments, that inspired loyalty, that commanded respect, that had a special gift of seeing what was important, and that had a sense of mission. Bass found that followers had complete faith in the leaders with charisma, felt proud to be associated with them, and trusted their ability to overcome any obstacle.

Tichy and Devanna (1986) undertook to publish a set of hypothesis relating to leadership. The authors start by pointing to the economic and moral pressures on leaders in the changing global market, including pluralistic workforces with scarce resources. Transitional leaders must help people overcome three reasons for resistance to change: 1) habit and inertia, 2) fear of the unknown, and 3) sunk costs (**transformation, trust**).

Roberts (1989) summarized research on leadership principles utilized by Attila the Hun as loyalty, courage, desire, stamina, empathy, decisiveness, anticipation, timing, dependability, credibility, and competitiveness among others (**trust, transformation, empathy,** and **power**). Roberts's points out that the Huns were a fiercely independent multiracial and multilingual group that was able to assimilate foreigners and integrate themselves into foreign nations. Roberts says that according to Attila the Hun accepted differences and diversities must be pooled into a common purpose worthy of the tribes and nations overtaken. This article was a very early connection to the notion of the triple bottom line plus one that has been suggested by Elkington (1997). That being that a company has a responsibility to be profitable to the shareholders, have a concern for the society within which it functions, environmentally sensitive and concerned, and to govern with sensitivity and concern.

The work by Yukl (1989) and Bass and Stogdill (1990) provide excellent overviews of the theory and research that have been performed relating to leadership. Their work provides the foundation for a literature review of leadership. This work only introduces their work, and only selects excerpts to illustrate the major themes on leadership discussed by both authors.

Yukl (1989) provides a thorough review of the research on leadership, and concludes that (Pg. 423): "several thousand empirical studies have been conducted on leadership effectiveness, but many of the results are inconsistent and inconclusive." This is part of the reason for the lack of codified leadership skills for Project Managers. He categorizes the dimensions of leadership into characteristics of the leader, follower, and situation as shown in Table 5.

Yukl also describes the types of **power** associated with leaders from French and Raven (1959), and Yukl and Falbe (1991):

Position **Power**

- Legitimate Power – power associated with title or authority
- Reward Power
- Coercive Power – punishment power
- Information Power – control over information
- Ecological Power – control over the physical environment or technology

Personal **Power**

- Referent Power – admiration, desire to obtain approval (**trust, transformation, empathy, communications**)
- Expert Power – special knowledge

Yukl also describes guidelines for transformation leadership as follows:

- Articulate a clear and appealing vision – **transformation, communication**
- Explain how the vision can be attained **- transformation, communication**
- Act confidently and optimistically – **trust, transformation**
- Express confidence in followers - **power**

83

- Use dramatic, symbolic actions to emphasize key values – **communications**
- Lead by example - **empathy**
- Empower people to achieve the vision – **power**

Table 5 - Leadership (Yukl modified)

Dimensions	Leader	Follower	Situation
Traits (motives, personality, values)	Yes	Yes	
Confidence and optimism (**transformation**)	Yes	Yes	
Skills and expertise (**communication**)	Yes	Yes	
Behavior	Yes		
Integrity and ethics (**trust, empathy**)	Yes		
Influence tactics	Yes		
Attributions about followers	Yes		
Attributions about the leader		Yes	
Trust in the leader		Yes	
Task commitment and effort		Yes	
Satisfaction with leader and job		Yes	
Type of organizational unit			Yes
Size of unit			Yes
Position **power** and authority			Yes
Task structure and complexity			Yes
Task interdependence			Yes
Environmental uncertainty			Yes
External dependencies			Yes

Yukl closes by providing his observations about the characteristics of leadership, by listing the ten most important leadership functions as:

- Help interpret the meaning of events (**trust, communication**).
- Create alignment on objectives and strategies (**communication**).
- Build task commitment and optimism (**communication, transformation**).
- Build mutual **trust** and cooperation.
- Strengthen collective identity (**transformation, empathy, communication**).
- Organize and coordinate activities (**communication**).
- Encourage and facilitate collective learning (**communication, power**).
- Obtain necessary resources and support (**power**).
- Develop and empower people (**empathy, power**).
- Promote social justice and morality (**trust, empathy, transformation**).

Bass (1990) sets forth the differences between transactional and **transformational** leadership as follows (Pg. 22 Exhibit 1):

Transformational Leader

- Charisma – Provides vision and sense of mission, instills pride, gains respect and trust.
- Inspiration – Communicates high expectations, uses symbols to focus efforts, expresses important purposes in simple ways.
- Intellectual Stimulation – Promotes intelligence, rationality, and careful problem solving.
- Individualized Consideration – Gives personal attention, treats each employee individually, coaches, advises.

Transactional Leader

- Contingent Reward – Contracts exchange of rewards for effort, promises rewards for good performance, recognizes accomplishments.
- Management by Exception (active) – Watches and searches for deviations from rules and standards, takes corrective action.
- Management by Exception (passive) – Intervenes only if standards are not met.
- Laissez-Faire – Abdicates responsibilities, avoids making decisions.

Bass & Stogdill (1990) provide a thorough and well referenced review of leadership in this handbook. The authors open their work by providing a brief review of the history of leadership. They cite the work of Smith and Krueger (1933) who concluded a review of anthropological research by finding that leadership occurs among all people regardless of culture, lifestyle, or location. They also cite the work of Lewis (Lewis 1974) who concluded that even societies without institutionalized chiefs, rulers, or elected officials there are always leaders who initiate action.

Bass & Stogdill provide a review of the pre and post 1947 leadership studies that were performed. In the post 1947 review, they provided of how many times particular leadership attributes were reported. The authors summarize this section of their work by stating that the mass of research finding about leadership traits of successful leader's points to activity level, rate of talk, initiative, assertiveness, aggressiveness, dominance, ascendance, emotional balance, tolerance for stress, self-control, self-efficacy, enthusiasm, and extroversion (**communication, transformation**, and **power**). From experience, some of these traits, for example aggressiveness in Thailand, are not universal or *etic* traits. Thus, the individual test group and findings must be reviewed to determine if the characteristics of the test group (e.g.

Western versus Eastern). A correlation matrix that relates various studies discovered in this work is provided in Appendix 7, that was begun with the work of Bass & Stogdill.

In a chapter on task competence, Bass & Stogdill describe studies on competence that intertwines with intelligence. The authors say that meaning competence is a mixture of intelligence, training, and experience (e.g. a military officer). They cite a study by Spencer and Winter ((undated)) that assessed 800 incidents of leadership behavior by naval officers, and concluded that there were 27 competencies. Spencer and Winter grouped these into five categories by factor analysis that distinguished between superior and average leadership and management performance: competence in achieving tasks, skillful use of influence, management control, and advising and counseling.

The results are illuminating for they intertwine competence with **communications, power, empathy,** and **trust**. Bass & Stogdill summarize this chapter by stating that competence is relative to the leader, follower, and the situation. Practice confirms that a leader does not necessarily need to be a knowledge expert in a field to be competent. According to the authors, being knowledgeable of the technical terminology, reasonably intelligent, intuitive, and good at listening are often adequate.

In a chapter on interpersonal competence, Bass & Stogdill describe empathetic (**empathy**) abilities, the ability to **communicate,** authenticity and **trust,** and the ability to handle conflict (Chapter 5 of this work addresses conflict management). Under **communication**, they discuss competence, quality, meaning, consistency, timing, style, linguistic forms, writing ability, and non-verbal communications. The authors indicate that the research is mixed on the issue of empathy, despite the general regard for the importance of empathy for leaders. They note that the research is complicated by the various definitions of empathy.

The definition of empathy cited by Bass & Stogdill is from Kilcourse (1985) (Pg. 118): "the ability to walk around in someone else's world." The authors clearly believe that empathy is a core competency for leaders despite the research. They summarize by saying that (Pg. 123): "new research designs are needed to provide definitive tests of the hypothesis that leadership and **empathy** are linked because any theory of leadership that is of consequence includes the notion that the leader fulfills some of the needs of the group by helping the members cope with the internal and external environment."

Bass & Stogdill discuss esteem, and charisma in two separate chapters of their text. They say that (Pg. 183), "the esteemed leader may achieve charismatic standing in the eyes of others." This work considers esteem to be an aspect of **transformation** and **power** (referent power). In the chapter on charismatic leadership the authors point to the work of Downton (1973) who suggested if a follower is drawn to the goals but not the leader, then the leader is inspirational (**transformation**) becoming the embodiment of the follower's aspirations. If however the follower gives god-like status to the leader and does not criticize, the follower emulates the leader possibly fulfilling a self-image. The contention being that an effective and sustainable leader will encourage people to question and criticize if and when necessary.

In the chapter on charisma (**transformation**), Bass & Stogdill refer to the work of Burns (1978) and his findings relating to transformational leadership. Burns found four aspects of transformational leadership emerged in his survey of military and industrial superiors:

- Charismatic leadership (complete faith) (**transformation, trust**)
- Inspirational leadership (communicates high performance expectations) (**communication**)
- Intellectual stimulation (enables one to think of old problems in new ways) (**trust, communication, power**)
- Individualized consideration (**empathy**)
- The authors also include the concept of vision in the category of transformational leadership skills (Ray 1989), as does this work.

In the chapter on **power** Bass & Stogdill refer to the initial work of French and Raven (1959) that was later refined by Hinken and Schriesheim (1986). The findings were similar to those noted above by Yukl and included expert power, referent power, reward power, coercive power, and legitimate power. When discussing referent power, Bass & Stogdill refer to the work of Podsakoff and Schriesheim (1985) who found that (Pg. 235): "the use of referent power by leaders usually contributes to their subordinates' better performance, greater satisfaction, greater role clarity, and fewer excused absences." Bass & Stogdill also provide a review and discussion of the power and structure of organizations and teams. This work argues that appropriate empowerment of individuals is one way to build **trust,** improve **communication,** demonstrate **empathy,** and **provide transformational** leadership.

Cohen (1990) provides a military combat model view of leadership. He states that a leader should: 1) take risks, 2) be innovative, 3) take charge, 4) have expectations, 5) maintain a positive attitude, and 6) get out in front. He references a large study (Service 1944) of soldiers, and what attributes they thought good leaders had. The top factors in order of importance were competence (**transformation, trust**), interest in the welfare of the soldier (**empathy**), patience and the ability to make things clear (**communication**), does not boss people around (**power**), and tells you when you have done a good job. Cohen states that a leader must take responsibility for the actions of those he/she leads. The author also says that to get people to follow a leader must make others feel important, promote his/her vision, treat others as you would wish to be treated, and take responsibility for yourself and your group.

Cohen states that to build and maintain morale and esprit de corps a leader must: 1) let others participate in the ownership of your ideas, 2) be cheerful, 3) know what is going on and take action to fix or capitalize on it, 4) lead by personal example whenever possible, maintaining high personal integrity, 5) demonstrate concern for your group, and 6) focus on contribution not personal gain. On the issue of charisma (**transformation**), Cohen suggests the following actions: show your commitment, look the part, dream big, keep moving toward your goals, do your homework, build a mystique, and use the indirect approach.

Süleyman the Magnificent, is considered to have been one of history's greatest leaders. Goltz (1990) notes that Süleyman said in a communiqué to a commander that all virtue flows from justice, and that whatever is done by an unjust person is an evil act (**trust**). Of course, the definition of justice and virtue vary by culture. A leader must have knowledge of how different cultures perceive justice and virtue.

4.3 Leadership Theory -1991 thru 1997

From a psychological perspective, Lord and Maher (1991) write that children can by the first grade, clearly differentiate leaders from non-leaders, and that they can articulate the factors that separate the two groups (Matthews, Lord et al. 1990). In other studies the authors (Lord, Foti et al. 1984) found that on a scale of 0 to 5 the leadership traits that ranked 4.39 or above were, in order of importance: dedication, goal orientation, informed, charismatic, decisive, responsible, intelligent, determined, and organized. The authors found that prototype leadership qualities were recognized to be present in leaders by followers. It should be noted that the Lord study was performed on Western individuals. Clearly if children by the age of six can identify leaders, the culture within which a person is raised (family and social culture) will serve as the context for defining leadership.

Manz and Sims Jr. (1991) contend that the *Superleader* (**transformation**) is another type of leader who is capable of proactively leading themselves. They indicate that there are four kinds of leaders: the strong man (action rests with the leader – John Wayne is the example), the transactor (focus on goals and rewards – example is Larry Phillips the King County Council Chair in the USA), the visionary hero (based on follower's desire to follow the vision – example is Lee Iacocca), and the *Superleader* (ordinary individuals).

Heifetz (1994), in a book that focuses on political and social leadership, begins by describing three biases: systems bias (study the parts for solutions), biological bias (organism's response to the environment), and authority relationships from a service perspective. Heifetz notes that in leadership as in music, dissonance is an integral part of harmony, and silences create moments so that something new can be heard. Heifetz points to four mainstream theories of leadership thinking, and observes that all leave out value judgments. He notes that most cultures consider leadership normative. The theories that the author reviews are as follows:

- Trait Theory – the great man concept.
- Situational Theory – times produce the person.
- Contingency Theory – appropriate leadership is contingent upon the requirements of the particular situation.
- Transactional Theory – the interaction between leader and follower.

Heifetz provides a prescriptive definition of leadership as an activity rather than a set of attributes so that anyone may engage in leadership. He includes the following considerations:

- The definition must sufficiently resemble current cultural understanding of leadership.
- The definition should be practical so that people can use it.
- The definition should point toward socially useful activities.
- The definition should offer a broad definition of social usefulness. Here the author points to Burns (1978) and the concept that socially useful goals must not just meet the needs of followers but should also elevate them to higher moral standards – transformational leadership. Thus, Burns concludes Hitler was not a leader.

Heifetz also points out that adaptive change is an activity of leadership where technology will not itself solve the problem. The author defines authority as conferred **power** to perform a service. Heifetz describes leadership as both active and reflective, and of taking action beyond bestowed authority. He says that leadership is a razor's edge of overseeing periods of social disequilibrium or change, and sets forth five strategic principles of leadership:

- Identify the adaptive challenge – diagnose the situation.
- Keep the level of distress within a tolerable range for doing adaptive work.
- Focus attention on ripening issues and not on stress-reducing distractions – counteract issues like avoidance and denial.
- Give the work back to the people – put the pressure on the people with the problem.
- Protect voices of leadership without authority.

Jones (1994) in a study of Jesus suggested that Jesus displayed three categories of leadership strengths: strength of self-mastery (**transformation**), the strength of action, and the strength of relationships (**empathy, communications, trust**).

Mayer, Davis, et al. (1995) hypothesize that a manager expressing a high level of cognitive-based trust would engage in little control over the subordinate, and would direct little defensive behavior toward the subordinate. They however hypothesized that in affect-based trust the manager would engage in a great amount of need-based monitoring of the subordinate, demonstrating personal concern (**empathy**).

Yeung and Ready (1995) focus on developing leadership capabilities of global corporations. More than 1,200 managers from ten major global corporations in eight countries responded to an international survey on the core capabilities required for competitiveness. While the results highlighted six leadership capabilities that are globally valued, a comparative analysis of the data shows that culture affects the relative importance given to a leadership capability requirement.

Cleland (1995) prepared a paper on the connection between leadership and the Project Management Body of Knowledge (PMBOK). Cleland opens by saying that (Pg. 83): "the limited description of leaders and leadership in the project-management body of knowledge is noted with the suggestion that a more expansive discussion of leadership is needed for the body of knowledge, particularly as it continues to provide guidance in the management of crossfunctional and crossorganizational initiatives." I argue that Cleland's statement also applies to cross-cultural issues. Cleland quotes an older version of the PMBOK that address leadership.

In the newest 3rd Edition of the PMBOK (2004), the word leadership does not appear in the index, and only occurs nine times in the PMBOK. Eight of those nine occasions use leadership as an adjective to thank a participant. The one and only reference to leadership as a topic of importance for Project Managers in the PMBOK is found under the under the heading of interpersonal skills (Pg.5): "Leadership. Developing a vision and strategy, and motivating people to achieve that vision and strategy." As Cleland notes, in the new world economy leaders emerge on teams, and then return to a follower role in flat organizations. The ability to create cross-functional and a nimble organization is greatly facilitated by people who learn cross-cultural leadership skills.

Bartholomew and Adler (1996) provide an overview of cross-cultural research. They begin with the view that technology and the transnational firm is changing the way businesses compete. They note that in the business journals reviewed, 71% of the articles included the concept of culture, and of those 94% concluded that culture makes a difference. The authors also note that there are three major trends in research: cross-cultural interaction in transnationals (Ghoshal and Bartlett 1990), cultural differences (managerial behavior in most of the research), and integration of academia and business (the need for just-in-time research in the future).

Bennis and Nanus (1985) built their leadership view on four strategies: 1) attention through vision (creating focus)(**transformation**), 2) meaning through **communication** (a commonwealth of learning), 3) **trust** through positioning (accountability, predictability, reliability), and 4) the deployment of self through positive self-regard and the Wallenda factor[11] **transformation**). The authors state that leadership is a transaction between leaders and followers.

Fiedler (1996) reports a pessimistic review of the research on leadership stating that the advances in knowledge gained relating to leadership are:

- Emergent leadership, there is no evidence for specific leadership traits, people seen as good leaders are seen as good followers.
- Leadership effectiveness depends upon how the leader's personality matches with the followers.
- Stress and control primarily drive the leader's uncertainty or lack of **power**.
- Leader behaviors are as evaluated by others, or as structured by the leader.

---

[11] Wallenda was a tight-rope walker in the circus, and was fearless until he started to think about what he was doing.

- Charismatic leaders are blindly obedient and unquestioning.
- There are no gender or ethnic biases as for who may be a leader.
- Attributed abilities, skills, and motivation affect the leader relationship to the followers.

Luthans and Hodgetts (1996) take a view of American management from a global perspective. They indicate that some American firms are going beyond learning organizations and are creating what are known as *World-Class Organizations* (WCO's) that are able to change paradigms and develop competencies that permit them to exceed customer expectations (Hamel and Prahalad 1994). The six pillars of this new WCO described are customer focus, continuous improvement, flexible organizations, creative HR management, egalitarian culture of mutual respect, and technological support.

Pitt, Berthon et al. (1996) refer to the Wayzata World Factbook (Wayzata 1993) that is produced annually by the Central Intelligence Agency (CIA) in a cluster analysis of world economies. This view of the world is useful for marketing and from the perspective of transnational firms, could be an added dimension for cross-cultural considerations (relative economic prosperity).

Tollgerdt-Anderson (1996) in an article about her review of job advertisement for senior executives, refers to an article by Skapinker (1989) in reviewing 1,500 executives from the USA, Western Europe, Japan, and Latin America finding that there are substantial variations in attitudes relating to leadership. This is confirmed by the research in this work as well.

Turner and Henry (1996) described their research relating to relocation of executives from 26 countries. Fisher and Muller (2005) identify the traits, characteristics and skills of leadership as: loyalty, excellence, assertiveness, dedication, enthusiasm, risk management, strength, honor, inspiration, and performance (**trust, transformation, power,** and **communication**). The authors contend that if the leadership attributes match with the life cycle of the company there are synergies that will exist. Wilson, Hoppe, and Sales provide a view of the cultural orientations that ranges from the extreme of individualism to collectivism for one example. The authors point out that leadership is viewed differently in different countries, and as a result, the testing and training must be adjusted accordingly (1996).

In a study of trust, McAllister (1995) indicates that interpersonal **trust** has cognitive and affective foundations. Cognitive in that we choose whom we will trust and under what circumstances, and affective because trusting relationships consist of emotional bonds including care and concern. The authors state that the antecedents for cognitive-based trust (reliability), from the trustor's perspective, will be based upon past reliability and performance, culturally or ethnically similar backgrounds, and high professional credentials. Regarding affect-based trust, the authors indicate that interpersonal care and concern may be critical to the development of affect-based trust (Clark and Mills 1979), and that affect-based trust may indeed depend upon the creation of cognitive-based trust. Interestingly they also posit that once affect-based trust is created, it tends to remain even if actions belie the underlying belief.

Bennis and Biederman (1997) referred to a study by Korn-Ferry and the Economist that confirmed the authors' concept that that tomorrow's organizations will be managed by teams of leaders. The authors describe how great groups, and individual leaders, direct their creative genius to create miracles. There are fifteen take home lessons for great groups. A few of them are 1) Start with superb people, 2) Great groups and leaders create each other, 3) Great groups are on a mission from God, and 4) Great groups have an enemy.

Mullavey-O'Brien (1997) in an article about training for cross-cultural communications and empathy defined **empathy** to be the ability to put oneself in another's place and to know another's from their perspective. The authors also added that there was a need to communicate this understanding in a meaningful way, while recognizing that the source of one's experience lies in the other person. She also subdivides empathy as follows:

- Empathic Understanding – experiencing another's feelings and experiences.
- Empathic Communications – used to describe empathic understanding in a meaningful way.
- Accurate Empathy – an empathic response that reflects the content and feelings in the **communication**.
- Generalized Empathy – the ability to extend the empathic understanding to a group beyond the current one-to-one.
- Relational Empathy – also called meta-empathy or looking through your eyes at me with you.
- Cultural Empathy – the ability to understand others within the framework of their cultural background. Intercultural Empathy describes between members of different cultural groups, whereas cross-cultural empathy describes differences in empathy across cultural groups.

Greenleaf (1997) indicates that a true natural servant automatically responds to a problem by listening, and that to become a leader one must learn to listen effectively and automatically. Greenleaf introduced the concept of *servant leadership*.

In recent years management research has witnessed a surge in interest in cross-cultural and multinational management, and international joint ventures (IJV).[12] Special issues have been devoted to cross-cultural or foreign research in the *Academy of Management Journal, Organizational Science, and Leadership Quarterly*. Theoretically, cross-cultural and IJV research contributes to generalizability of theories and more importantly, creates a difference in perspectives that can deepen our understanding of the cultures being compared.

Currently, we are experiencing an increasing global collaboration between partnerships and between people of different national origins. Research on cross-cultural and multinational management can contribute heavily to the effectiveness that Project Managers can bring to their trade.

4.4 Leadership Theory - 1998 thru 2000

Corporate culture is an important consideration for cross-cultural leadership for a variety of reasons. First, the issue is that corporate culture to some extend subjugates or modifies the societal cultures that are resident within people. Second, the mobility of labor today often brings a wonderful diversity to the corporate workplace. For example, an Indian raised in Los Angeles, working in Tokyo will be absorbent when it comes to the uptake of a global corporate cultural design than would an individual working in a local manufacturing facility in Bangalore.

The structure of an organization will change the calculus of the five Hofstede transactions. Take power distance as an example. If the firm is a transglobal enterprise, then a leader in Belgrade, Serbia and Montenegro, would have significant (Power Distance Index 76 – i.e. significant distance to power tolerated) latitude in empowering local team members, but may choose not to do so. In a global firm, the center-of-gravity of **power** would be located in the home country, say Germany, and little empowerment would be possible in the local Belgrade

---

[12] See also (Beamish, Glaister & Wang, 1993, Gray & Yam 1992; Hamel, Doz & Prahalad, 1989, Brett, Tinsley, Janssens, Barsness & Lytle, 1997; Graen, Hui, Wakabayashi & Wang, Child, Markoczy & Cheung 1995 Graen & Wakabayashi, 1994)

office.   If the transglobal firm has a culture of empowerment, then the first case may prove a difficult adjustment for the Belgrade office, whereas the second would perhaps not.

Bartlett and Ghoshal (1998) discuss different structures of companies that do business in multiple countries, and categorize the different structures as shown in Figure 16.   Ghoshal and Bartlett (1990) proposed a theory for global firms, that being that they function more as an inter-organizational entity than an intra-organizational entity.

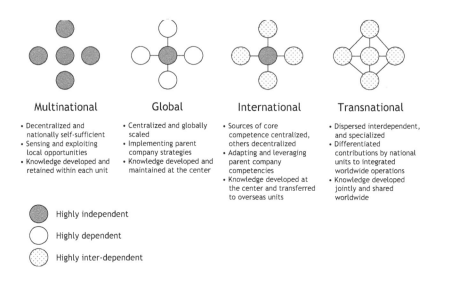

Figure 16 – Corporate Structures (Bartlett & Ghoshal modified)

Mobley, Gessner et al. (1999) edited a book that explores global leadership topics including competencies, gender, psychological perspectives on leadership, and values.   Most of the articles are from a Western European perspective, with a few from Asia.   The book explores a range of theories on global leadership, and it includes a Chapter on the GLOBE research program (see Section 2.6).   The majority of materials are addressed in the text of this work, so they will not be repeated here.

Avolio and Bass (1999) revisited the original MLQ (multifactor leadership questionnaire) and its six areas of: charisma/inspiration (**transformation**), intellectual stimulation, individualized consideration (**empathy**), contingent reward, active management by exception, and passive-avoidant leadership. The authors reconfirmed their earlier testing and state that leaders need to utilize both transformational and transactional skills.

Baron (1999), in a book about Moses, concluded in his work that there were ten words that summarized leading people in difficult times: accept (accept the role of leadership), assess (**communicate**), connect (**empathy**), deliver (**trust**), persevere, solve, search, enforce, endow (**power**), and depart (**transformation**). Baron says that we tend to expect great leaders to be charismatic, eloquent, and most of, and all eager to lead. The author concluded that regardless of this expectation, Moses was actually none of these.

Bennis (1999) stated that there are five leadership traits, with a sixth added in a subsequent article:
- Passion and purpose (**transformation**).
- Generate and sustain trust - Bennis (2002) suggests in a later article that there are five attributes of **trust**:

     Competence – someone to rely on

     Constancy – security

     Caring (**empathy**)

     Candor (**communications**)

     Character (**transformation**)
- Purveyors of hope and optimism (**transformation, empathy**)
- Manifest bias for action
- Keep learning and growing
- Courage – Later article by Bennis (2004) (**trust, transformation**)

Black, Morrison et al. (1999) researched 130 senior executives in 50 firms in Europe, North America, and Asia found that characteristics of global leaders are:
- Inquisitiveness – the foundation (**transformation**)
- Perspective – manage uncertainty, balance tensions (**trust**)
- Character – connect emotionally, personal integrity (**transformation**)
- Savvy – global business and global organizational (**power**)

The authors indicate that these characteristics represent 33% of what makes leaders successful. The authors say that 22% are made up of the business-specific dynamics of country affiliation, industry, company affiliation, and functional responsibility. The final 44% are made up of the

96

global dynamics of dispersion and duality. Dispersion being the synergy between perspective, inquisitiveness and savvy (shrewdness). Duality being the synergy between character, inquisitiveness, and savvy.

The authors indicate that only 40% of US firms offer their ex-pats any cross-cultural training, whereas this percentage is about 80% in Japan, Korea, and Europe. The authors also reference the Global Explorer[TM] assessment tool for evaluating global leadership competencies, and the Global Assignment Preparedness Survey (G-A-P-T-S[TM]). This is resonant with my personal experience on expat assignments.

According to Wofford (1999) (Pg. 524): "the MLQ assesses behaviors such as making personal sacrifices, handling crises, instilling pride, displaying extraordinary talent and competence, and building respect. The C-K (Conger and Kanungo 1998) assesses twenty nine behaviors in six categories of charisma: (1) vision and articulation. (2) environmental sensitivity, (3) unconventional behavior, (4) personal risk, (5) sensitivity to member needs, and (6) change from the status quo" (**trust, transformation** and **empathy**).

Ledeen (1999) points to Machiavelli (1983) as having said that what makes a leader despised is being considered changeable, frivolous, effeminate, cowardly, irresolute. Machiavelli concluded that a leader must strive to make everyone recognize in his actions greatness, spirit, dignity, and strength. In *The Prince,* Machiavelli (1961) sets forth leadership qualities as generosity, compassion, faithfulness, courageousness, and religiousness (**power, trust, empathy, transformation**).

Ledeen goes on to say that, a strong leader must balance the use of **power** with that of **empathy**, and that without fear of punishment men will not obey laws that force them to act against their passions. Ledeen also says that both virtue and corruption flow from the top down. Ledeen also points to Plutarch who said that the greatest talent of a leader is to secure obedience through the affection he/she inspires. According to Ledeen, the Zulu King Shaka as said that the Zulus are parts of two hundred and more unruly clans which had to be broken up and reshaped, and that only fear and death will hold them together. The lessons from history, according to Ledeen, point to the need for a strong leader to wield **power** from a wellspring of virtue - what I call an iron fist in a velvet glove. The lessons from history about leaders suggest that a leader must be **trusted**, demonstrate **empathy**, be **transformational**, **communicate** effectively, and wield power appropriately (see Figure 4).

Baum (2000), in writing about change, indicates that opportunity exists in conflict, and that it offers a chance to practice inclusive rather than exclusive behavior. He also says that the key to leading others through change, tragedy, and turmoil is inspiration (**transformation**). Baum quotes one translation of the Tao Te Ching (newer translations differ (Hendricks 1989)) as saying (Pg. 207): "true Leaders are hardly known to their followers; next after them are the leaders the people know and admire; after them, are those they fear; after them, those they despise. To give no **trust** is to get no trust." Part of the reason that a true leader is hardly known is that their leadership is unobtrusive, and is confirmed voluntarily by the follower (see Figure 5).

Coleman (2000) begins an article on power by quoting Bertrand Russell (1938) as having said that (Pg. 109): "the fundamental concept in social science is power, in the same sense in which energy is the fundamental concept in physics." Coleman sets for the following **power** factors:

Personal Factors

- Cognitive – radical, pluralist, and unitary ideologies; implicit theories; social dominance orientation
- Motivational – need for power, authoritarianism
- Moral – moral development, egalitarianism, moral scope

Situational Factors

- Deep structures – history, roles, norms, hierarchy, distribution of wealth
- Goal interdependence
- Culture - power distance

Leadership development is summarized well by Day (2000). Day concludes by stating (no page number HTML document article begins on Pg. 581): "The proposed distinction between leader development and leadership development is more than mere semantics. At the core of the difference is an orientation toward developing human capital (leader development) as compared with social capital (leadership development). Orientation toward human capital emphasizes the development of individual capabilities such as those related to self-awareness, self-regulation, and self-motivation that serve as the foundation of intrapersonal competence (McCauley 2000). Orientation toward social capital emphasizes the development of reciprocal obligations and commitments built on a foundation of mutual trust and respect (Drath 1998); (Whitener 2000); it rests on a foundation of interpersonal competence, but ultimately, it requires enactment. Leadership is developed through the enactment of leadership."

Earley and Singh (2000) indicate that (Pg. 2): "there is a paucity of theory that can be drawn on concerning the conduct of sophisticated international research in management." The authors identify a number of scholars that are building the conceptual foundations including:

- Original Foundations of Study – Haire, Hofstede (most research built upon his work), Trompenaars, Schwartz, Markus and Kitayama, and Ting-Toomey and Gudykunst.
- Industry/Organizational Researchers - Dyer, Ghosal, Hennart, Kobrin, Kogut, Zaheer.
- Organizational Behavior – Adler, Bond, Brett, Brewer, Brislin, Child, Erez, Gannon, Hofstede, House, Miller, Porter, Schuler, Schneider, Steers, Triandis, and Westney.
- Foreign direct investment and multinational corporations – Hymer, Kindleberg, Knickerbocker, Vernon, Buckley, Casson, Hennart, Rugman, and Kogut.
- Administrative process within multinational corporations – Arvey, Bhagat and Sales, Bartlett and Goshal, Black, Gregerson and Mendenhall, Boyacigiller, Doz, Hedlund, Prahalad, Schuler, Dowling, and CeCieri.

Earley and Singh outline a typology, initially introduced in the *Academy of Management Journal,* that categorizes cross-cultural research into four categories or forms that address the dimensions of international management systems, and cross-cultural management considerations:

- Unitary Form – Understand a phenomenon in a particular circumstance on its own terms. Understanding of group but not for establishing universal principles (*emic*) – examples: Berry, Earley and Mosakowski, Mead, Barley.
- Gestalt Form - Examination of a system, comparative to similar systems (*etic*) – examples: Erez; Lincoln, Hanada and McBride.
- Reduced Form – Break down a system into component parts. Assumes cultural systems can be broken down and that individual relationships are meaningful out of context (*emic/etic*) – examples: Earley; Tornblom, Jonssons, and Foa.
- Hybrid Form – Combination of Gestalt and Reduced Forms (*emic/etic*) – examples: Van Maanen and Barley; Schwartz and Bilsky.

Heil, Bennis et al. (2000) wrote a book to revisit the theories of Douglas McGregor on leadership, and on a humanistic view of the workplace. The authors revisit the example of Lincoln Electric Company and say that (Pg. 38): "at Lincoln, trust is the lynchpin to their management systems, tying together five interrelated qualities that make up the company's organizational design: commitment, conflict management, learning, systems thinking, agility...**trust** is the key." One of the quotes from McGregor applies to empowerment is (Pg.

63): "we have learned that if we push decision making down in an organization as far as we possibly can, we tend to get better decisions, people tend to grow and develop more rapidly, and they are motivated more effectively" (**power**).

Heil, Bennis et al. (2000) note that in the future more companies will organize in teams (Project Management as it is being called) because it is (Pg. 66): "the most efficient way to customize and deliver value in an era where specialization, speed of delivery, and rapid learning are keys to organizational success."

In an article on **communications** and conflict Krauss and Morsella (2000)[13] review four basic paradigms of communications, and set forth principles associated with each:

Encoding-Decoding Paradigm (sender and receiver)
- Avoid communications with low "signal to noise" ratios, or increase redundancy

Intentionalist Paradigm (intention)
- Listen and try to understand the intended meaning
- Consider how your message (words) will be received

Perspective-Taking Paradigm
- When speaking take account of the perspective of the listener

Dialogic Paradigm
- Be and active listener
- Focus on creating conditions for effective communications
- Pay attention to message form

Many of the authors cited in this work emphasize the importance of effective communications regardless if the topic is leadership, culture, conflict, cross-cultural leadership, or organizational structure.

Marquardt and Berger (2000) suggest that leaders in the twenty-first century will need to be *Systems Thinkers*, or people who have the ability to see connections between issues, data, and the wider environment (Senge 1990). In the practice of Project Management, more often than not companies are seeking people who demonstrate the ability. The authors point to an article by Robert Greenleaf (1997) that introduced the idea of *servant leadership* (if one is to lead one

---

[13] See also Krauss, R. M. and M. Deutsch (1966). "Communication in Interpersonal Bargaining." Journal of Personality and Social Psychology **4**: 572-577.

first must serve), and a later work by Spears (1995) that set forth characteristics of a servant leader. The characteristics included listening (**communication**), **empathy**, healing, awareness of self and others, persuasion (**trust**), conceptualization, foresight (**transformation**), stewardship, commitment to the growth of people (**power**), and building community. They point to Kofi Annan as an example of a leader that has vision, can see the big picture, has a sense of stewardship and spirituality, is dedicated to learning, systems thinking, and above all is a *servant leader*.

Morris, Podolny et al. (2000) point to two approaches for cultural research, subjectivist and structuralist. They argue that a blend of the two is the best technique for studying cultures based upon the work of Parsons (1951):

- Subjectivist – Generalizations about subjective psychological aspects of personalities and culture (*emic*) – examples of authors include: Benedict; Mead; Kardiner; Wrong; Cantril; Osgood; Yet; Geertz; Ronen; Triandis; Hofstede; Leung; Earley; Ho; Diaz-Guerrero, Lindsley, Sanchex-Burks, Nesbit and Yarra; Doi; Hsu;Pye; Schwartz; Bellah, Madsen, Sullivan, Swindler, and Tipton; Singelis, Triandis, Bhawuk, and Gelfand; Ross and Nisbet.

- Structuralists – Focus on external relations or social structure (*etic*). Examples of authors include: Marx; Lukes; Inkeles; Pascale and Athos; Mayhew; White, Boorman, and Breiger; Lincoln, Burt, Ibarra, Emerson; Podolny and Baron; Gross and Raynor; Fischer and Shavit; Giddens; Brint; Emirbayer and Goodwin; Dore; Rohlen; Gluckman; Kapferer, Triandis; Gudykunst; and Wheeler et al.

Socio-technical systems theory is used by Mumford, Zaccaro et al. (2000) to evaluate leadership's need to solve complex problems. The authors state that leadership problems are different from routine problems because of their complexity (multiple possible answers), novel nature, and ambiguity of information. The authors cite several examples of studies where a positive correlation was found between divergent thinking skills, and leader performance.

The issue of social judgment skills (understanding and monitoring social dynamics) is also addressed. The authors rely on research for the US Army, and take the general perspective that research focused on the leader's attributes rather than on the follower's perceptions of the leader are the way forward. The authors conclude that leaders are not born, nor are they made. The inherent potentials of leaders are shaped by experience that allows them to develop the capabilities needed to solve significant social problems.

Schmincke (2000) in an intriguing book, superimposes modern management terms on the Code of the Samurai, and offers insights into leadership from early Japan. Schmincke opens the book by saying that the *Art of War* (Tzu 1963) is about strategy, but the Code of the Samurai is about leadership. The code indicates that leadership is built on integrity (family duty, social responsibility, and the concept of shame - **trust**), bravery (**power**), and honor (including respect for others - **empathy**). The premise of the Code of the Samurai is that leaders must at all times keep their mortality in mind, and must compare the choices that manifest themselves to this benchmark. The Code of the Samurai also states that reliability (doing what one promises), continuous learning, and information acquisition and sharing (**communication**) are critical aspects of leadership. Still sage advice in the international marketplace.

4.5   Leadership Theory - 2001 thru 2005

Lipman-Blumen (2001) states that we cling to leaders to repress our awareness of our mortality, that change causes anxiety in people and organizations, and that people desire meaning to their actions and existence (**trust**). The author argues that these are reasons people tolerate bad leaders.

Csikszentmihalyi's (2001) research shows that creativity never happens in the mind of a person exclusively, it requires *domain* or information, *field* or all the individuals in a group, and *person* or a single person. He asserts that leaders must become connoisseurs who can recognize good ideas (**transformation**).

Lawler III (2001) states that leaders in the era of human capital need to self-manage so as to lead others involved in the project – as in a *flat* organization (an organization that has minimal layers of management). Lawler also states that individuals often need to move from being leaders to being followers and back to being leaders. This is particularly the case in flat organizations in changing international market conditions. As the projects change and different knowledge sets are needed, followers become leaders, become followers.

Lord (2001) undertook a review of ten years of cognitive research in psychology on leadership to uncover the underlying assumptions. The research was organized into three central themes for each of two sections. For individual and dyadic cognition, they identified metacognitive processes and leadership, implicit leadership theories (ILTs), and network based models of

ILTs as central themes. For collective cognition, they identified charisma, organizational performance and sensemaking, and **transformation** and change as central themes.

Lord provides a view of the research on cross-cultural leadership and concludes by saying that more than two decades have passed since Eden and Levitan (1975) concluded (Pg 741): "leadership factors are in the mind of the respondent. It remains to be established whether they are more that that." This work agrees with the idea that the follower's perceptions are the key in leadership transactions. As the definition for leadership indicates (see Figure 5), a leader must inspire the desire to follow.

Stewart (2001) argues that in flat organizations **trust** needs the support of competence, communities of practice (CoP's), commitment, and **communication**. Flat organizations are far more prevalent today, and will continue to increase as competitive pressure increases.

Dalton, Ernst et al. (2002) identify what they call four *pivotal capabilities*: international business knowledge, cultural adaptability, perspective-taking, and ability to play the role of innovator (**empathy, transformation, communication**, and **power**). This was the result of a three-year study of 211 global and local managers in four major multinationals. The authors reference the work of Bass (1997) and the four universal leadership characteristics: charisma, inspirational motivation, intellectual stimulation, and individual consideration.

Garlow (2002) provides a religious view of leaders. Three of the principles that Garlow espouses are: 1) if you want to lead others, master yourself first, 2) time is a friend of those with character, but an enemy of those with flaws, and 3) if you touch their minds you have their respect, if you touch their hearts you have their lives (**trust, empathy, transformation, power,** and **communications**). The second point bears repeating, for from practical experience, people often hear more clearly with their hearts.

Goleman, Boyatzis et al. (2002) believe that primal leadership operates through emotionally intelligent leaders. The authors believe that such leaders can create a resonance within the followers. By resonance, the authors mean a synchronous vibration that enables an emotional, spiritual, or non-verbal connection to be forged – hearing with hearts. The authors look at leadership from the perspective of the business leader, and claim that Emotional Intelligence (EQ) competencies are learned not innate. The authors describe Emotional Intelligence competencies as follows:

Personal Competence (**transformation**)

- Self-awareness
- Emotional self-awareness
- Accurate self-assessment
- Self confidence

Self-Management

- Emotional self-control
- Transparency
- Adaptability
- Achievement
- Initiative
- Optimism

Social Competence

- Social Awareness
- **Empathy**
- Organizational awareness
- Service (to others)

Relationship Management

- Inspirational leadership
- Influence (**power**)
- Developing others
- Change catalyst
- Conflict management (**trust, empathy, communications**)
- Building bonds
- Teamwork and collaboration

Heifetz and Linsky (2002) discuss the dangers that a leader must face. The authors state that dangers derive from the nature of the problems that require leadership and adaptive change, and include such things as challenge to habits, beliefs, values, uncertainty, loss, etc. (**trust, transformation,** and **communication**). Adaptive change may require people to express disloyalty to others and other cultures, to question aspects of their identity, and to question their competence. The authors say that leadership is an improvisational art that cannot be scripted. It requires the leader to see what is happening to them and their initiatives and adjust as they are happening. An interesting connection can be made to the work of

Kubler-Ross and Kessler (2005) on death and grieving – the ultimate change. She says that people go through five phases when a person dies: denial, anger, bargaining, depression, and acceptance. In managing change, fear and danger will be issues that people will face. A leader must act as a guide and anchor during such times.

George (2003) describes what he calls *authentic leaders*. *Authentic leaders* genuinely desire to serve, and are more interested in empowering people than they are in power, money, or prestige. The author says that leaders are as guided by the qualities of the heart, passion and compassion, as they are by the qualities of the mind (**trust**, **power, empathy, transformation, and communication**). George also advocates a single worldwide standard for ethics. George defines the five dimensions of *authentic leadership* as:

- Understanding their purpose - Passion
- Practicing solid values - Behavior
- Leading with heart - Compassion
- Establishing connected relationships - Connectedness (George quotes Krishnamurti (1996) as saying "relationship is the mirror in which we see ourselves as we are."
- Demonstrating self-discipline – Consistency

Goldsmith, Greenberg et al. (2003) performed a survey of 200 future CEO's in 120 international companies to elicit their attitudes and insights relating to global leadership. Their approach was to ask people how they saw the future of leadership. One of the findings was that future global leaders would need to have a financial understanding of the world economy, an understanding of different cultures, an understanding of global/regional markets, and a comfort with *diversity tension* – the ability to channel this energy effectively.

Goldsmith, Greenberg et al. point to the necessity to forge and nurture partnerships through belief in the partner's capabilities, **trust**, and accountability. They suggest that in order to keep leaders firms must shown respect, create thriving environments, provide training, provide coaching, provide feedback, reward achievements, and listen. According to the authors (Pg. 201): "listening is possibly the one absolutely necessary skill for a global leader to be successful, because listening leads to learning – learning about self, others, the organization, and the industry." The authors point to the work of Bennis (1989) as said that followers need direction, **trust**, and hope (**transformation**) from a leader. Goldsmith, Greenberg, et al. say that the following items emerged from their research as most important for the future:

- Thinking globally

- Appreciating cultural diversity
- Developing technological savvy
- Building partnerships and alliances
- Sharing leadership

Hetland and Sandal (2003) used a sixteen dimension personality questionnaire and an MLQ (multifactor leadership questionnaire) to evaluate transformational leadership in Norway.[14]

Table 10 provides the summary table that the authors provide to describe the dimensions of transformational leadership including idealized influence (**trust**), inspirational motivation (**transformation**), individualized consideration (**empathy**), and intellectual stimulation (**transformation**). The authors also correlated the MLQ with the Sixteen Personality Factors Questionnaire[15] four traits of warmth, reasoning, openness to change, and tension. The authors found support for their hypothesis that **transformational** leadership was positively correlated with how effective a manager was perceived to be, and that transformational leadership is more motivational that transactional leadership.

However, the authors did not find support for the hypothesis that the personality factors would be correlated with the MLQ. They did find that warmth (**communication, empathy, power**) was the strongest personality correlate. Transformational leadership was positively correlated with how effective a manager was perceived to be, and that transformational leadership is more motivational that transactional leadership.

Schneider and Barsoux (2003) of INSEAD open their book by saying that those concerned with managing across cultures are no longer just the jet-setting elite, the corporate trouble-shooters, and battle-scarred expatriates. The business world of today consists of people of many different cultures working together. Appreciating (**empathy**) and being able to manage cultural differences is becoming a part of everyone's job. This reflects my personal experience as well. They also discuss the idea of professional cultures, and networks of specialists, and built their work on that of Kluckhohn and Strodtbeck.

---

[14] See also Bass, B. M., & Avolio, B. J. (1995). Transformational leadership development. Manual for the Multifactor Leadership Questionnaire. Palo Alto, CA: Consulting Psychologists Press.
[15] See also Russel, M. T., & Karol, D. L. (1994). The UK edition of the 16PF5: administrator's manual. Windsor, UK: NFER-Nelson.

The authors also provide a humorous organizational chart to illustrate the differences in corporate culture in different social cultures. The figures provide examples of how different cultures perceive organizational structure. For example, consider the Chinese example showing a massive hierarchical structure. One key in leading is such a culture is the notion of a need for structure. Alternatively, consider the Arabian model showing no structure. Leaders in the Middle East must come to accept that structure is not a desirable attribute for a leader.

Schneider and Barsoux state that the competencies for managing differences abroad are: interpersonal skills, linguistic ability, motivation to live abroad, tolerance for uncertainty and ambiguity, flexibility, patience and respect, cultural empathy, strong sense of self, and a sense of humor (**communication, empathy, trust,** and **transformation**). They also provide a solid list of strategies for managing multicultural teams, and for managing virtual teams. The closing chapters of the book address the issues of ethics and sustainability.

Hunter (2004) in a book about *servant leadership* points to Jesus Christ as the greatest leader ever, for the reason that he was able to build authority and influence by serving. The author belives that love is a requirement for the servant leader and defines it as the acts of extending yourself for others, by identifying and meeting their legitimate needs, and by seeking their greatest good.

Hunter reports that participants in his seminars list leadership qualities as being honest (**trust**), respectful, firm but fair, appreciative, and having good **communication** skills. Hunter points to Greenleaf (1997) as having said that a non-servant leader who wants to be a *servant leader* must undertake the arduous discipline of learning to listen, which must be sufficiently sustained so that the automatic response to any problem is to listen first. Hunter describes the four stages of creating habits in people as being unconscious and unskilled, conscious and unskilled, conscious and skilled, unconscious and skilled (skilled implementation like an athlete). He describes this in the context of change and of fostering an organization, which welcomes change.

McCauley and Van Velsor (2004) provide an excellent review of leadership development and training at the Center for Creative Leadership. One chapter in the book focuses on the cross-cultural issues in leader development, and begins by indicating that leadership development is happening in all societies. The authors use culture to mean a set of shared values, beliefs, and preferred actions. Therefore, it is applicable to personal, societal, and business culture.

McCauley and Van Velsor point to the work of Leslie and Fleenor (1998) who stated regarding 360 degree testing instrument validity that much is unknown about the international validity and reliability of instruments developed and used in the U.S – meaning their potential extrapolation to the international areana. Furthermore, McCauley and Van Velsor point to the issue of multi-cultural groups, and they question which group's norms and culture should apply. The authors suggest that an organizational norm might be more appropriate to guide leader development. This is a critical consideration for cross-cultural leadership, and its importance is determined in part by the structure of the corporate entity (global, international, multinational, transnational), and the cultures that the cross-cultural leader must blend.

McCauley and Van Velsor also bring into question the issue of change. They state that there is sound empirical evidence that people worldwide value variety and challenging tasks, but that the acceptance to change varies across cultures. This is a critical consideration for cross-cultural leadership regardless of the structure of the firm. The authors point out that support from others (mentors/coaches) is another variable for consideration and is accepted differently in different cultures. This is a view also espoused by Goldsmith, Greenberg et al.

McCauley and Van Velsor state that organizations can have a capacity for leadership, with leadership being defined as the collective activity of organizational members to accomplish the tasks of setting direction, creating alignment, and gaining commitment. In a flat organization, potentials must exist in all individuals for leadership to become a skill. In practice, this is a big challenge. If a firm is a transglobal entity, local cultural values will vary and with them the application of global principles – like gender equality or gratuities. In such firms an atmosphere of trust must be in place if people are to be coaxed to accept values for work that are likely different from those utilized in their private lives.

The authors reference the 4MAT learning model (McCarthy and Keene 1996) to be helpful in designing challenge based training. Table 11 shows the learning cycle with the L mode cognition relating to language, logic, sequential analysis, and stepping back from the flow of experience; the R mode cognition relates to patterns, nonverbal intuition, emotional and physical intelligence, and being immersed in the flow of direct experience.

McCauley and Van Velsor (2004) point to the issue of the word leader itself. *Chun-tzu* in ancient China described a person who was a cultured and accomplished scholar-administrator, in modern China *ling dao* (leaders) means persons of high administrative position, and *gan bu* (cadres) staff and managers, according to the authors.

There are many programs designed to train people to be leaders, and many of these have been designed and developed to improve the abilities of a company's employees. Development activities, case studies, simulations, games, experience, mentoring, and coaching are a few of the techniques utilized to provide leadership training. The best method(s) must be fitted to the individual, and must take into consideration their experience, training, cognitive complexity (Streufert, Pogdash et al. 1988), social complexity (Hooijberg, Hunt et al. 1997), behavioral complexity (Denison, Hooijberg et al. 1995), and personality. In the last decade, the research has moved toward accepting the complexity of leadership, and models such as those proposed by Denison and Hooijberg are embracing the notion that leadership qualities are not linear, and are not easy to assess.

Mäkilouko (2004) looked at multicultural projects from a Finnish perspective with teams that included Finnish, Chinese, Europeans, and Americans. The author found that forty of forty-seven project leaders utilized a task oriented leadership style. These people indicated cultural blindness, ethnocentrism (the tendency to look at the world primarily from the perspective of one's own ethnic culture), parochialism (selfishness, narrowness, pettiness), or in-group favoritism were challenges that they faced.

In the survey, the remaining seven leaders that indicated the almost total use of relationship orientation indicated cultural sympathy (**empathy**) was recognized and facilitated, and three of these leaders attempted to maintain synergy (**transformation**), group cohesion, and conflict avoidance (see Chapter 5). The conclusion of the study indicated that relationship oriented project leaders (Project Managers) may have a higher potential for success. The conclusion also indicated that the acquisition of cultural knowledge may help project leaders to avoid avoiding conflict, and that relying on personal influence alone should be eschewed with more emphasis placed on coaching.

Christenson and Walker (2004) address the concept of vision in a study about information technology and Project Management. The authors addressed four characteristics of vision being:
- that it must be understood
- that it must be motivational

- that it must be credible
- that it must be demanding and challenging.

The authors linked vision to **transformational** leadership and argued that projects are in fact transformations, and as such should benefit from transformational leadership. According to the Project Management body of Knowledge (PMBOK), a project is (Pg. 5): "a temporary endeavor undertaken to create a unique product, service or result." Projects are transformations in conventional matrix or functional type organizations.

Thamhain (2004) studied 80 technologically intensive projects, and in his concluding remark he notes that effective project leaders are (Pg. 45): "social architects who can foster a climate of active participation by involving people at all organizational levels in the planning, formation, and execution of projects. They also can build alliances with support organizations and upper management to ensure organizational visibility, priority, resource availability, and overall support for sustaining the team effort beyond its start-up phase" (**power, transformation, communication**). From practical experience, alliances require a very heavy reliance on trust, empathy, transformation, power, and communications.

Wheatley (2005) offers a humanistic and spiritual view of leadership. She contends that leaders help people better understand themselves by the way they lead. She also points to the last works of Deming, and that of Greenleaf, both of whom focused on the human spirit according to the author. As she says about leaders that they (Pg. 30): "trust our humanness; they welcome the surprises we bring to them; they are curious about our differences; the delight in our inventiveness; they nurture us; they connect us" (**trust, empathy, transformation, power**, and **communication**). Wheatley also states that knowledge is born in a chaotic process, and that that process takes time. A leader must recognize that the creation of slack time to interact is an essential commodity that must be addressed.

Mayo and Nohria (2005) undertook an effort to provide a historical view of business leadership in the United States in the 20th century. They used a survey of 7,000 business leaders to produce a list of 1,000 potential candidates. The initial survey asked the business leaders to describe how they interpreted what it meant to be a great business leader. The results of the survey were that great business leaders would have strategy and vision (**transformation**), would be a pioneer or innovator (**transformation**), would have an impact on industry (**power**), would deliver financial performance, would have an impact on society (**trust** and **empathy**),

110

and would develop people's abilities (**transformation**). The authors found that there were three types of business manager prototypes that emerged - entrepreneurs, managers, and leaders. They then sorted the results into decades (the approach taken for the organization of this work), and found that the context of the time in which each worked made a difference in how they approached the business world. In some useful charts, the authors summarize what they describe as *Context-based Leadership*, and they provide a brief description of the differences between entrepreneurs, managers, and leaders. To emphasize the importance of Mayo & Nohria quote Klapp (1954) as saying (Pg.xxix): "the same act performed too soon or too late or in the wrong scene may make a person a fool rather than a hero." This work considers context to be of primary importance in cross-cultural leadership. To make the connection between context-based leadership and this work, I would re-describe the social mores aspect of the context as culture.

Wang, Chou et al. (2005) surveyed three-hundred of the five-hundred largest companies in Taiwan that had implemented enterprise resource planning (ERP) systems. Their results confirmed that leaders should demonstrate more charismatic (**transformation**) behavior to improve cohesiveness, and team performance.

Turner and Müller (2005) were commissioned by the Project Management Institute (PMI) to conduct research to determine if a projects manager's leadership style was a success factor on projects, and if it was different on different types of projects. The authors started with a literature review and found (Pg. 49): "surprisingly, the literature on project success factors does not typically mention the project manager and his or her leadership style or competence as a success factor on projects. This is in direct contrast to the general management literature, which views effective leadership as a critical success factor in the management of organizations, and has shown that an appropriate leadership style can lead to better performance."

In their review, Turner and Müller concluded that the Project Management literature has (Pg. 59): "largely ignored the impact of the project manager, and his or her leadership style and competence, on project success."

Time and space will not permit further study of the literature at this time. During the course of this research, there have been a number of papers discovered that offer areas for future study including:

111

- ((Burke and Russell 1986); (Shamir and Howell 1999); (Powell 1990)) social networks
- (Hodgetts and Luthans 1994)world organizational structure
- (Goleman 1998) emotional intelligence
- (Atwater and Waldman 1998) published a study on 360 degree feedback
- (Podsakoff, MacKenzie et al. 1995) leadership moderators
- (Podsakoff, MacKenzie et al. 1996) transformational leaders
- (Graen and Uhl-Bien 1995) LMX theory
- (Scandura, Graen et al. 1986) LMX theory
- (Ashkanasy and O'Connor 1997) value congruence leader-follower
- (Keller 1999) implicit leadership theories
- (Mintzberg 1998) covert leadership
- (Pfeffer 1977) ambiguity of leadership
- (Hamel, Doz et al. 1989) collaborative learning
- (Niven 2002) Balanced scorecard (NGO's and development banks)

4.6 Chapter Summary

This Chapter has provided a review of the literature on leadership from 1862 through 2005. As with the previous chapters on culture and metaphor, I have highlighted the connections between the works referenced and the hypothesis of this work. There is a very rich body of knowledge in leadership that has been explored by psychologists, sociologists, anthropologists, religious scholars, political scientist, business management thinkers, and many more. I have attempted to provide a wide range of perspectives on leadership rather than an exhaustive study of a limited number of authors, for I believe this approach is better suited to a study of cross-cultural leadership. It provides diversity of opinion and viewpoints.

As noted by Turner and Müller, the literature on Project Management has largely ignored the topic of leadership. Likewise, the Project Management Body of Knowledge (PMBOK) only provides a brief mention of leadership. This work is intended to help fill those gaps.

In the next Chapter I will explore another aspect of cross-cultural leadership, and management, that requires a specific set of skills and sensitivities, that of conflict management.

5. Conflict Management
5.1 Chapter Introduction

Conflict is an integral part of human interaction between people, groups, cultures, sects, firms, and countries. Conflict can, if guided, be healthy and productive. However, if ignored may lead to disastrous consequences, and the deterioration of long-term relationships. In the international marketplace, the potential for conflict is extremely high as cultural beliefs and customs collide with regularity. Therefore, cross-cultural leadership must attend to the inevitability of conflict with guidance, knowledge, patience, and a celebration of diversity. Part of cross-cultural leadership intelligence XLQ, is the ability to manage conflict. A strong leader will avoid avoiding conflict, and will imbue this attitude in her followers.

There is a close correlation between **trust, empathy, power, transformation,** and **communications**, and conflict resolution.

5.2 Conflict Theory 1973 thru 1993

Bass & Stogdill (1990) discuss conflict in a chapter along with legitimacy. They summarize by saying that leaders face many conflicts from such things as roles, resources, perceptions, and more. Personal experience shows that conflict is a daily reality in the international marketplace and includes cultural, ethnic, gender, racial, and managerial issues. Leaders must have the ability to confront and manage or resolve (depending upon the circumstances) conflict effectively. Conflicts managed or resolved gracefully, leaving face in tact for the participants, is a skill set that is essential for leaders. Conflict management or resolution requires a number of skills, but from experience in the legal and dispute resolution industries, communications skills are critical and essential.

Deutsch (1973) describes a theory of cooperation and competition that considers interdependence among goals, and the type of action taken. The author considers how these dimensions affect three major social psychological processes that affect cooperation and competition: substitutability, attitudes, and inducibility. Substitutability means how a person's actions can satisfy another's intentions - critical to the functioning of social institutions. Substitutability enables one to accept the activities of others in fulfilling one's needs (**trust**, and **empathy**). Attitudes are the predisposition to respond favorably, unfavorably, or evaluatively to one's environment or self - we respond positively to stimuli that are beneficial, and negatively to that which is harmful. Inducibility refers to the readiness to accept another's influence (**empathy**), being willing to be helpful to those that are helpful.

Deutsch explains that cooperative relationships differ from competitive relationships through the display of the following characteristics:

- Effective **communications**
- Friendliness, helpfulness, and less obstructiveness
- Coordination of effort, orientation to task achievement, orderliness in discussion, and high productivity
- Feeling of agreement with the ideas and of others and a sense of basic similarity in beliefs and values
- Willingness to enhance the other's **power** (e.g. Knowledge)
- Defining conflicting interests as a mutual problem

Deutsch believes that rapport building, conflict resolution (listening, **empathy**, identifying creative means to resolve disputes, etc.), and group process and decision making (leadership, **communications**, clarifying, summarizing, integrating, etc) skills are necessary for effective conflict resolution.

Kilmann and Thomas (1978) provide a four perspective model of conflict. Their view considers external and internal sources for conflict and events and conditions:

External

- Events (processes) – behavior is shaped by events outside of the individual like threats, negative evaluations, or encroachment. The authors suggest interaction management (change behaviors) as the strategy to manage this type of conflict.
- Conditions (structure) - behavior is shaped by conditions outside of the individual like social pressure, conflict of interest, or procedures. The authors suggest contextual modifications (change the objectives) as the strategy to manage this type of conflict.

Internal

- Events (processes) – behavior is shaped by events outside of the individual like frustration, strategies, or defense mechanisms. The authors consciousness raising (change cognitions, perceptions, or emotions) as the strategy to manage this type of conflict.
- Conditions (structure) - behavior is shaped by conditions outside of the individual like

motives, attitudes, or skills. The authors suggest selection and training (screening for the right people and training in techniques) as the strategy to manage this type of conflict.

Sullivan, Peterson et al. (1981) studied 156 Japanese and 100 American managers in joint ventures in Japan. They state that **trust** plays a crucial role and is the essential requirement for the Japanese partner, and if trust exists, written arbitration clauses in contracts can in fact lead to distrust. Tinsley and Brett (1997) studied 60 US American and 30 Hong Kong Chinese students, and found that US Americans prefer an *integrating interests* (low context) approach while Hong Kong Chinese prefer the *relational bargaining* (high context) approach.

Burley-Allen (1982) states that 40% of a person's time is spent listening, and that people listen at three levels: listening in spurts, hearing sounds and words but not really listening, and active listening. In active listening people put themselves into the other person's position and listen from their point of view. I argue that this is essential in cross-cultural situations and goes to the issue of knowledge on the part of a leader. An early mentor of mine told me repeatedly that one cannot listen when their mouth is open. The lesson being that one should default to listening rather than speaking. When I teach and mentor, I recommend that the percentage of time spent, listening should be closer to 70% as a goal.

Rahim (1983) in an article about interpersonal conflict (strong methodology) cites the work of Blake and Mouton (1964) who classified styles of resolving interpersonal conflicts as shown in Figure 17. As the figure shows, the view of Blake & Mouton was one of concern for others (people in their context), and concern for performance of the group. Blake & Mouton's book, *The Managerial Grid*, provided a grid for evaluating and training management skills, with one consideration being how to manage conflict. The Rahim model builds upon the work of Blake & Mouton by looking at the issue of conflict through the lens of self concern and concern for others. This generalized version is more appropriate for use in this discussion for it better reflects the conditions of society and culture in conflict. The Blake & Mouton work takes a more western perspective of performance or corporate success.

Rahim's article represents a view of these aspects based upon a conceptualized two-dimensional model for conflict as concern for self and concern for others. He contends that the tests confirmed the acceptability.

115

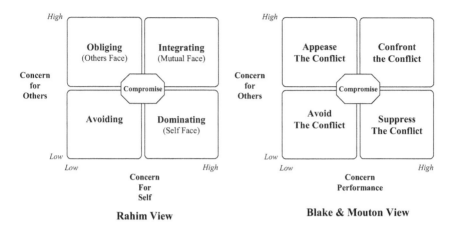

Figure 17 – Negotiation Styles (Rahim/Blake & Mouton modified Fig. 1)

Habib (1987) measured manifest conflict in multinational joint ventures. He indicates that conflict is a dynamic process consisting of the following stages (Pondy 1967):

- Latent - potential conflict such as role deviance, resource conflict, divergence of goals, bad communications, drive for autonomy
- Perceived - Cognitive
- Affective – stress, tension, hostility, anxiety
- Felt - cognitive perceptions of the situation
- Manifest – behavior from passive to aggressive
- Aftermath

Figure 18 is taken from the Pondy article. Pondy indicates that conflict can be considered as *disequilibrium* in an organization. In personal experience, I would describe it as cacophony, or noise. It is contagious, infectious, and debilitating if not managed.

In a book that addresses the socio-psychological aspects of conflict and cultures, Augsburger (1992) provides numerous interesting folk tales to illustrate the theories drawn from academia and testing regarding conflict. He begins by noting that in cross-cultural disputes, the basic propositions to be considered are: 1) either-or thinking must be set aside, 2) the parties in the dispute are the least able to solve it, 3) cross-cultural conflict confronts us with our ignorance, and 4) using conflict wisdom of each culture is preferable to creating a world view (*etic*) approach.

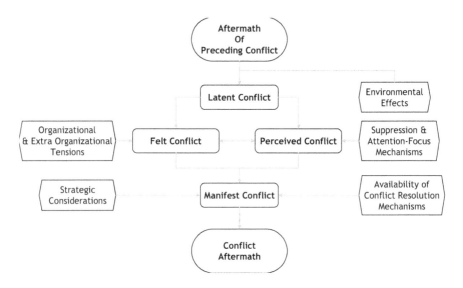

Figure 18 – Disequilibrium (Pondy modified Fig. 1)

Augsburger states that while conflict is universal, the way it is perceived is distinct and unique in every culture, and with every person. Augsburger addresses what he calls the where, why, what and which of conflict:

- Where- the considerations are for the type of culture (high-context, low-context).
- Why – the considerations are for expressive (desire to release tension, express. frustration, etc), and instrumental which deal with goals. He notes that triggering events will differ widely in different cultures (individual offense versus group –offense; low-context & high-context cultures for example).
- What – the attitude and action will be.
- Which – pattern of communication will be utilized.

The author suggests three types of **communication** patterns (Glenn, Witmeyer et al. 1977): factual-inductive (begins with facts), axiomatic-deductive (begins with general principles), and affective-intuitive (begins with relational/emotional perceptions).

Augsburger suggests that mediation can be conducted from the *medi-etic* (begins with theory from another culture) or *medi-emic* (begins with local approach) approaches. He then quotes Morton Deutsch's crude law of social relations, as (Pg. 50): "the atmosphere of a relationship will foster certain acts and processes." Deutsch also offered two corollaries to this law. The first being (Pg. 50): "the processes and acts that are characteristic of a given social atmosphere will induce that very atmosphere if introduced into a newly forming relationship." The second corollary being that (Pg. 50): "a firmly developed atmosphere can be rapidly changed to the negative if one party acts in a contradictory manner (Deutsch 1973)."

As a trained mediator, both *etic* and *emic* considerations must explored. A mediator must build a bridge of trust between herself and each party. To do this requires that the mediator develop an understanding of the parties, their cultures (business and social), and the ways that they receive and process information.

Augsburger provides an entire chapter on the issue of face. In it, he describes the concept of face in the West as being personal face, the *I-identity*, self-esteem, guilt, dignity, and pride. By contrast, face in the East Augsburger describes as being group face, the *We-identity*, esteem for others (**empathy**), shame, honor, and solidarity.

Augsburger also describes what he calls the *triangulation* process of having a third party to assist in resolving disputes being as old as civilization itself. He provides a number of insightful tales, and one Nepalese proverb to open the chapter (Pg. 143): "when the first wife fights with the second, the husband gets his nose cut off." Augsburger concludes with what he calls his Cyclical Conflict Model.

Corne (1992) provides a number of culturally specific suggestions for resolving disputes between Japanese and Americans. The author says that basic negotiating principles (Fisher and Ury 1983) must be coupled with sensitivity, **empathy**, and thorough preparation to be successful. In personal experience, preparation is the key. Many conflicts go unresolved due to a lack of time spent in understanding the other party's needs and wants, values, face, and communication preferences. Oddly, in many cases I find that parties do not fully understand their own needs and wants.

Agee and Kabasakal (1993) undertook a study of US and Turkish students to determine how they resolve conflicts. First they reviewed the literature on conflicts by citing the work of Habib (1987) on overt conflict action in international corporations, and Filley (1978) on problem solving as a dispute resolution technique. Agee and Kabasakal also cite the work of Ruble and Thomas (1976) and their five conflict resolution modes as:

- Competing – focused on one's position while neglecting the others' needs.

- Avoiding – failure to satisfy either one's or another's needs.

- Accommodating – failure to satisfy one's own needs in order to satisfy those of others.

- Collaborating – problem solving, information exchange, mutual decisions.

- Compromising – parties each give up something to make a mutually acceptable decision.

Agee and Kabasakal also reference the cross-cultural conflict research of ((Sullivan, Peterson et al. 1981), (Kozan 1989), and (Leung 1987)). The authors make use of what they call a convenience sample (Sekaran 1983). The authors found in their study that there were no significant differences in the approach of Turkish and American students in personality conflicts, but that there were in different work style conflicts. The authors speculate that the situation seems to make the difference (Kozan 1989).

5.3 Conflict Theory 1994 thru 1999

Levinson (1994) provides a broad overview of aggression and conflict. He describes conflict as a dispute between two or more individuals or groups over access to or control of resources, and includes economic, political (**power**, leadership), social (prestige or status), and personal esteem (**transformation**) in the definition of resources. The book is based upon worldwide surveys of 3,000 cultures, and is organized into 90 sections. A select listing of sections follows:

- Advisors - The first section discusses advisors using the example of the San of Botswana who rely upon advisors to settle disputes. The section on aggression by women referenced work by Burbank (1987) who found that of a sample of 317 societies, 137 had instances of aggression by women (82% of which were verbal).

- Aggression in folktales - Levinson references the work of Cohen (1990) in describing how folktales express indirectly desires, wishes, fears, anxieties shared by members of the society.

- Apology - Levison notes that in a study of 56 societies (Hickson 1986) only 14% utilize apology as a means of resolving conflict, but where it is used there are specific requirements (e.g. Korea, Japan, Taiwan, Iran, Fiji).

- Avoidance and Withdrawal – Levison points to research on the Javanese use of *satru*, people cease talking to one another, and to the Thai who consider withdrawal to be an appropriate response. Another study found that Jamaicans will withdraw and focus their anger on others, or themselves in silence, and that the Zapotec rely upon denial that a dispute exists.

- Combative Sports – Social scientists argue that combative sports are more common in societies that are warlike (Worchel 1974).

- Conflict Resolution – Levinson cites the work of Newman (1983) who defines eight types of legal systems for resolving disputes as: self-help, advisor, mediation, elder's council, restricted council, chieftainship, paramount chieftainship, and state level systems (judicial systems and courts). Levinson notes that complex societies like the USA use all eight types.

- Ethnic Conflict – Levinson describes ethnic conflict as springing from culture, religion, and physical features of language, and lists 41 countries that had ethnic conflict ongoing in 1994. Levinson points to the work of Horowitz (1985) as having said that ethnic solidarity is powerful, permeative, passionate, and pervasive, and that the consensus among experts is that ethnic conflicts must be managed for they cannot be resolved. This is also a critical issue for cross-cultural leadership, intra-culture or country. Leaders must be aware of the cultural and ethnic backgrounds of people working on their teams (e.g. Spanish and Basques, or Turks and Armenians).

- Gossip – Levinson says that gossip is the most common form of verbal aggression, that it is usually derogatory, and that the person talked about is normally not present. Levinson points to the work of Haviland (1977) as having said that what people gossip about is a good index of what they worry about. Levison also indicates that gossip is especially prevalent in conflicts involving two political factions within a single culture (see also (Rosnow and Fine 1976)).

- Humor – Levinson says that humor is a cultural universal, and can play a role in controlling aggression. He notes that psychological interpretations reveal that humor is a mechanism for meeting human needs to express aggressive drives and feelings. In cultures where aggressive behavior is controlled, humor is less aggressive. Examples provided include the San of Botswana who use joking as an alternative to loosing one's temper, Chicanos who use word play as a sort of cultural indictment (Casimiro Flores rendered as *I almost see flowers* in English), or Liberian boys' use of insults to mimic men even if they don't understand what they are saying (Apte 1985). This is also a critical issue for cross-cultural leadership, intra-culture or country. Leaders can learn about people from the humor common in a culture

- Machoism – Levinson indicates that machoism is found mainly in cultures where male and female roles are clearly differentiated, and where boys spend large amounts of time with their mothers and other women until the passage to manhood. He notes that aggressive male behavior in such societies is expected (see also (Munroe, Munroe et al. 1981).

Tse and Francis (1994) studied 101 executives from Canada and China and determined that negotiators do not significantly change their approach when conducting inter and intra cultural conflict negotiations. The study also explores how personality related and task related conflicts generate different resolution styles.

Coleman (1995) hypothesized that the degree of concern for others, the degree of concern for self, and separation represent the strategies people use to cope with cultural diversity (**empathy**).

In an article on counseling, Coleman (1997) focuses on conflict in multicultural environments. In his review he points to the work of LaFromboise, Coleman, et al. (1993) who found five methods that people use to develop competence in a second culture: assimilation, acculturation (**empathy**), alternation, integration, and fusion (**transformation**).

Singelis and Pedersen (1997) provide an excellent training view of resolving conflict and mediation across cultures. Their assumptions are summarized as follows:
- Conflict – Micro can become macro, constructive can become destructive, necessary become unnecessary, can lead to innovation, sometimes the result of wrong inferences.
- Mediation – Win-win outcomes, mediators not necessarily neutrals, complex and dynamic, fluid and adaptable, related to counseling.
- Culture – People have multiple cultures, shared and learned, includes norms, values and structures, identity is dynamic not fixed, provides guidelines for behavior, is complex but not chaotic, provides assumptions about others' behaviors.

Spicer (1997) performed a study on 30 Americans and Russians working in multi-national organizations in Moscow, and found that the transfer of culturally specific tacit knowledge was the main source of interpersonal conflict in all four dimensions (American/American, Russian/Russian, Russian/American, and American/Russian). Spicer notes that there is a need to bridge the gap between cross-cultural research and cultural knowledge research.

121

Avruch (1998) describes the review of a book on Interactive Conflict Resolution (ICR) by Ronald Fischer (1997). Fischer describes the contingency approach to conflict resolution and links the intervention (conciliation, consultation (ICR), arbitration, and peacekeeping) to the stage of the conflict (discussion, polarization, segregation, destruction).

Avruch (Avruch 1998) introduces a series of articles by concluding that there is a need to place conflict resolution in the larger socio-cultural context and not isolate it from the meanings in which conflict is embedded – an understanding of the cultures in conflict is essential. This work contains a very strong reference list.

Avruch (1998) sets out to review the different views of culture, and to assess how they are used in conflict resolution. His opening definition is that culture (Pg. 5): "is a derivative of individual experience, something learned or created by individuals themselves or passed on to them socially by contemporaries or ancestors." The idea being that it is an individually based definition. He argues that *generic culture* is particular to Homo sapiens, and that *local cultures* are specific to individuals within a culture.

Avruch says that conflict occurs when (Pg. 24): "two related parties – individuals, groups, communities, or nation-states – find themselves divided by perceived incompatible interests or goals in competition for control of scarce resources." He points to the work of Ruth Benedict (1946) in persuading the US government not to drop the atomic bomb on Kyoto during World War II, with consideration for it being the cultural soul of Japan. Along these lines, he suggests that metaphors are an approach that scholars in anthropology, international relations, and conflict studies are now focusing more and more ((Johnston 1995); (Fernandez 1991); (Nudler 1990)). In describing the considerations of diplomacy, the author quotes the definition created by Wynn Catlin as, "diplomacy is the art of saying *nice doggie* till you find a rock."

Avruch quotes Napoleon as having said that **power** trumps everything, but it is only a temporary solution to negotiations. He references the work of Cohen (1990) on the Egyptian-Israeli conflict where Egypt continued to retaliate to save honor, whereas the Israeli's considered disproportionate force to be a deterrent. This failure to understand culture caused the conflict to escalate. Avruch warns that one major concern is to see cultures as monolithic, homogenous, uniformly distributed and timeless. He argues that an *emic* approach is literally indispensable when considering cultures and conflict.

On the *etic* side, Avruch points to the work of Hofstede, and quotes his answer to the question of how much cultural variation the four dimensions of his work define (Pg. 67): "the four dimensions together account for 49 percent of the country [national culture] differences in the data…The remaining half is country [national culture] specific: it cannot be associated with any worldwide factor…"

As Avruch indicates, most of the research conducted at the university level is extremely thin, usually compares a USA institution with a similar institution in another country, and usually comes from the Western perspective. He goes on to note that studies have shown how mutually entangled reasoning and culture can be, and how little work in cross-cultural studies of human reasoning have been performed (Hamill 1990). With regard to the theory of culture and conflict, Avruch quotes Jim Laue as saying (Pg. 94): "well it seems to work in practice – let's see if it works in theory."

Avruch also quotes Marc Ross as saying (Pg. 94.): "modifying psycho-cultural interpretations, is a crucial step before effective joint problem-solving can occur in many polarized conflicts…The emphasis is on facilitating participation in situations that challenge previous interpretations…It is hoped that new metaphors will develop, allowing adversaries to view each other differently…"

Avruch reiterates that the importance of negotiators with cultural sensitivity, who knows that there is much to learn about the specific individuals that are to take part in negotiations, not just their cultural background. He quotes a Moroccan proverb to this end: *men resemble their times more than their fathers*. In closing he notes that experienced people from the USA State Department suggests that once a person better understands other cultures, the better they are able to understand their own. This last quote succinctly summarizes a theme that has been discussed in this work. That being that because of the mobility of our time, people have moved from their homelands and have become citizens of the world. The world and their environment shape to a large degree their values and perspectives, perhaps as much as their lineage.

Bailey (1998) notes that the cultural knowledge at the disposal of any particular individual is an *idiocosm* (an individualistic view of the world). An idiocosm is an individual selection from what is available in a culture. The process of translating culture into action is either one of caricature (to excite an attitude in the viewer) or a mask (presenting in a way to persuade).

The warning here is that a leader must take care in learning to **empathize** that he or she does not impose excessive personal views on the information being acquired.

Clarke and Lipp (1998) propose a seven step conflict resolution model for cross-cultural conflict (strong advice for facilitators):

- Problem identification – statement of problem, difficulties, and explanations. Suggestion that each cultural group do each independently first, then reach mutual understanding. (**communication**)
- Problem clarification – statement of intentions and perceptions. Suggestion that each cultural group do each independently first, then reach mutual understanding. (**communication, empathy**)
- Cultural exploration – hidden expectations and assumptions. Explore and discuss.
- Organizational exploration – global and local considerations. Guide discussions on methods.
- Conflict resolution – set goals, achieve harmony, set plan. Explore the standard values through facilitation.
- Impact assessment – monitor the results and assess the benefits.
- Organizational integration – lessons learned.

The authors base their hypothesis on the foundation of that extensive knowledge in the other culture and prolonged contact with the culture is essential. They also believe that the use of a bi-cultural facilitation team is important. The authors also suggest that one of the results of this seven-step approach is to develop what they call a *unique third culture*. By this, they mean a blending of the two to form a third that is designed and constructed for the negotiation by the parties.

Connors (1998) did an experiment with a group of education students in a workshop to explore the use of art in resolving conflicts. Her conclusions were that using art, visual metaphors, and storytelling was an effective and efficient means of learning about creative conflict resolution. Section 3.5 of this work explored the issue of metaphor, as did a recent paper (Grisham 2006).

Levine (1998) provides a perspective from his experiences in the USA legal system. He suggests ten principles that foster dispute resolution:

- Believing in abundance – negotiations from the view that there is enough for all through creativity

- Using resources efficiently – be mindful of the use of resources in getting to resolution. It creates a mindset of attention to thrift
- Being creative – look for win-win solutions (**transformation**)
- Fostering Resolution – nurture collaboration between the parties
- Becoming vulnerable – drop the bravado barriers. The author describes the use of the *truth circle*. The participants form a circle and pass around a *talking stick*, which permits the person with the stick to speak uninterruptedly while the others listen attentively (**trust, power, empathy**)
- Forming long-term collaborations – moving the mind set from short term quick hit solutions to long term thinking
- Relying on feelings and intuition – working beyond the proven five senses
- Disclosing information and feelings – share information more fully (**communication**)
- Learning throughout the process
- Becoming responsible – responsible for solving the conflict

Levine also sets forth a model for conflict resolution in seven circular steps:
- The attitude of resolution – internalizing the ten principles above, and listening effectively. The author indicates that there are many truths. As a colleague, Dr. William Ma often says from his experience, "there are a thousand ways of telling a truth."
- Telling your story – effective communications and listening (**communication**)
- Listening for a preliminary vision of resolution – thinking about a resolution that honors the concerns of all parties (Dawson 1995)
- Getting current and complete – saying the difficult things that include emotional issues
- Reaching agreement in principle – defining a vision of the future
- Crafting the new agreement
- Resolution – the act of unraveling a perplexing problem

Nader (1998) argues that there is a harmony model of law which has developed over time that differs from the conventional conflict model. She illustrates her point by comparing the differences between villagers in Protestant New England and urban dwellers. The urban dwellers tended to rely on laws whereas the villagers tended to rely on interpersonal harmony in the community. The author states that (Pg. 43): "the rise of economic and social stratification, industrialization, commerce and trade, increased immigration, and declining church membership...the conflict model replaced the [harmony] model."

Nader points to the work of Chanock (1987) who reports that missionaries introduced the idea of punishment and conflict on societies that were previously inclined toward a harmonious approach. Thus, calling into consideration how other societies that experienced colonialization modified their approach. Nadir concludes her article by saying that harmony is heavily influenced by religion, and that in most parts of the world law and religion are not separated as they are in the west.

Oetzel (1998) did a study of Latinos and European Americans. The study found:

- Self-construal (**transformation**) is a better predictor of conflict styles than ethnic/cultural background (self-construal is self-image, or how we see ourselves).
- Dominating conflict styles are associated positively with independent self-construal while avoiding, obliging, and compromising conflict styles are associated positively with interdependent self-construal
- Integrating conflict styles are associated strongly and positively with interdependent self-construal and weakly and positively with independent self-construal.

Scimecca (1998) states that the field of conflict resolution lacks a theoretical base, and that there are only two theories that predominate: game theory (assumption that both parties to a conflict have perfect information), and human needs theory (people seek to supply their basic human needs). The author then goes on to state that both are flawed. Nader added the harmony model to game theory and human needs theory discussed by Scimecca.

Xie, Song et al. (1998) performed a study of 968 marketing managers from Japan, Hong Kong, the United States, and Great Britain. The authors hypothesize that there is a relationship between performance and the level of inter-functional conflict. They found that in Western culture the conflicts in new product development suffered from inter-functional conflict, while the reverse was true for Eastern cultures. They also found that competition was a counterproductive method in Japan, and the reverse to be true in the West. The article provides some interesting findings relating to products.

Adams (1999) reports on an article that reviews the work of Tinsley (1998) which sets forth three strategies for dealing with conflict: defer to **power**, focus on existing rules or laws, or seek a solution that satisfies self-interests. Tinsley found that the Japanese group sought to defer to power, the German group sought to resort to rules and regulations, and the American group chose to use the last approach of self-interest.

Liu (1999) describes the principle arguments relating to inter-cultural studies by argumentation theorists who maintain that conflict resolution must be based upon shared interests and reasons. Liu argues that people are more aware of other value systems (Lee Kuan Yew as an example of a western-educated leader), that they prefer to frame arguments in these terms, and that they do not suffer a disadvantage for doing so. Liu postulates that arguments are increasingly using intra-cultural wedges to cast doubt within the opposition or cross arguing.

5.4 Conflict Theory 2000 thru 2005

Deutsch (2000) sets forth a number of unanswered questions that remain for knowledge and practice in conflict resolution through what he calls conflict resolution training (CRT) including:

- Nature of the skills involved in constructive conflict resolution
- What determines when a conflict is ripe for resolution
- What are the basic dimensions along which cultures vary their response and management of conflict
- What are the differences and similarities of conflict between individuals, groups, and cultures
- What are the most effective ways of dealing with difficult people and conflicts

Fischer (2000) describes the types of intergroup conflicts as being: resource, value, **power**, and needs. Fischer points to the research on groups and social identity theory to emphasize that the self-esteem of people is linked to group membership and that group membership can lead to ethnocentrism, nationalism, or professionalism – what the author calls attribution errors. The possible excesses that can occur lead easily to groupthink, and the desire to escalate the conflict. The author then suggests that in such conditions an independent third party is the most viable option.

Kimmel (2000) presents the concept of *micro cultures* in an article on culture and conflict as commonalities in meaning, norms of **communication**, and behavior, shared perception and expectation that develop among individuals from varying cultural backgrounds as the interact over time. Kimmel notes that Hall (1976) hypothesized that cultural categories, plans and rules are unconscious. Moreover, as Avruch and Black (1991) contend, as societies become more complex and fluid, ethnographic markers become less reliable. The author argues that training in cross-cultural communications must get to the emotional level if it is to be successful. Kimmel describes five levels of cultural awareness:

- Cultural chauvinism – little knowledge or interest in others
- Ethnocentrism – belief in superiority and stereotyping
- Tolerance – behavior is not seen as inherent, but as living in a different society
- Minimization – differences are acknowledged but trivialized
- Understanding – recognition and acceptance of differences

The author contends that the ability of people to shift their mindset, and the ability/desire to learn, are critical to the process of cultural awareness. For building peace and negotiations, Kimmel indicates that the skills required include **empathy**, imagination, innovation (**communication**), commitment (**trust**), flexibility, and persistence (strong reference for training). In addition, modesty and graciousness are key personal attributes in intercultural considerations (Etheridge 1987).

In a study of 150 Jordanian managers, Kozan (2000) studies a demographic base that is not western, that isolates authority and the topic of conflict. The study showed that there was a high level of correlation between collaboration and compromise (Blake and Mouton 1964). The author suggests that this apparent contradiction may lie in the sequential nature of negotiations, in that compromise is just an opener for collaboration. Kozan also notes that managers guard their **power**, but are not forceful in applying it, and that there is a general aversion to forcing people in the culture. The author points to the work of Ali (1987) who said that familiarity with sociocentric and family-tribal orientations is essential for understanding how decisions are made in Arab society. The author concludes that process rather than content theories should be utilized in developing countries.

In an article on communications and conflict Krauss and Morsella (2000) review four basic paradigms of **communications**, and set forth principles associated with each:

Encoding-Decoding Paradigm (sender and receiver)

- Avoid communications with low *signal to noise* ratios, or increase redundancy

Intentionalist Paradigm (intention)

- Listen and try to understand the intended meaning
- Consider how your message (words) will be received

Perspective-Taking Paradigm
- When speaking take account of the perspective of the listener

Dialogic Paradigm
- Be an active listener
- Focus on creating conditions for effective communications
- Pay attention to message form

Lederach (2000) writes about the central American perspective on conflict. One example of his use of cultural metaphor is (Pg. 168): "Perhaps the term that best indicates and describes the folk concept of conflict is *un enredo*, or *estamos bien enredados* (we are all entangled). A simple translation, however, does not transmit the full significance of the term. This is a fishing metaphor in its roots. It is built around the Spanish word red, a fisherman's net. To be *enredado* is to be tangled, caught in a net. The image is one of knots and connections, an intimate and intricate mess. A net, when tangled, must slowly and patiently be worked through and undone. When untangled it still remains connected and knotted. It is a whole. A net is also frequently torn leaving holes that must be sewn back together, knotting once again the separated loose ends. Nothing describes conflict resolution at the interpersonal level in Central America better than this folk metaphor."[16]

In an article that addresses the constructive use of controversy, Lewicki and Wiethoff (2000) suggest that there must be cooperation, and propose the following sequence:
- Initial problem – people categorize and organize incomplete information to form an initial conclusion (freeze the epistemic process)
- Presentation of conclusion – a cognitive rehearsal to deepen their own understanding
- Confrontation of different conclusions – different conclusions from others create uncertainty (unfreeze the epistemic process)
- Curiosity – search for more information and different perspectives
- New conclusions – re-conceptualized and re-organized conclusions

Ravlin, Thomas et al. (2000) describe multicultural conflict in groups with a focus on cultural values. The authors state that values are learned early in life and are relatively stable over time. For a Chinese-American, the implication is that they would have acquired more

---

[16] See also Lakoff, G. and M. Johnson (1980). Methphors We Live By. Chicago, University of Chicago Press.

emphasis on American attitudes and values if they left China at the age of twelve for example. This article has a wealth of strong references.

Avruch and Black (2001) state that culture is the *sine quo non* (something that is an essential part of the whole) of being human, and that conflict is a natural part of that essence. They use the metaphor of grammar for culture, and the requirement that conflict requires an understanding of the party's grammar.

Donaldson (2001) in an article on ethics notes that there is no black and white for ethical standards but rather what he calls *moral free space*, or the *gray zone*. He describes conflicts of relative development, and conflict of cultural tradition as two types of conflict that should be considered. Conflicts of relative development arise when countries have different levels of development and differences in wages and standards of living. Conflict of cultural tradition means attention to cultural standards that are not practiced in the expatriate manager's home country.

Greenberg (2001) provides a good review of the research that has been conducted on the concept of justice. He discusses distributive (norms of fairness) and procedural (the process itself) justice. Greenberg also addresses the issue of trust as being calculus based (i.e., trust based on fear of getting punished) and identification-based **trust** (i.e., trust based on accepting another's wants and desires) (Lewicki and Wiethoff 2000), and notes that this constitutes a limitation as it ignores fundamental differences in the construct of trust (Lewicki, Mcallister et al. 1998). Greenberg states that (no page number HTML document): "in a study of cultural differences, a limitation is posed by the inherent tendency for national cultures to be interdependent, leading to cultural diffusion. This, in turn, creates spuriously inflated correlations between culture and various dependent measures, a phenomenon known as Gallon's Problem (Naroll, Michik et al. 1980)." As the world becomes more mobile, this problem becomes more intransigent.

Gurevitch (2001) describes the effects of what he calls the *circle of understanding* (**communication, empathy**) as enumerated in the circular four step process below:

- Inability to understand – use of stories, explanations, and information provide a means of communication between the parties from a common world (e.g. culture).
- Ability to understand – adequate information is received and internalized from step 1 (e.g. common culture).

- Inability to not understand – new understanding is a version of some old understanding like a preconceived dogmatic idea. Similar to an intransigent position.
- Ability to not understand – ability to listen and understand communications as if the other person. The author suggests techniques for opening effective dialogue in workshops.

Lederach (2001) provides a graphical view of his work in Central America where, *confianza* reflects the concept of **trust** and confidence, *platicar* reflects more than conversation but a cultural "being" with another, *consejo* reflects the idea of a counselor or mentor, and *ubicarse* reflects the idea of getting advice or finding out where one is. Finding a way out of the situation or putting things back together is *arreglo*. Lederach's article addresses the prescriptive and elicitive models of conflict resolution.

In an article with an Arab view of the west, Salem (2001) describes a comfort culture in the West. He states that western conflict resolution is based on the assumption that pain is bad and comfort is good, whereas other cultures consider bad to be *bad* and good to be *good*. The author maintains that Western culture eschews discomfort, and that other cultures consider discomfort to be part of natural life.

Oetzel, Ting-Toomey et al. (2001) performed a study of 768 students from China, Germany, Japan, and the USA to investigate *face* and *facework* during conflicts. By *face* the authors mean an individuals sense of positive image (respect, honor, status, reputation, credibility, competence, family/network connection, loyalty, **trust**, relational indebtedness, and obligation issues), and by *facework* they mean **communication** strategies used to keep face or cause another to loose face.

Prescriptive	Elicitive
Training as transfer	Training as discovery and creation
Resource: Model and knowledge of trainer	Resource: Within-setting knowledge
Training as content: Master approach and technique	Training as process oriented: Participate in model creation
Empowerment as learning new ways and strategies for facing conflict	Empowerment as validating and Building from context
Trainer as expert, model, and facilitator	Trainer as catalyst and facilitator
Culture as technique	Culture as foundation and seedbed

Figure 19 – Conflict Modes (Lederach data modified)

The authors use a definition of conflict as (Pg. 235): "the interaction of interdependent people who perceive opposition of goals, aims, and values, and who see the other party as potentially interfering with the realization of these goals (Putnam and Poole 1987)." Chinese face consists of *lien* (or *lian*) and *mien-tzu* (or mianzi) ((Gao 1998); (Chang and Holt 1994)) *Lien* refers to the moral character of an individual while *mien-tzu* refers to the social status achieved through success in life.

In Japan face (**empathy, trust**) consists of *mentsu* and *taimen* (Morisaki and Gudykunst 1994). *Mentsu* is similar to the concept of moral character, and *taimen* refers to the appearance one presents to others. In Germany *gesicht* means face and the United States of course, face. Oetzel, Ting-Toomey et al. describe face theory as (Pg. 238): "in a nutshell, the face negotiation theory argues that: (a) people in all cultures try to maintain and negotiate face in all **communication** situations; (b) the concept of 'face' is especially problematic in uncertain situations (such as conflict situations) when the situated identities of the communicators are called into question; (c) cultural variability, individual-level variables, and situational variables influence cultural members' selection of face concerns over others (such as self-oriented face-saving vs. other-oriented face-saving); and (d) subsequently, cultural variability, individual-level variables, and situational variables influence the use of various facework and conflict strategies in intergroup and interpersonal encounters."

Oetzel, Ting-Toomey et al. consider face in three categories: self-face, other-face, and mutual-face. In referencing their theory to Hofstede's dimensions, they contend that *individualists* have high self-face, *collectivist* have high other face and mutual-face. Their study includes the separate work by the authors that found different types of facework behavior during conflicts with best friends or relative strangers:

- Dominating Facework - aggression and defend-self, express feelings
- Avoiding Facework – avoid, give in, involve third party, pretend
- Integrating Facework - apologize, compromise, consider the other, private discussion, remain calm, talk about the problem, express feelings

Oetzel, Ting-Toomey et al. also describe the work of Brown and Levinson (1987) on politeness theory. Politeness theory focuses on positive and negative face, with five strategies: do not perform the act, go off the record, mitigate the threat of negative face, mitigate the threat of positive face, then go on the record. While the theory has been criticized widely, much research has been done using it as a starting point.

In an article on communications, Singh (2001) states that dialogue is a means of containing inter-cultural conflict through an attitude of discovery, exploration, and interrogation. Singh points to the work of Burbules and Rice (1991), who argue for *communicative* *virtues* that include:

- Tolerance
- Patience
- Respect for differences
- Willingness to listen to others
- The inclination to admit one may be mistaken
- The ability to reinterpret or translate one's own concerns in a way that make them comprehensible to others
- The self-imposition of restraint in order that others may 'have a turn' to speak
- The disposition to express oneself honestly and sincerely

According to Singh, Burbules (1993) argues that (Pg. 349): "if dialogue is to have a chance of success, it must ride on participants' mutual feelings of concern (**empathy**), **trust**, respect, appreciation, affection and hope as well as on cognitive understanding (**communication**)."

Ting-Toomey, Oetzel et al. (2001) did a study to explore effects of ethnic background, sex, and self-construal types (see (Singelis and Brown 1995) and (Gudykunst and Matsumoto 1996)) on conflict styles among African Americans, Asian Americans, European Americans, and Latin Americans in the USA. The authors start with two aspects of self-construal, independent and interdependent, and then combine these into four dimensions of self as biconstrual, independent, interdependent, and ambivalent. They predicted and found that self-construal (self-image) provides a better explanation of conflict styles than does ethnicity or sex.

Ting-Toomey, Oetzel et al. state that the theory of face (2001) defined eight styles of responses during conflict that were clustered in this study into (**empathy, trust**) Self-face, Other-Face, and Mutual-Face, and that conflict styles are learned within the primary socialization of an individual's cultural group (Ting-Toomey and Kurogi 1998). The authors also point to other work on gender (Gillian 1998) that found males tend to be individualistic and females collectivist. The authors also state (Pg. 91): "ethnic identity salience is the strength with which one identifies with their ethnic group, whereas cultural identity salience is the strength with which one identifies with the larger culture. Ting-Toomey, Yee-Jung et al. (2000) found that ethnic and cultural identity have stronger effects on conflict styles than ethnic background."

Figure 20 was constructed from the Rahim model and the information from the Ting-Toomey, Oetzel et al. article.

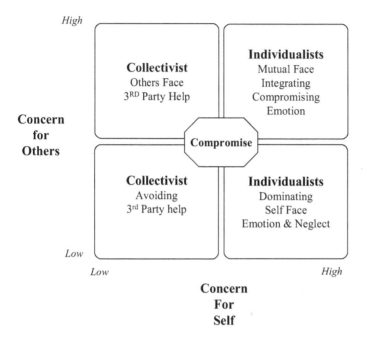

Figure 20 – Face (Ting-Toomey, Oetzel et al. modified)

Gesteland (2002) looks at culture through the lens of practical experience negotiating in numerous cultures. Gesteland's book provides numerous practical tips relating to communications across cultures, and many do's and don'ts. He proposes a scale that ranges from deal focused (DF) (transactional) to relationship focused (RF) and categorizes cultures as adapted in Ayoko, Härtel et al. (2002) argue that the type and course of conflict in culturally heterogeneous workgroups is impacted by the communicative behaviors and strategies employed by group members during interactions using **communication** accommodation theory (CAT) (Giles 1973). The study groups were heterogeneous but from a single national community. Ninety percent of the participants indicated that cultural differences underpinned most of the conflicts, occurred daily, and were intense; also 84% of participants indicated that poor **communication** skills underpinned conflicts. The authors also state that (no page numbers, HTML document): "there is substantial evidence that diverse workgroups experience more conflict and higher turnover, less **trust**, less job satisfaction, more stress, more absenteeism, and more communication problems," citing the work of others.

Table 6.

Ayoko, Härtel et al. (2002) argue that the type and course of conflict in culturally heterogeneous workgroups is impacted by the communicative behaviors and strategies employed by group members during interactions using **communication** accommodation theory (CAT) (Giles 1973). The study groups were heterogeneous but from a single national community. Ninety percent of the participants indicated that cultural differences underpinned most of the conflicts, occurred daily, and were intense; also 84% of participants indicated that poor **communication** skills underpinned conflicts. The authors also state that (no page numbers, HTML document): "there is substantial evidence that diverse workgroups experience more conflict and higher turnover, less **trust**, less job satisfaction, more stress, more absenteeism, and more communication problems," citing the work of others.

Rahim (2002) argues that organizations do not need conflict resolution, but conflict management (strong reference for organizational conflict). That means to minimize the disfunctionality of conflict, and maximize the attributes. He states that the criteria for conflict management should be organizational learning (**communication**), needs of stakeholders (**empathy**), and ethics. In addition, some strategies for conflict management include:

- Minimization of affective conflicts or interpersonal conflicts. The author quotes from Jehn (1997) who said that (Pg. 210): "relationship conflicts interfere with task-related effort because members focus on reducing threats (**trust**), increasing **power**, and attempting to build cohesion..." Rahim says that affective conflict diminishes group loyalty, commitment, job satisfaction, and intention to stay in the organization.
- Maintain moderate substantive conflict or task and content conflict. The author quotes from Jehn again (1995) who says that (Pg. 210): "groups with an absence of conflict may miss new ways to enhance their performance, while very high levels of task conflict may interfere with task competition." Rahim adds however, that substantive conflict can diminish group loyalty, commitment, job satisfaction, and intention to stay in the organization.
- Use appropriate strategies (behavior such as integrating, obliging, dominating, avoiding, and compromising).

Table 6 – Negotiating Focus (Gesteland data modified)

Relationship Focused Formal			
Polychronic Reserved	**Monochronic Reserved**	**Polychronic Expressive**	**Polychronic Variably Expressive**
Indian	Japanese	Arab	Russian
Bangladeshi	Chinese	Egyptian	Polish
Vietnamese	Korean	Turkish	Romanian
Thai	Singaporean	Greek	Slovak
Malaysian			
Indonesian			
Filipino			

Moderately Deal Focused Formal		Deal Focused Moderately Formal	Deal Focused Informal
Monochronic Variably Expressive	**Monochronic Variably Reserved**	**Monochronic Reserved**	**Monochronic Variably Expressive**
French	Lithuania	British	US
Belgian	Estonia	Irish	Canada
Italian	Baltic States	Danish	Australia
Spanish		Norwegian	
Hungarian		Swedish	
		Finnish	
		German	
		Dutch	
		Czech	

Rahim states that according to management scholars there is no one best way to make decisions, and that leadership requires matching the leadership style (from autocratic to participative) to the situation or contingency theory. He suggests that a conflict contingency theory could be constructed from a similar view (Rahim and Bonoma 1997). Rahim describes the styles available for handling interpersonal conflict in Figure 17. In this figure, Rahim redefines the dimensions Blake and Mouton provided earlier. In addition, Rahim adds his own metrics for calculating his Rahim Organizational Conflict Inventory-II (ROCI-II).

He uses a 5-point Likert scale for each of the dimensions, and then the Problem Solving dimension (PS=IN-AV) and the Bargaining dimension (BA=DO-OB) can be calculated.

Listening is a mutualistic art that by its very practice enhanced equality. The empathetic listener becomes more like his interlocutor as the two bridge the differences between them by conversation and mutual understanding. Indeed, one measure of healthy political talk is the amount of silence it permits and encourages, for silence is the precious medium in which reflection is nurtured and empathy can grow" (**communications**).

Brislin and Liu (2004), in a paper that emphasizes the financial aspects of diversity, point to the work of Pettigrew (1998). Pettigrew identified four key components for positive, non-conflict, intercultural contact: equal status, common goals, cooperative effort, and support from authority figures (**empathy, power**, and **communication**). According to the authors, cross-cultural education is the key to avoiding and resolving conflicts. They recommend the use of critical incidents or stories that force people to deal with the conflicts that can arise. In the same Brislin and Liu text, Lee, Moghaddam et al. point to the work of researchers represented in *Culture & Psychology* as having had adopted a normative model of behavior and has preferred qualitative methods shared with the *new social psychologies* of Europe.

Kim, Lee et al. (2004) point to the work of Ting-Toomey, Gao et al. (1991) as one example of the *national culture* approach to conflict management studies, and Kim and Leung (2000) for limitations due to conceptualizations of conflict styles. Kim, Lee et al. study the intra-cultural variability of people to examine links between individualistic and collectivistic values, using the Rahim Organizational Conflict Inventory-II (1983). They found only three discrete dimensions of conflict styles emerged: compromising/integrating, obliging/avoiding, and dominating. Table 7 provides a detailed description of the appropriate times and conditions to utilize each of the contingency theory styles.

Rahim goes on to set forth a process for managing conflict. The process begins with a diagnosis, followed by intervention, conflict, learning and effectiveness, and feedback.

In his article on listening, Welton (2002) quotes from a book by Barber (1984) who says that (Pg. 200): "an emphasis on speech enhances natural inequalities in individual's abilities to speak with clarity, eloquence, logic and rhetoric.

Listening is a mutualistic art that by its very practice enhanced equality. The empathetic listener becomes more like his interlocutor as the two bridge the differences between them by conversation and mutual understanding. Indeed, one measure of healthy political talk is the amount of silence it permits and encourages, for silence is the precious medium in which reflection is nurtured and empathy can grow" (**communications**).

Brislin and Liu (2004), in a paper that emphasizes the financial aspects of diversity, point to the work of Pettigrew (1998). Pettigrew identified four key components for positive, non-conflict, intercultural contact: equal status, common goals, cooperative effort, and support from authority figures (**empathy, power**, and **communication**). According to the authors, cross-cultural education is the key to avoiding and resolving conflicts. They recommend the use of critical incidents or stories that force people to deal with the conflicts that can arise. In the same Brislin and Liu text, Lee, Moghaddam et al. point to the work of researchers represented in *Culture & Psychology* as having had adopted a normative model of behavior and has preferred qualitative methods shared with the *new social psychologies* of Europe.

Kim, Lee et al. (2004) point to the work of Ting-Toomey, Gao et al. (1991) as one example of the *national culture* approach to conflict management studies, and Kim and Leung (2000) for limitations due to conceptualizations of conflict styles. Kim, Lee et al. study the intra-cultural variability of people to examine links between individualistic and collectivistic values, using the Rahim Organizational Conflict Inventory-II (1983). They found only three discrete dimensions of conflict styles emerged: compromising/integrating, obliging/avoiding, and dominating.

Slate (2004) reported the comments of Mr. Ahmed El-Kosheri saying (Pg. 98): "in general, the legal community throughout the Arab world is still manifesting its hostility to transnational arbitration .... the continuing attitude of certain western arbitrators being characterized by a lack of sensitivity towards the national laws of developing countries and their mandatory application, either due to the ignorance, carelessness, or to unjustified psychological superiority complexes..." Slate then suggests that the dispute resolution profession should explore the issues of verbal miscommunications, non-verbal miscommunications (**communications**), cultural mores of negotiation and mediation, cultural biases and stereotypes, and religion and politics.

In an article on creating high performance teams through leadership coaching, de Vries and Manfred (2005) discusses the importance of constructive conflict resolution. De Vries begins by looking at the executives doing the coaching and recommends that they assess their own personalities and roles (martyr, scapegoat, cheerleader, peacemaker, hero, or clown) as a starting point for helping teams seek effective conflict resolution. Communications were critical in seeking to manage conflicts effectively based on frank, open, and honest engagement. The ability to build trusting relationships through open exchange of information was a critical component.

Table 7 – Conflict Styles (Rahim modified Table 1)

ROCI-II	Conflict Style	Situations where appropriate	Situations where inappropriate
IN	Integrating	1. Issues are complex. 2. Synthesis of ideas is needed to come up with better solutions 3. Commitment is needed from other parties for successful implementation 4. Time is available for problem solving. 5. One party alone cannot solve the problem. 6. Resources possessed by different parties are needed to solve their common problems.	1. Task or problem is simple. 2. Immediate decision is required. 3. Other parties are unconcerned about outcome. 4. Other parties do not have problem-solving skills.
OB	Obliging	1. You believe that you may be wrong. 2. Issue is more important to the other party. 3. You are willing to give up something in exchange for something from the other party in the future. 4. You are dealing from a position of weakness. 5. Preserving relationship is important.	1. Issue is important to you. 2. You believe that you are right. 3. The other party is wrong or unethical.
DO	Dominating	1. Issue is trivial. 2. Speedy decision is needed. 3. Unpopular course of action is implemented. 4. Necessary to overcome assertive subordinates. 5. Unfavorable decision by the other party may be costly to you. 6. Subordinates lack expertise to make technical decisions. 7. Issue is important to you.	1. Issue is complex. 2. Issue is not important to you. 3. Both parties are equally powerful. 4. Decision does not have to be made quickly. 5. Subordinates possess high degree of competence.
AV	Avoiding	1. Issue is trivial. 2. Potential dysfunctional effect of confronting the other party outweighs benefits of resolution. 3. Cooling off period is needed.	1. Issue is important to you. 2. It is your responsibility to make decision. 3. Parties are unwilling to defer, issue must be resolved. 4. Prompt attention is needed.
CO	Compromising	1. Goals of parties are mutually exclusive. 2. Parties are equally powerful. 3. Consensus cannot be reached. 4. Integrating or dominating style is not successful. 5. Temporary solution to a complex problem is needed.	1. One party is more powerful. 2. Problem is complex enough needing problem-solving approach.

De Vries summarizes by saying that (Pg. 70): "**trust** is a delicate flower: it doesn't take much to crush it, and once destroyed, it takes a very long time to nurture it back into bloom. However, if trust is honored and protected, it flourishes and bears good fruit. Trust makes for constructive conflict resolution; constructive conflict resolution makes for genuine commitment; and commitment makes for accountability—all factors that have an enormous impact on the bottom line of an organization."

5.5   Conflict Theory LeBaron

Michelle LeBaron (2003) wrote about the intersection of culture and conflict with emphasis on *cultural fluency, mindful awareness,* and *dynamic engagement* (**empathy, communication**). This is a very strong reference for those interested in training for conflict resolution. LeBaron notes that cultures give our lives shape, and are formed from our upbringing, ancestors, stories, metaphors, rituals, myths, and of course experiences (**empathy, communication**). Early in the book, she describes the common metaphors for the USA as a *melting pot,* and for Canada as a *salad bowl.* Her suggestion being that metaphors provide us with starting points, and that they can help reveal the complexities and paradoxes of cultures – what she called *mindfields.* She also suggests that we can explore the cultural differences through the eyes of poets, novelists, historians, artists, philosophers, and musicians.

LeBaron considers cultural fluency internalized familiarity with the workings of a culture. In other words, knowing the vocabulary and the grammar (idioms, symbols, history, art and experience with those that speak it), or what she calls the underground river. The example she uses is one of literal translations that have no meaning, where an idiom is the only way to convey the true meaning. LeBaron insists that one must suspend defensiveness and replace it with a spirit of inquiry, and points to three main considerations for starting points: high-low context, individualism & communitarianism, and specificity & diffuseness. She also described the importance of respect in cultural conflicts – with the starting point being the platinum rule *do unto others, as they would have you do unto them.*

On the issue of time, she points to an Indian description of an eon as being the time required to wear away the Himalayas with a delicate touch each year from a monk. In addition, she describes the Arab perception of time from the desert as a *constant everydayness.*

LeBaron describes a training technique for sensitizing people how they respond to unfamiliar circumstances. The room is split into two groups, and each selects a cultural consultant who leaves the room to prepare a strategy for gathering information about the culture of Alphaville. The consultants are outsiders and can only ask yes or no questions. The residents remaining in the room are instructed to respond yes to any question asked with a smile, and no to any question asked with a non-smile (strong resource for cultural training).

LeBaron summarizes her ideas on cultural lenses with an interesting chart that shows the relationship between core values, personality, and the way we see cultures[17]. The exterior divisions are intended to represent cultural identity groups, which can be numerous, and the radial lines indicating their influence on the personality and core values. The author also provides a good chart to summarize the three dimensions of conflict, and show how they intertwine.

LeBaron suggests that dynamic engagements are animated by a spirit of dialogue with the following components: attend/assess, suspend judgments, receive from the other side, create circles of shared experience, design a resolution that makes cultural sense, reflect, integrate, and quest.[18]

After the introduction to culture and conflict, LeBaron describes the ways of knowing about cultural conflict resolution as shown in Table 14. She begins with the personal practices that we can do by ourselves. Writing into clarity helps remove us from a problem by changing our focus, and helps surface those parts of us that *whisper:*

- By shapeshifting, she draws on the folklore of tricksters that are wily and can change shape, by suspending common sense and exploring ideas.
- By sitting with resistance she means to explore those feelings that one would prefer to push away.
- By writing a letter, she suggests writing a letter to someone dear explaining your issues.
- By listening with your body, she means to use the natural skills to read body language openly.
- By catching and releasing, she means the creative process of intense focus on a problem, then putting it out of the conscious mind.
- By shifting frames, she means frames of reference, like our cultures; and by continuing inquiry, she means putting ourselves in unfamiliar cultural territory, exploration.

---

[17] See also Novinger, T. (2001). Intercultural Communications: A Practical Guide. Austin, University of Texas Press.

[18] See also Palmer, H. (1990). The Enneagram: Understanding Yourself and Others in Your Life. San Francisco, Harper San Francisco.

Table 8 – Knowing (LeBaron data modified)

Ways of Knowing	Practices for Attention	Personal Practices	Interpersonal Practices	Intergroup Practices
Intuitive & Imaginative	Release Given's	Writing into clarity & Shapeshifting	Dancing on a dime & noticing magic	Discovering common futures & composing shared images
Emotional	Emotional Fluency (EQ)	Sitting with resistance & writing a letter	Exchanging three minutes of passion & enacting rituals	Cultivating emotional intelligence & facilitating conversational learning
Somatic	Physical Attunement	Listening with the body & catching releasing	Using metaphors & embracing paradox	Learning through adventure & applying participatory action research
Connected	Spiritual Understanding	Shifting frames & continuing inquiry	Partnering & sharing songs	Dialoguing & metaphor journeying

Under interpersonal practices, LeBaron describes dancing on a dime as critical for bridging cultural differences. She describes it as being graceful and poised under change and uncertainty, springing from a solid relationship that can sustain such fluctuations:

- By noticing magic, she means to uncover the gems in intercultural situations.
- By exchanging three minutes of passion, she means describing for three minutes things about which one is passionate.
- By enacting rituals, she means to put sensations and feelings ahead of thought and analysis.
- By using metaphors, she means making strong use of images and symbols.
- By embracing paradox, she means to accept those actions that are contradictory.
- By partnering she means having someone act as a coach or mentor.
- By sharing songs, she means to share music as a way of opening a different personal world.

142

Under intergroup practices, LeBaron begins by describing discovering common futures. By this, she means imagining alternative futures and the use of open space technologies,[19] future searches, and dialogue:

- By composing shared images, she means a way of exploring a gestalt.
- By cultivating emotional intelligence, she means expanding personal understanding of cultures.
- By facilitating conversational learning, she means paying attention to the spaces where conversations take place.
- By learning through adventure, she means to share excursions.
- By applying participatory action research, she means bringing people together in groups to explore cultural differences.
- By dialoguing, she means setting structures into place where people share personal opinions not those of groups.
- By metaphor journeying, she means sharing and exploring cultural metaphors.

5.6 Negotiation

Due to the limitations set for this work, the following is a very brief overview of some basic literature on the topic of negotiation theory. The following would serve as a point of commencement for a more thorough review of the literature.

Brett (2001) indicates that there are distributive agreements (distribute a fixed set of assets – smaller *pie*) or integrative agreements (distribute a differentially valued set of assets – bigger *pie*). Brett distinguishes between interests (needs underlying the negotiator's position), priorities, and strategies (set of behaviors). The author points out that within a culture there is a wide range of diversity and behavior that can be thought of as normal distribution curves. She says (Pg. 9): "negotiation strategies are linked with culture because cultures evolve norms to facilitate social interaction. Norms are functional because they reduce the number of choices a person has to make about how to behave and because they provide expectations about how others in the culture will behave. Functional norms become institutionalized, meaning that most people use them and new members of the culture learn them because they make social interaction efficient."

---

[19] See also Weisbord, M. and S. Janoff (2000). Future Search: An Action guide to Finding Common Ground in Organizations and Communities. San Francisco, Berrett-Koehler.

In Figure 21, Brett summarizes negotiation strategies, and discusses how different cultures deal with issues such as confrontation and motivation. When discussing influence, the author emphasizes the importance of *fairness standards* (contract, law, precedent, norms, etc.) in negotiations to provide a benchmark for perceived fairness. Regarding the transfer of information, Brett makes the point that cultural issues can make large differences in the **communication** of information and intent.

Brett states that there are three features of cultural study related to the variability of negotiation strategies across cultures: individualism/collectivism (Hofstede 1980), egalitarianism/hierarchy (Leung 1997) (Hofstede's power/distance), and low/high context (Hall and Hall 1990). On the issue of individualism/collectivism negotiators may choose or avoid confrontation, and their motivation may be individually focused or group focused. In egalitarianism/hierarchy negotiations, the author notes that the participants will use confrontation and influence in different ways depending, for example, on the respect the culture provides for social status (**power**). In high/low context situations, negotiators will use distinct confrontational and information styles. Brett then sets forth the following considerations:

- Research is only beginning to understand the characteristic cultural negotiation strategies.
- Individual cultural members may not act like a cultural prototype.
- Negotiators change their strategies.

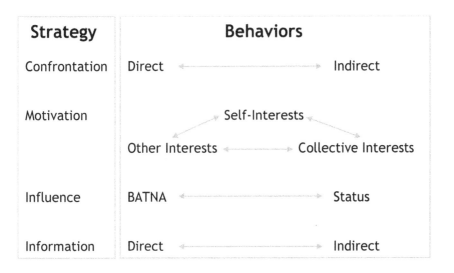

Figure 21 – Behaviors (Brett modified Exhibit 1.3)

Brett rightly observes that it may in fact be a disadvantage by knowing too much about the other party's culture, as it may lead to an oversimplification and stereotyping. In addition, experience indicates that transnational corporate culture will alter all of these aspects as well. On the issue of conflict in multicultural teams Brett indicates that there are three basic types: task conflict (difficult tasks), procedural conflict (how to do a task), and interpersonal conflict. Interestingly, she notes that research indicates that conflict is very detrimental to routine tasks, but that it can actually enhance performance on non-routine tasks or tasks with uncertainty.

Chaiken, Gruenfeld et al. (2000) focus on attitude change and persuasion in conflict resolution. The authors describe the heuristic-systematic theory of persuasion. The systematic approach is one of being careful, deep thinking, research intense, and carefully reasoned. The heuristic approach is one of being based upon easily comprehended cues (stored knowledge and memory). The authors argue that when concerns for accuracy are great, then the demand for systematic processing increases. The authors also contend that when their knowledge capacity is limited, then the use of heuristics increases (defense or impression motivation). Chaiken, Gruenfeld et al. indicate that persuasion research indicates that systematic processing is engaged by a defense motivation, then parties seek out information that supports their point of view, and resist information that runs counter (**communication**).

A review of Fisher and Ury (1983), and Thompson (1998) also provide a rich review of negotiation, and excellent references for those wishing to learn more about negotiation skills. In addition research on culture and conflict should also include: (Bordon 1991), (Cohen 1986), (Kimmel 1995).

5.7 Hourglass Model

It is critical that a leader have the ability to understand the sources of conflict, recognize conflict early, manage the conflict, and do this in a constructive way that pulls people together.

The sampling of the literature in cross-cultural conflict is rich and diverse, and I find common themes that resonate well with experience and practice. As indicated in the introduction, leadership requires the ability to manage conflict. Deleterious conflict needs to be resolved, but other forms of conflict can encourage the exploration of ideas and creativity. A leader must be able to understand the difference, and to have the capability to keep active conflict balanced – to manage it.

145

5.7.1 Origin of Conflict

According to LeBaron (2003) conflict emerges when people have difficulties dealing with *differences*. According to Levinson (1994) a conflict is a dispute over resources, and Rahim (2002) believes that they are either interpersonal or task oriented. The concept of differences is perhaps a better starting point as it allows the diversity of conflict than can occur in international relationships. At one extreme, consider two people in conflict over the appropriate way to greet each other and at the other extreme a war over the ownership of oil rich property. Clearly, differences in culture (religion, customs, folklore, music, art, literature, philosophy, language, history, and geography), ethics, power, and economic status cause friction, and friction causes conflict. LeBaron (2003) suggests that conflicts can be considered as material, **communicative**, or symbolic.

Consider the metaphor of friction for conflict. In the physical world, friction changes the speed at which water and airflow, the fuel efficiency of an automobile, or the ability of a person to climb rocks. However, it is often used to describe interpersonal relationships as well, as in the saying *there is a lot of friction in the room*. It can be a good thing in the case of climbers, and a bad thing in the case of low fuel economy. In the practice of Qigong and Yoga, one strives to eliminate friction blockages, thus improving the laminar flow of energy. Pondy (1967) describes this as disequilibrium, Nader (1998) describes the opposite as harmony.

Conflict is similar to change in that it has been with humankind for thousands of years, and will be with us for thousands more. It cannot, and should not, be eliminated but rather managed to benefit from the advantages, and minimize the disadvantages - this is the task of leaders.

5.7.2 Knowledge Lens

As with all leadership issues, there is a *chicken and egg* conundrum of what comes first. In an ideal world, the starting point is knowledge, for it determines the degree of *difference* that people perceive. Knowledge will change the *friction* (increase or decrease) that is present in the interactions that occur, and requires the careful understanding of a leader to guide and balance it.

Cohen (1990) describes how folktales express indirectly desires, wishes, fears and anxieties. Levinson (1994) suggests humor is a universal balm that can be applied. Most authors ((Brislin and Liu 2004); (Clarke and Lipp 1998); (Avruch 1998)) agree that cross-cultural training is a very strong mediator for avoiding and diminishing destructive conflict. Many suggest that the use of art and storytelling is a good method of exploring and extending knowledge of another culture. Spicer (1997) found for example that the major source of interpersonal conflict was a lack of tacit cultural knowledge. LaFromboise, Coleman et al. (1993) found that people use five methods to develop competence in a second culture: assimilation, acculturation, alternation, integration, and fusion (**empathy, transformation**).

Kimmel (2000) describes five levels of cultural awareness: cultural chauvinism, ethnocentrism, tolerance, minimization, and understanding. It is clearly in the best interest of the leader to see that individuals (including themselves) have reached as high a level of awareness as is possible. He concludes that **empathy**, imagination, innovation (**transformation**), commitment (**trust**), flexibility, and persistence are skills needed to achieve awareness. Etheridge (1987) adds modesty and graciousness to this list.

Metaphors ((Lederach 2000); (Augsburger 1992); (Avruch 1998); (Benedict 1946); (Johnston 1995); (Fernandez 1991); (Nudler 1990); (LeBaron 2003)), stories, and using the conflict wisdom of various cultures can help to educate people in the richness of a culture more effectively and rapidly. Michelle LeBaron (2003) wrote about the intersection of culture and conflict with emphasis on *cultural fluency*, *mindful awareness*, and *dynamic engagement*.

5.7.3   Diagnosis Lens

As people begin to participate and interact conflicts will develop, sometimes rapidly, sometimes slowly. As the conflict begins to take shape and becomes discernable, a diagnosis of the conflict will be required.

A number of authors ((Blake and Mouton 1964), (Rahim 2002), (Oetzel, Ting-Toomey et al. 2001)) argue that conflicts can be categorized as either interpersonal (affective) or task/goal (substantive). Interpersonal conflicts are clearly more intractable than task/goal conflicts and can lead to imbedded *friction* short and long term. Rahim (2002) contends that interpersonal conflict diminishes group loyalty, commitment, job satisfaction, and intention to stay in the organization. Both Rahim and Jehn (1995) suggest that while task/goal conflict may enhance performance under certain circumstances, the downsides are the same as for interpersonal conflicts. For interpersonal conflicts they set forth a model that has as its two dimensions concern for self, and concern for others (see Figure 17). This concept connects the work of *emic* and *etic* studies into a model that provides insights in how to manage specific conflicts, and the tools that may be most effective. It should be emphasized that this figure speaks to both the diagnosis and intervention sides of the model.

Krauss and Morsella (2000) contend that **communications** is critical in conflict management and set forth four paradigms for effective communications: encoder-decoder, intentionalist, perspective-taking, and dialogic.

5.7.4   Intervention Lens

It has been argued that trust (see also (Sullivan, Peterson et al. 1981);(Greenberg 2001); (Lewicki and Wiethoff 2000); (Kramer and Tyler 1996); (Rousseau, Sitkin et al. 1998)), empathy, communications, and power ((Coleman 2000); (Avruch 1998) power trumps everything)) are necessary dimensions for cross-cultural leadership. When intervening into a conflict the level of each dimension achieved by the leader will determine the effectiveness and the durability of the solution achieved.

As noted above, Rahim (2002) constructed a systematic method of diagnosing conflicts, and of dealing with them. This basic structure must then be extended to consider the *cultural individuality* of the contestants. *Cultural individuality* means the psychological, social, and business context each person has. Leaders must consider the use of culture only as a trail marker on the way to understanding an individual. Consider the following examples of people of the same educational, economic, social, and cultural status:

- A person who is raised in Hunan province has never traveled outside of China, or of the province, and who speaks no English.
- A person who is raised in Beijing and who moved to Montreal when 12 years old and speaks both Chinese and English.
- A person raised in Los Angeles who speaks English but not Chinese.

Consider the examples if the person in question has a Chinese lineage, and then a British lineage. Now consider that the person has worked for a transnational firm for 10 years, and then one who has only worked in a local firm. If one changes the mix and considers education, economic status, social status, cultural status, professional status, parental involvement,

148

ethnicity, and gender, an infinite diversity emerges. However, knowing the trailhead enables a leader to begin the journey to acquiring detailed knowledge about the persons involved in the conflict. Other authors have come to this same conclusion ((Kim, Lee et al. 2004); (Greenberg 2001); (Oetzel, Ting-Toomey et al. 2001) called ethnic identity salience; (Kimmel 2000) micro cultures; (Avruch 1998) generic and local; *etic* only accounts for 49%; (Hamill 1990)).

As Deutsch (1973) observes, the processes and acts that are characteristic of a given social atmosphere will induce that very same atmosphere if introduced into a newly forming relationship. Thus in a corporate environment, the culture of the people will adjust, and can be molded.

The dimensions set forth in Figure 17 provide five general means of addressing conflict as integrating, obliging, dominating, avoiding, and compromising. Clarke and Lipp (1998) suggest that conflict resolution be conducted by problem identification and clarification, cultural and organizational exploration, conflict resolution, and organizational integration. These phases are subsumed in the model proposed: knowledge, diagnosis, intervention. Oetzel, Ting-Toomey et al. (2001) describe facework as a key ingredient in conflict management. Facework is categorized by them as self-face, other-face, and mutual-face. If one considers Figure 20 self-face and other-face are resonate with the two primary dimensions, and mutual-face (compromise) with one option.

There are numerous techniques that can be utilized in the process of intervention as argued by other authors ((Burbules and Rice 1991); (Slate 2004); (Levine 1998); (Ting-Toomey, Gao et al. 1991)). These authors suggest *communicative virtues* that include tolerance and patience, and rides on trust, respect, appreciation, and affection. Of course, *communicative virtues* span each dimension of the model: knowledge, diagnosis, and intervention. Welton (2002) concludes that listening is a critical in that it provides a mutualistic art that enhances understanding. Greenberg (2001) concludes that the way people perceive justice is also an important consideration.

Gurevitch (2001) describes the problems associated with the failure to discard preconceived ideas about others and other cultures. Lewicki and Wietoff (2000) believes that rapport building, conflict resolution (listening, **empathy**, identifying creative means to resolve disputes, etc.), and group process and decision making (leadership, **communications**, clarifying, summarizing, integrating, etc) skills are necessary for effective conflict resolution.

149

Coleman (2000) quotes Bertrand Russell (1938) as saying (Pg. 109): "the fundamental concept in social science is power, in the same sense in which energy is the fundamental concept in physics." The concept of **power** is a key consideration in conflicts for it helps to explain some of the imbalances or differences – and how to deal with them.

The use of a third party as a mediator is suggested by a number of authors including Fischer (2000) and Augsburger (1992) triangulation. LeBaron (2003) provides the ways of knowing as described above. Her approach is preferred for a model of how to approach intervention.

5.7.5   Model Description

As noted, the lenses of the *hourglass model*, Figure 22 start with knowledge, progress through diagnosis, and then intervention. From intervention will flow lessons, through diagnosis again, and extend knowledge. The model is a general process and is not intended to be a dogmatic or static approach. For example, as knowledge is consulted there will be a possible recognition that more information is required and therefore some diagnosis may be required. Following this same approach there may be a need to engage (subtle intervention) in preliminary dialogue to facilitate the diagnosis and knowledge. The perfect world would be 100% knowledge at the start, with a mindset to acquire as much knowledge as possible. The size of the ellipses represents the amount of time that should be applied to each of the lens. On the output side, lessons are learned and they need to be diagnosed, and then the knowledge base can be increased - this could be from an individual to an institutional perspective.

It is suggested that the model be applied using a preventive approach, but it may be utilized just as well in a responsive way. The key is that the acquisition of knowledge and diagnosis of the conflict are the most important lenses. Many conflicts occur from a lack of understanding or a failure of communications. Both of which can be moderated by increasing the knowledge and diagnosis prior to a formal or structured intervention.

The *hourglass model* will be extended to define a list of tools and techniques that can be applied to facilitate improvement. For example, in the knowledge lens the use of metaphors is a critical technique for developing a richer knowledge of cultures (personal, societal, commercial, etc.). A cultural knowledge of the cultural individuality of the contestants including religion, customs, folklore, music, art, literature, philosophy, language, history, geography, ethics, power, gender, and economic status are critical. Knowledge of the structure of the economic agreement is also important to know whether it is a fixed price contract or an al*liance*.

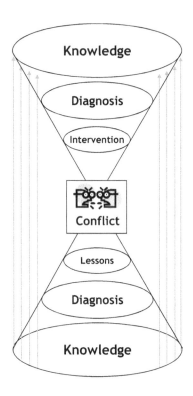

Figure 22 – Conflict Model (Grisham)

For diagnosis, an example of a necessary technique would be to employ active listening skills to increase the knowledge of the details or feelings of the contestants. This would also be a skill of great importance with the intervention lens. During intervention, negotiation skills are primary, after **communication** and effective listening.

The hourglass model is proposed for use by in conflict of any kind. This approach is particularly useful in the context of cross-cultural leadership for it provides a process that can be utilized formally or informally to approach the most intransigent types of conflict. As the research confirms, the issues of trust, empathy, power, and communications are critical in assessing, diagnosing, and engaging in disputes.

5.8 Chapter Summary

This chapter has addressed the issue of conflict in cross-cultural settings. Much of the conflict theory is useable in any cultural or legal environment, as are many of the negotiations skills. However, as this work has described, there are cultural nuance strategies about which a leader must be cognizant. Conflict, like change, is an integral part of what leaders must manage. If they are experienced and trained leaders, they can use these two issues to advantage. A leader must have the ability to deal effectively with conflict.

In the next Chapter, I will discuss in more detail the hypothesis of this work.

6. Cross-Cultural Leadership Hypothesis
6.1 Chapter Introduction
There are core leadership dimensions that are universally effective regardless of the ethnicities, the culture, the economic environment, the structure of the firm, or the complexity of a project or program. Those dimensions are:

- Trust
- Empathy
- Transformation
- Power
- Communication

This work defines leadership as the ability to inspire the desire to follow, and to inspire results that surpass expectations (Figure 5). Leadership can be displayed from a children's playground to the most complex transnational corporations and from humanitarian efforts to wars. Therefore, a broad definition has been selected to condense a complex attribute, yet to provide flexibility of application.

As discussed in Section 2.2, I find that Mead's (1955) definition of culture is best suited to the discussion of universal leadership. Therefore, I have adapted her definition for use in this work as follows:

Culture Definition

a body of learned behavior, a collection of beliefs, habits and traditions, shared by a group of people and successively learned by people who enter the society

---

Figure 23 – Culture (Mead modified)

As noted earlier, this definition provides the versatility required to address intra/inter cultures, organizations, or groups, and it is the definition adopted for this work.

To lead effectively in a cross-cultural environment requires the acquisition and cultivation of basic human (emotional, social, and cultural), business, and cultural skills. Taken as a whole, I have called this Cross-Cultural Leadership Intelligence (XLQ) in this work. Most of the authors cited in this work believe that leadership is a learned set of skills that can be effectively translated into other cultures. I hold the same view from experience.

As the research review in this work confirms, much of the testing has been narrowly focused, and is often difficult to correlate. Yukl (1989) put it well when he observed that (Pg. 423): "the confused state of the field can be attributed in large part to the sheer volume of publications, the disparity of approaches, the proliferation of confusing terms, the narrow focus of most research, the preferences for simplistic explanations, the high percentage of studies on trivial questions, and the scarcity of studies using strong research methods." Regardless, there are patterns that exist in the multitude of theories and research that seem to describe a condensing consensus of the major qualities of leadership listed above. To explore this potential consensus, an exegetical approach has been undertaken to search for commonalities in the existing body of knowledge, and to compare the leadership dimensions hypothesized to this existing research. This has provided a rich tapestry of research methods and theories, and a benchmark to demonstrate that there is published support for the hypothesis.

Hofstede's (2001) *onion diagram* shows that at the center of each individual are core values, and that practices cut across the outer levels of rituals, heroes, and symbols. I believe that the core leadership dimensions must be synchronistic with core values, and that leadership qualities must be displayed through the appropriate cultural lens. For example, trust is a universal value and a leadership quality, regardless of culture, based upon a review of the published research. To build trust, however, requires an understanding of how trust is perceived in each particular culture. Certainly, the reputation of a leader will often be known, but she or he must earn the trust of the individuals and groups served, every day.

The culture of the countries and organizations on a project can be diverse. Consider a global matrix firm with offices in 50 countries (here I mean branches that are fully staffed with a significant number of nationals), paired with a small projectized firm that has offices in a 51st country, doing a project for a political bureaucracy. Then assume that the project is conducted 50% virtually (on-line with no face-to-face contact. Bass and Stogdill (1990) suggest that when adopting or implementing the following styles of leadership proper sensitivity to cultural differences are required:

- Autocratic or democratic
- Participative or directive
- Relations oriented or task oriented
- Considerate or structuring
- Active or laissez-faire.

The underlying concept is that a leader not only has the ability to implement some or all of these styles, but also must select the appropriate style to fit the circumstance and organizational structure. To take one example, consider power. A leader will know how and when to exercise the power that she has, and the type of power (e.g. participative or directive) that the circumstances, structure, and culture require. The application of authorized power would be quite different in autocratic and democratic cultures, and quite different in corporate cultures that are participative versus directive.

The economic environment (business sector, geographical location, and the market timing) associated with a project must also be understood by a leader. Imagine a power generation project, located in Thailand, during a period of economic contraction for the country. This environment will force a leader to adapt the communication and empathetic qualities to fit the potentially pessimistic attitudes of the project team and stakeholders. Under circumstances such as these, the leader will potentially have less influence on superior stakeholders because the pressure to complete the project may have dissipated, and the influence to move problems ahead faster may have diminished. This then can affect trust.

Project complexity is a major consideration relating to leadership. IT projects with a value of US$100,000, single sourced, updated product, with duration of four months need a project manager, but not necessarily a person with leadership skills. A US$2 billion project with cultural complexity, structure, and economic environment as described above must have a project manager, but more importantly a project manager that has strong leadership skills. The point being that the conditions and complexity of a project will determine the amount of XLQ required.

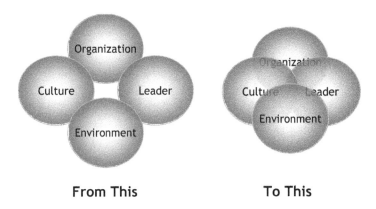

From This   **To This**

Figure 24 – XLQ (Grisham)

Figure 38 provides a graphic representation of the interrelationship between the major factors for consideration of leadership and XLQ. A leader will not, indeed cannot, and should not change the culture, environment, or organization of a project. What the leader can do is to bring a common inspiration to each, and celebrate the inherent characteristics of each dimension. One measure of the effectiveness of a leader is the extent to which she or he can overlap in the circles. As the figure shows, what a leader can do is to cause a blending or coming together of the different considerations, voluntarily, in the minds and hearts of the various participants.

The next sections of this work discuss the hypothesis for the individual dimensions of leadership.

6.2 Trust

Trust is the foundation of Cross-Cultural Leadership Intelligence (XLQ). Trust is a consistency of ideas, communication, and action, which inspire people to transcend or allay their fears. At its most basic, trust is the absence, or transcendence, of fear. Fear is an emotion that has many faces: death, punishment, loss of sustenance, loss of face, loss of respect, and loss of power to mention a few. It is also specific to an individual at a given time.

In an article on trust and risk management Earle (2004) quotes a definition for trust proposed by Rousseau, Sitkin, et al. (1998) as (Pg. 169): "Trust is a psychological state comprising the intention to accept vulnerability based upon positive expectations of the intentions or behavior

156

of another." Bachman (2001) suggests that power and trust are linked. He says that power exists at the structural level (organizational structure), and that it can be conducive to the development of trust – but that one or the other dominates.

In their consideration of inter-organizational virtual teams Kasper-Fuehrer and Ashkanasy (2001) focus in part on the issue of trust. The authors propose that communication of trustworthiness, establishment of a common business understanding, and strong business ethics are the essentials for creating and maintaining trust in virtual organizations. Their view of ethics is largely from the IT perspective however.

Trust as defined by Webster's Ninth New Collegiate Dictionary is *assured reliance on the character, ability, strength, or truth of someone or something.*

In an article on trust, Mayer, Davis et al. (1995) define trust as being (Pg. 712):

Trust Definition

the willingness of a party to be vulnerable to the actions of another party based on the expectation that the other will perform a particular action important to the trustor, irrespective of the ability to monitor that other party

---

Figure 25 – Trust (Mayer, Davis et al.)

This definition is described by the authors as a follower perspective of the leader-follower transaction. It is based on the notion that the follower is vulnerable in the transaction, and must feel comfortable with this vulnerability. This definition is used in this work for it captures the vulnerability, inability to monitor (leap of faith) and the willingness to expose oneself.

Lewicki and Wiethoff (2000) note that there has been attention given to the issue of trust from several social sciences ((Lewicki and Bunker 1995); (Kramer and Tyler 1996); (Rousseau, Sitkin et al. 1998)). These authors help to illustrate the categorizations of the major themes as personality theorists (readiness to trust, deeply engrained into the personality), sociologists and economists (institutional phenomena), and social psychologists (interpersonal transactions). Lewicki and Wiethoff adopt a definition of trust as being (Pg. 87): "an individual's belief in, and willingness to act on the basis of, the words, actions, and decisions of another" (Lewicki,

Mcallister et al. 1998). Lewicki and Wiethoff maintain that implicit in the definition are three elements that contribute to the level of trust: chronic disposition, situational parameters, and the history of the relationship.

Lewicki and Wiethoff point to a previous article (Lewicki and Bunker 1995) that posits professional relationships have three types of trust: calculus-based trust (CBT or CBD for calculus-based distrust), knowledge-based trust, and identification-based trust (IBT or IBD for identification-based distrust). Calculus based trust is grounded in the potential rewards and punishments for not violating or violating the trust (the authors use the metaphor of the children's game *chutes and ladders*). Identification-based trust is based upon the ability of the parties to understand the other's wants and needs, and to identify with them (the authors use the metaphor of singing together or harmonizing). The authors note that knowledge-based trust is a dimension of relationships and confidence in the other party.

The authors build a matrix of types of trust and distrust to illustrate their theory, and to show how trust may change over time. They contend that trust is the first potential casualty of conflict, and must be present if the parties are to manage conflict. They then propose the following strategies for building trust:

Calculus-based Trust

- Agree explicitly on expectations of tasks and deadlines
- Agree upon procedures to monitor the other person's performance
- Cultivate alternative ways to have needs met
- Increase awareness of how other see one's performance

Identification-based Trust

- Share common interests
- Share common goals and objectives
- Share similar reactions to common problems
- Share values and integrity

Building trust requires patience, consistency, and time whereas destroying trust can be instantaneous. The published research that has been reviewed for this work provides a near unanimous agreement that trust is essential for leadership. One study actually indicates that when trust is present, culture differences decrease in importance (Jarvenpaa, Knoll et al. 1998).

Buskens (2002) begins his book with an overview of trust, and the sociological literature on trust has been extensively reviewed by Misztal (1996). Misztal identifies trust as having three functions. First, the *integrative function* of trust, or system-level trust in normative systems as the main source of social order. This means that social order is a result of norms prescribing trustful and trustworthy behavior. Second, the *reduction of complexity* where Luhmann (1988) argues that actors increasingly need trust because of the growing complexity of modern society and because the consequences of decisions are becoming more uncertain. Third, *trust as a lubricant for cooperation* (Arrow 1974).

The GLOBE survey has been utilized as a benchmark to correlate the findings of this research to a recent broad study of cross-cultural leadership. Appendix 1 provides a correlation between the terminology used by the various authors referenced in this work and the GLOBE survey dimensions. The hypothesis descriptors are set forth in the column titled "Work," and the column titled "Question" indicates that this descriptor was a question posed to the Delphi panel (see Section 7.6).

The process undertaken for trust, and each of the other dimensions was to perform the exegetical exploration of the literature, and then compare it to the GLOBE dimensions. This was followed by an inspection of the data and addition of my personal experience. The combination of these factors led then to the *Work* column descriptors. Once the descriptors were established, a question was posed to the Panel that represented each of the descriptors. The questions posed to the Delphi panel for Trust are shown in Appendix 6.

This work proposes the hypothesis for the leadership dimension of Trust, and its descriptors, and sub-descriptors, as summarized below:

1. Trust Hypothesis

Leadership requires the creation and maintenance of Trust, regardless of culture.

2. Trust Descriptor Hypothesis

The following are descriptors of trust:

- Care and Concern

    Esteem

    Face

- Character

    Honesty & Integrity

    Duty & Loyalty

159

Admiration

- Competence

    Technical

    Judgment

- Dependability

    Predictability

    Commitments

- Fearlessness

    Confidence

    Self-Sacrifice

- Humaneness

    Tolerance

    Respect

- Integrator

    Goals

    Cohesiveness

- Integrity & Ethics

    Values

    Ethics

- Truth & Justice

    Fairness

    Candor

6.3 Empathy

Empathy is the ability to think, feel, and communicate from another's perspective - or as the saying goes the ability to *walk in another's shoes*. There is a strong connection between trust, empathy, and communications as well. Trust requires the removal of fear, and empathy is one tool for accomplishing that goal. To empathize with another, one must first understand the other person's perspectives, and must communicate effectively (listen actively). The interplay between these attributes is subtle, concurrent, and heavily influenced by education. Without a cultural education, and some language skills, it would be difficult or impossible to understand another person's perspective. In any knowledge transfer there must be explicit information (dialogue, body language, etc.), context (education about a culture for example), reflection, and externalization before tacit knowledge may grow.

Education about other cultures is a critical ingredient in many of the attributes of XLQ, and the work of Gannon (see Section 3.5) on cultural metaphors can be of great assistance in this regard. The concept of cultural metaphors rests on the idea that an understanding of history, politics, art, religion, geography, philosophy, ethics, language, customs and rituals is required to appreciate a person's perspective.

Empathy, as defined by Webster's Ninth New Collegiate Dictionary is: "the action of understanding, being aware of, being sensitive to, and vicariously experiencing the feelings, thoughts, and experience of another of either the past or present without having the feelings, thoughts and experiences fully communicated in an objectively explicit manner."

Harrington (2002) begins an article on compassion with a quote from Victor Weisskopf (Pg. 18): "knowledge without compassion is inhuman. Compassion without knowledge is ineffective." Harrington explores the ethical and scientific considerations of compassion - a synonym for empathy. Harrington says that (Pg. 68): "I believe that at the most fundamental level our nature is compassionate, and that cooperation, not conflict, lies at the heart of the basic principles that govern our human existence." In another work, the Dalai Lama (1995) defines compassion and love as (Pg. 64): "positive thoughts and feelings that give rise to such essential things in life as hope, courage, determination, and inner strength."

Rinpoche (1994) says of compassion (Pg. 191): "it is not simply a sense of sympathy or caring for the person suffering, nor simply a warmth of heart for the person before you, or a sharp clarity of recognition of their needs and pain, it is also a sustained and practical determination to do whatever is possible and necessary to help alleviate their suffering."

Eisenberg (2002) defines empathy as (Pg. 135): "an affective response that stems from the apprehension or comprehension of another's emotional state or condition, and that is similar to what the other person is feeling or would be expected to feel." She suggests that sympathy is a response that stems from empathy and elicits feelings of concern or sorrow. While a through review of Eisenberg's work is well beyond the scope of this work, her work provides a rich study on the issue of empathy. Her work included sessions with the Dalai Lama in Dharamsala where he contended that children are born loving and caring, and she cites research that shows children at age 1 or 2 exhibit prosocial and empathetic behavior. The suggestions are that societal interactions alter and change the ability of a person to empathize.

As noted earlier, Mullavey-O'Brien (1997) defined empathy. Their definition has been adopted for use in this work:

Empathy Definition

the ability to put oneself in another's place, to know others' experiences from their perspective, and to communicate this understanding to them in a way that is meaningful, while at the same time recognizing that the source of one's experience lies in the other

---

Figure 26 – Empathy (Mullavey-O'Brien)

To have empathy one must first be informed and knowledgeable about oneself and the other person. There must also be a genuine desire, not feigned, to listen effectively and compassionately with all of the senses. As indicated in Section 3.6, the level of training that a person has achieved will determine how well she or he can *put oneself in another's place* with regard to culture. As to the person themself, this requires the desire to listen and learn about the other person.

The GLOBE survey has been utilized as a benchmark to correlate the findings of this research to a recent broad study of cross-cultural leadership. Appendix 1 provides a correlation between the terminology used by the various authors referenced in this work and the GLOBE survey dimensions. The hypothesis descriptors are set forth in the column titled *Work*, and the column titled *Question* indicates that this descriptor was a question posed to the Delphi panel (see Section 7.6).

The process undertaken for empathy, and each of the other dimensions was to perform the exegetical exploration of the literature, and then compare it to the GLOBE dimensions. This was followed by an inspection of the data and addition of my personal experience. The combination of these factors led then to the *Work* column descriptors. Once the descriptors were established, a question was posed to the Panel that represented each of the descriptors. The questions posed the Delphi panel for Empathy are shown in Appendix 6.

This work proposes the hypothesis for the leadership dimension of Empathy, and its descriptors, as summarized below:

1. Empathy Hypothesis

Leadership requires the creation and maintenance of empathy, regardless of culture.

2. Empathy Descriptor Hypothesis

The following are descriptors of Empathy:

- Cultural Intelligence (CQ)
- Humaneness
- Servant Leadership

6.4 Transformation

In transaction theory, there is a requirement for the presence of a leader and a follower. Alternatively, said another way, without a transformation, there is no transaction to be accomplished. A leader must transform a goal to be achieved, with an understanding that transcends the explicit information available. This is illustrated in a recent article in the Washington Post (2005) reported by Lynette Hart of the University of California-Davis. She reported that elephants likely sensed the tsunami in Asia recently by laying their trunks on the ground to feel seismic vibrations, and determine which direction to use for escape. Therefore transcending the explicit information available.

The example of Moses is often used to illustrate the idea of transformation. Moses kept focused on the long-term goal despite the short term challenges that arose. He maintained the transformation through many life and death trials, without which the Israelites would have lost their way – in all senses of the word. Transformation may be intuitive, inspirational, mandated, or derived from power. However, it requires, as with trust, a constancy and fortitude to stay with the transformation. As with the other attributes described for XLQ, transformation plays an important role in the creation and maintenance of trust for it can help to remove or mitigate fear.

Conger and Kanungo (1987) explore the issue of charisma and provide a model to suggest future study. They conclude that the leader's behavior forms the basis of the followers attitudes and perceptions

In a chapter addressing charismatic leadership, Boal and Bryson (1988) indicate that the essence of transformational leadership is to lift ordinary people to extraordinary heights. Similarly, Bass (1985) says that it is the ability to get people to perform beyond the level of expectations. The definition of leadership used in this work, the ability to inspire the desire to follow, and to inspire achievement beyond expectations, was based in part on this quote from Bass (see Figure 4). For transformational leadership, it would further include the ability to inspire people to risk change.

Bass provides a solid framework for transformational leadership as described in the leadership section of this work (see Chapter 4). Bass then provides the basis for the definition of transformation for this work:

Transformation Definition

demonstrating charisma (vision, instilling pride, gain respect and trust), inspiration (high expectations, uses symbols storytelling and metaphors to express important principles and purposes), intellectual stimulation (promotes intelligence, knowledge, creative problem solving), consideration (personal attention, coaching, mentoring), and the pursuit of change

---

Figure 27 – Transformation (Bass)

Podsakoff, MacKenzie et al. (1996) used six dimensions of transformational leadership, from the literature, in a study that they performed. The six dimensions identified were articulating a vision, providing an appropriate model (role model), fostering the acceptance of group goals, high performance expectations, providing individualized support (mentoring & coaching), and intellectual stimulation.

In an article on Implicit Leadership Theory, House, et al. (1999) generally confirmed the concept that charismatic/transformational leadership are universally endorsed (*etic*), but that the attributes must be adjusted based upon the culture involved. Their conclusion relating to culturally contingent elements of charismatic/transformational leadership summarize perfectly the hypothesis of this work regarding far more than just this attribute (no page number HTML document): "Several of the culturally contingent attributes are also seen as part of charismatic/ transformational leadership by different authors. Examples include risk taking, compassionate, unique, enthusiastic, and sensitive. In the current study, I found that in some cultures these attributes are seen to contribute and in others to impede outstanding leadership. However, not only are these attributes culturally contingent, the behaviors reflecting them may also take on different meanings in different cultures. What is perceived as sensitive or compassionate in one country may be seen as weakness in another. Similarly, behavior that is risk taking may be seen as reckless in one country, but may be perfectly normal, expected behavior in another."

This work adds the notion that a conventional cultural view must be tempered heavily with the specifics of the individual and the situation.

Of the XLQ attributes, transformation is perhaps one of the more straightforward to learn. In many instances, a transformation is the result of a published set of goals and objectives. In these cases, the effectiveness of the transformation is related to the leader's ability to communicate effectively, and in a manner that people believe the leader believes. Likewise, in those undertakings where the goals are intuitive, inspirational, or mandated, the transformation is likely to be more greatly affected by the personality skills of the leader.

As with Trust and Empathy, the GLOBE survey has been utilized as a benchmark to correlate the findings of this research to a recent broad study of cross-cultural leadership. Appendix 1 provides a correlation between the terminology used by the various authors referenced in this work and the GLOBE survey dimensions.

This work proposes the hypothesis for the leadership dimension of Transformation, and its descriptors, as summarized below:

    1. Transformation Hypothesis

Transformation is a characteristic of leadership, regardless of culture.

    2. Transformation Descriptor Hypothesis

The following are descriptors of Transformation:

- Inspiration
- Charisma
- Risk Change
- Vision

6.5 Power

There is an abundance of research on power and historical examples that extend back to the beginnings of recorded time. Arrien's (1993) work indicates that there is the power of presence or charisma (mental, emotional, spiritual, and physical), the power of communication, and the power of position. Heifetz' (1994) work describes authority as conferred power to perform a service or the concept of servant leadership. There is also the power of reward and punishment, the power of knowledge, and referent power. Power can be used, and misused, to support leadership, but does not of itself create or maintain leadership. Despots and dictators wield power, and people will obey the rules and requirements imposed. However, wielding power does not inspire the desire to follow, and results that surpass expectations (see Figure 5). Likewise, in organizations it does not follow that people who have position power are recognized as leaders.

Power is an essential part of leadership. Power that is voluntarily offered up (referent, knowledge, charisma, etc.) by a follower to a leader is the most potent and lasting form of power. As an extreme example, followers may give a military leader the power of life and death over them – extreme trust and sacrifice. Power can evaporate if trust in the leader has been jeopardized. Trust can create power, but power in and of itself cannot produce trust. From this research, power can be considered on a metaphorical basis as the fuel that drives leadership.

As described in the leadership section of this work Yukl and Falbe (1991) provide a thorough overview of power as listed below that accounts for the dimensions put forward by French and Raven as well (1959). Tracy Gross adds an additional dimension as noted:

Position Power

- Legitimate Power – power associated with title or authority.
- Reward Power
- Coercive Power – punishment power
- Information Power – control over information
- Ecological Power – control over the physical environment or technology

Personal Power

- Referent Power – admiration, desire to obtain approval
- Expert Power – special knowledge
- Impossible Dream Power - To make something impossible happen (Gross 1996)

Yukl says that (1998)(Pg. 142): "in this book, the term power is usually used to describe the absolute capacity of an individual to influence the behavior or attitudes of one or more designated target persons at a given time." Bass and Stogdill (1990) warn that power is not synonymous with influence, though it is often used interchangeably, but that all power yields influence. Bass and Stogdill cite the definition of power by Russell (1938) (Pg. 225) as: "the production of intended effects." For this work, the definition of power is a blend of the foregoing:

Power Defined
The capacity to influence behavior and attitudes to achieve intended results.

Figure 28 – Power (Grisham)

As with Trust, Empathy, and Transformation, the GLOBE survey has been utilized as a benchmark to correlate the findings of this research to a recent broad study of cross-cultural leadership. Appendix 1 provides a correlation between the terminology used by the various authors referenced in this work and the GLOBE survey dimensions.

This work proposes the hypothesis for the leadership dimension of Power, and its descriptors, as summarized below:

1. Power Hypothesis

Power is a characteristic of Leadership, regardless of culture.

2. Power Descriptor Hypothesis

The following are descriptors of Power:

- Knowledge Power
- Position Power
- Power Distance
- Referent Power
- Reward & Punishment Power

6.6 Communications

Effective communications begins with effective listening. Grisham's Second Law of Project Management is: *Listen, Question, Think, then Act.*[20] A leader must be an effective listener first and foremost, and must imbue this desire in followers. Grisham's Laws follow closely with those proposed for Knowledge Management. Explicit information is provided (listen), information is placed into context (listen & question), information is internalized and reflected upon (think), and then the information is acted upon (practice).

---

[20] Thomas Grisham circa 1990

167

According to Peter Drucker (2000) (Pg. 339): "what can be learned cannot be taught, and what can be taught cannot be learned." In the context of education and knowledge transfer, the concept is that tacit knowledge cannot be taught, and explicit knowledge cannot be learned. In communications this concept is critically important for the ability to communicate complex tacit knowledge, like cultural attitudes, cannot be taught. In the global marketplace it is therefore essential that time is available for the translation of explicit information into tacit knowledge.

In a book authored by two people with over 40 years of cross-cultural communication experience, Carté and Fox (2004) suggest the following checklist for effective communications:

- keep an open mind
- try to put yourself in the other person's position
- ask carefully chosen open questions (ones that start with who, what, why, where, how etc);
- really listen to the answers
- ask closed questions (ones that invite a Yes or No answer) to check that any deductions you've made are correct

Pearce (2003) contends that one's (preface xix) "ability to manage is measured by what you know and what you get done, but your ability to lead is measured not only by your competence but also by your ability to communicate who you are and what you stand for." The author contends that leadership communications must offer credibility, trustworthiness, confidence, passion, facts, and faith - competence and trust. To do this Pearce contends that there are four principles that must be employed: discovering what matters, applying courage and discipline, deciding to lead, and connecting with others (resonance). He suggests a framework that includes assuring that communications include:

- Establish confidence and build trust – removal of the filters of fear and suspicion, establish a clarity of purpose
- Create shared context – tell the story of how everyone came to be at the same place - their history. Facilitates the decision to change, presents a broader context, and builds trust.
- Declare and describe a compelling future – declaration as an *act of creation*. Pearce quotes Saint-Exupéry (1950) as saying (Pg. 110): "If you want to build a ship, don't drum up the men to gather wood, divide the work and give orders. Instead, teach them

168

to yearn for the vast and endless sea. As for the future, your task is not to foresee it, but to enable it."

- Commitment to action – organizational support, personal commitment (the leader must act), involvement of others

From a practice point of view, Pearce suggests the use of *invested listening* which includes:
- Answering the stated and unstated question
- Acknowledging feelings
- Finding common intent
- Distinguishing between your context, or point of view, and the questioner's point of view
- Checking in: making sure that you have been responsive

Gundykunst, Ting-Toomey et al. (1991) present considerations for designing courses in intercultural communications. This is a very strong reference on inter-cultural communications. The authors point to the work of Spitzberg and Cupach (1984) and their three components of communication competence: knowledge (cognitive), motivation (affective), and skills (behavioral).

Baldoni (2003) begins his book with a quote from Drucker (1973) on communications that (Pg. 8): "it is less about information that it is about facilitating kinship within an organization." Baldoni' own overview of leadership communications is that (Pg. 4): "effective messages are built upon trust. Trust is not something that we freely grant our leaders; we expect them to earn it. How? By demonstrating leadership in thought, word, and deed. Credible leaders are those who by their actions and behaviors demonstrate that they have the best interests of the organization [and people] at heart." He says that the traits of leadership communications are:
- Significance. Messages are about big issues that reflect the present and future of the organization (e.g., people, performance, products, and services)
- Values. Messages reflect vision, mission, and culture
- Consistency. Messages exemplify stated values and behaviors
- Cadence. Messages occur with regularity and frequency

From a trial attorney's point of view, Spence (1995) argues that there is power in credibility (the ability to stand naked), and that the trick is to abandon trickery and use the truth. From his experience, he says that communications occur with words, rhythms, silences, hands, and bodies. He also says that if one is required to choose the single essential skill it would be the ability to listen. In describing his technique for listening, he says that sometimes when he is listening to the final argument of his opponent he lays his head back and listens only to the sounds. The author contends that sounds betray, and always carry the argument better that the words. Because they betray the urgency, the sense of caring, anger, ring of truth, and the power that can change the jury's mind. He also believes that words should be from what he calls the *heart zone* rather than sophisticated vocabulary. One key issue for cross-cultural communications is to use simple basic words that are commonly understood.

In a fascinating book, Ekman (2003) provides the results of his research on expressions. In international groups, he found that nature not nurture accounted for an *etic* set of expressions. He says that his tests confirm that there is a difference between what he calls *managed* expressions versus the *alone* expressions. His example is that of Japanese and American responses to films of surgery and accidents being the same when alone, but when in a public setting the Japanese giving expression of a smile. He developed the Facial Action Coding System (FACS) that is used now widely by scientists to measure facial expression.

In his novel book titled Squirrel Inc., Denning (2004) explores the issues of change and leadership. He believes that storytelling is a way to communicate vision, values, knowledge, group cohesion, and so forth. He suggests that there are nine steps for constructing what he calls a "springboard story" that enables an audience to make a leap in understanding:

- The leader defines the specific change idea to be implemented in the organization
- The leader identifies an incident (either inside or outside the organization, community, or group) where the change idea was in whole or in part successfully implemented.
- The incident is narrated from the perspective of a single protagonist who is typical of the target audience.
- The story specifies when and where the incident happened.
- In telling the story, the leader ensures that the story fully embodies the change idea, extrapolating the idea from the story if necessary.
- The story makes clear what would have happened without the change idea.
- The story is stripped of any unnecessary detail.
- The story has an authentically happy ending.
- At the conclusion of the story, the leader links the story to the change idea with phrases such as "What if . . ." or "Just imagine . . ."

Effective listening includes reading body language, intonation, cultural signals, professional signals, corporate language, and patience. It requires that the listener turn-off preconceived notions and opinions, and hear the other person's perspective as well. There is time to consider and respond but only after questioning (in a non-aggressive, non-threatening, face saving manner) to make sure that the message received is the one intended to be sent – common context. In cross-cultural interactions, the issue of language must be considered as well. Even when speaking a common language, people have wildly different levels of ability. It is easy to assume that a person has a deeper level of understanding in a language than actually exists. If a translator is used, then the listener must rely heavily on other clues and signals that need to be read and interpreted correctly.

Communications are conducted differently in different cultures (corporate and social). Some cultures are more gregarious and some more subtle, some prefer logic and some intentions, and some engage in more formality and some less – high context and low context cultures. As a leader, it is necessary to design a communications system that considers the needs of each participating group (corporate or social), and balances the expectations. Each group will require a different approach, and the leader must rely upon her or his skills, abilities, and XLQ to improvise a system that will strike a balance.

Issues that are more mundane include knowledge management systems to make certain that everyone knows everyone, and that everyone knows what everyone knows. Policies for communication frequency and distribution are also necessary to assure that frequency is provided and assumed. Virtual teams rely heavily upon frequent contact, and need a way to develop a level of personal understanding absent physical interaction. In addition, people in teams need to know when another person is away from their work.

Harkins (1999) describes effective communications in a book devoted to the subject. His definition is adopted for this work (Pg. xii):

Communication Definition

an interaction between two or more people that progresses from shared feelings, beliefs, and ideas to an exchange of wants and needs to clear action steps and mutual commitments. Specifically, a Powerful Conversation produces three outputs: an advanced agenda, shared learning, and a strengthened relationship.

Figure 29 – Communication (Harkins)

As with Trust, Empathy, Transformation, and Power, the GLOBE survey has been utilized as a benchmark to correlate the findings of this research to a recent broad study of cross-cultural leadership. Appendix 1 provides a correlation between the terminology used by the various authors referenced in this work and the GLOBE survey dimensions.

This work proposes the hypothesis for the leadership dimension of Communication, and its descriptors, as summarized below:

1. Communication Hypothesis

Effective Communication is a characteristic of Leadership, regardless of culture. .

2. Communication Descriptor Hypothesis

The following are descriptors of Communication:

- Adaptability
- Competence
- Creativity
- Patience
- Sensitivity
- Wisdom
- Conflict Management – Conflict management has its roots in effective communications, thus it is included here.

6.7 Culture

As noted in the leadership dimension section, the GLOBE survey has been utilized as a benchmark to correlate the findings of this research. The dimensions of leadership are considered to be *etic* in nature, and apply regardless of the culture(s) with which a leader must work. The breadth of the GLOBE survey offered another interesting opportunity to connect the research of this work to the cultural dimensions of the GLOBE survey.

I believe that a leader must adjust his or her leadership dimensions to the individual cultures that are present on international multi-cultural projects. Since one part of the GLOBE survey explored cultural dimensions, I decided to see if the leadership dimensions of this work would map onto the GLOBE cultural dimensions. Again, those dimensions are shown in the Figure 30 below (see also Figure 12):

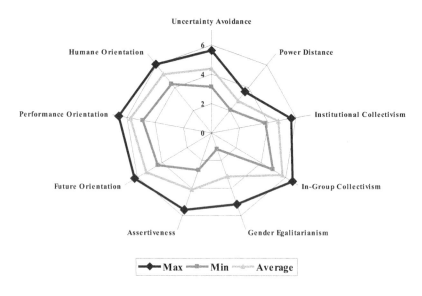

Figure 30 – Cultural Dimensions (GLOBE modified)

I was interested to discover if, for example, the Delphi panel would see a stronger connection between Humane Orientation and Empathy, rather than Humane Orientation and Power. In addition, I wanted to explore the concept of multi-cultural individuals, or people like Chinese Americans who may have a blend of values. The GLOBE survey focused on specific cultures in their surveys, it looked at people inside different cultures.

A number of Delphi panel members had difficulty with this group of questions, for they required a multi-dimensional set of considerations as the following examples illustrate:

- Does Trust map to Power Distance
- How strong is the connection between Trust and Power Distance in Ecuador (3.65) compared to Turkey (2.66)
- How strong is the connection between Trust and Power distance if the person has been raised in Turkey, but trained in the West.
- How strong is the connection if the team contains individuals from Turkey and Ecuador

I recognized that these were very difficult questions to answer, but I considered the Delphi panel of experts to be the perfect group to ask. One of the panel members, Alan Gilham, re-phrased the questions in the following light: "Which leadership dimension (trust, empathy, transformation, power, communication) would I expect to focus on most often (as a leader) to achieve success in societies/groups displaying the different (Globe) cultural dimensions?"

This work proposes the hypothesis for mapping the leadership dimension of trust, empathy, transformation, power, and communications onto the GLOBE cultural dimensions, as summarized below:

1. Articulation of Hypothesis

The following is how the hypothesis was introduced to the panel members:

The hypothesis is that the dimensions of Leadership (trust, empathy, transformation, power, and communications) are universal regardless of culture. An experienced leader will know that she/he must apply these dimensions in different degrees depending upon the culture(s) involved. The following questions explore the idea of how important each Leadership dimension is to each of the GLOBE cultural dimensions that will be described.

One such GLOBE dimension, Uncertainty Avoidance, means the extent that members of a culture, society, group, corporation, etc., (Pg 603): "seek orderliness, consistency, structure, formalized procedures, and laws to cover situations in their daily life." Clearly different cultures view this in different ways. If you are a leader with a team that includes a Singaporean and a Russian, the Russian is more likely to be interested in few rules and the Singaporean perhaps demanding of strict rules. So the question is how important are the Leadership dimensions in balancing the acceptance or rejection of rules.

The questions that are posed in this next section ask your opinion on how important the leadership dimensions are in balancing, normalizing, centering, etc. the needs of any culture regardless of where those needs are located on the GLOBE scale. Effective Communication is a characteristic of Leadership, regardless of culture.

2. Hypothesis Questions

The panel members were asked to evaluate each of the leadership dimensions against each of the GLOBE dimensions with a similar question: Rate each of the dimensions of leadership below on how strong you see the connection between it and the concept of Uncertainty Avoidance (for example).

3. The Cultural Mapping

The correlation, or mapping, was then performed by asking the Delphi panel members to rate the strength of the connection between each of the five leadership dimensions, and each of the eight GLOBE cultural dimensions. Table 9 provides a matrix of the GLOBE dimensions mapped onto the dimensions of this work.

Table 9 - Culture Mapping (Grisham)

GLOBE Dimension	Trust	Empathy	Transformation	Power	Communication
Uncertainty Avoidance					
Power Distance					
Institutional Collectivism					
Group Collectivism					
Gender Egalitarianism					
Assertiveness					
Future Orientation					
Humane Orientation					

6.8 Chapter Summary

This Chapter has presented the hypothesis of this work, and that there are leadership dimensions that are essential regardless of culture. Those dimensions are trust, empathy, transformation, power, and communication. I have described how the strength of each of these dimensions was mapped onto the GLOBE survey to connect the research back to a benchmark.

The dimensions of leadership are one of the foundations for XLQ, along with cultural knowledge. The next Chapter provides a discussion on the strategy and approach for testing the hypothesis.

7. Research Design for Hypothesis Testing

7.1 Chapter Introduction

The research approach to a topic as broad and deep as cross-cultural leadership presents significant challenges both in the research and in the testing methodology. This chapter will describe the perspective that was adopted for the testing strategy, the approach that was selected, and the justification for the approach. The Delphi technique, utilized for the testing, will also be described.

7.2 Ontological & Epistemological Overview

The idea for this research came from my experience working in multi-cultural environments, and witnessing the techniques that people from diverse backgrounds employed in managing and leading others. I felt that there were general patterns and similarities, blended with cultural and personal individuality, but that they were subtle and difficult to define. From my reading of business literature, I was not satisfied that the subject had been sufficiently codified to provide me with the connections and understanding that I thought the subject of cross-cultural leadership deserved. What I recognized that I needed was to engage in a program of education and research to study the issue, and learn more from those who had explored it.

Thus, the ontological approach of this work was to use my experience as a starting point to formulate and attempt to answer my questions. At the beginning, I had a crude outline of aspects for cross-cultural leadership, and that outline evolved as I completed the course work, reflective learning, and research. I sought to find multiple disciplinary views from a diversity of authors around the globe, and to investigate each one looking for connections and new paths to explore. As with many journeys, the end is the beginning, and I found my initial hypothesis to be rather durable. Thus from an ontological perspective, I began the journey with a goal in mind, sought expert advice and directions along the way, and found the goal (model) described in somewhat different terms.

From an epistemological perspective the question was if the model discovered was in fact valid: How much bias was introduced because of my experience?; Did my research embrace enough of the published literature?; How would I test the hypothesis in the most unbiased way possible? The answers to these questions lie in the basic approach to the research. From the beginning, I sought to find literature from as many disciplines as possible. This avoided the bias of focusing only on Project Management literature or on what I thought would be a fit for the hypothesis. I pursued the various disciplinary pathways by attempting to spot connections, and to follow the leads out to other disciplines. Once I found the references pointing back to previous pathways, I moved on to other disciplines.

Once there was a rich diversity of research, I used the exegetical approach to look for the threads and connections, and this evolved into the structure for the empirical testing. I connected this back to the GLOBE survey, the benchmark, and sought to discover the correlations if they existed. The Delphi technique then minimized any bias from the panel members. Once the survey was completed and analyzed, I then used my experience to give the results a sanity check.

By following this approach I immersed myself in the trees, so as not to see the forest until the end of the process.

7.3   Selecting a Testing Method

At the beginning of the Doctorate of Project Management (DPM) program, I began considering how to best structure the research for this topic. The first area to be explored was the potential use of case study research. Yin (1994) provides an excellent review of this approach. He also provides a table that sets forth five different research strategies, including the case study approach, and discusses the appropriate usages of each – see Figure 31.

The primary focus of this research was to establish what the dimensions of cross-cultural leadership are, and secondarily to explore how and why they apply to Project Management. As the Figure 31 indicates, the survey and archival analysis strategies offer approaches to answer the what (dimensions) and the where (cultures). In addition, Figure 31 shows that neither the survey nor the archival analysis requires control over behavioral events, and both permit focus on contemporary events.

Strategy	Form of Research Question	Requires Control of Behavioral Events?	Focuses on Contemporary Events?
Experiment	how, why?	Yes	Yes
Survey	who, what, where, how many, how much?	No	Yes
Archival analysis	who, what, where, how many, how much?	No	Yes/No
History	how, why?	No	No
Case study	how, why?	No	Yes

Figure 31 – Research Testing (Yin Fig. 1.1)

As indicated in Chapter 1, the exegetical approach to the research itself seemed to fit properly into a strategy for testing that also focused on answering the same questions.

The next major question was whether to take a qualitative or quantitative approach with the survey. At the outset, it was not entirely clear to me if the published work and existing research would provide adequate detailed information on the quantitative information available in the archives. Indeed, I was also not certain that an attempt to measure levels, how many or how much, would not be overly broad. The concern was, and is, that finding the dimensions of cross-cultural leadership would be challenging enough without attempting to determine the ranking of each on a numeric basis.

Coming from a six-sigma background at General Electric, I was familiar with quantitative measurements, and with the issues involved with obtaining dependable and consistent quantitative metrics on simple things like manufacturing processes. I also knew the inherent challenges of developing metrics for managerial, leadership, and customer satisfaction issues. My experience indicated that much of the social and managerial testing that was conducted began with qualitative data (strongly agree to strongly disagree), and was then transferred into a quantitative statistical analysis. Therefore, I looked to develop a qualitative methodology that could be analyzed in a quantitative manner.

Creswell (1998, pg 9) summarizes the use of qualitative research well (Pg. 9): "Qualitative inquiry represents a legitimate mode of social and human science exploration without apology or comparisons to quantitative research. Good models of qualitative inquiry demonstrate the rigor, difficulty, and time-consuming nature of this approach." Creswell uses the metaphor of a loom to describe qualitative research as a weaving together of minute threads that is not simply described. The author suggests that there are reasons to use a qualitative survey:

- Nature of the research – topics that begin with a how or what question.
- Need for exploration of the topic – as has been noted earlier in this work, there is a paucity of published data, and little or no testing of hypothesis, in the Project Management Profession.
- Need to present detailed views of the topic – the need to move from the macro view of generalities to a more detailed and functional view. The research provided in this work comes mostly from other disciplines (psychological, sociological, anthropological, etc) and the detailed studies are focused on issues specific to those fields of studies. The need for a cogent approach to cross-cultural leadership for the Project Management profession is desperately needed.
- Use a qualitative approach to study people in their natural setting – here a combination of my experience with international Project Management, coupled with the Delphi approach provide a natural setting in which practical knowledge meets with the research.
- Use a qualitative approach if personal involvement is desired – the nature of the DPM program is reflective, and is founded on the blending of sound research, practical experience, and testing. My involvement is essential in the process.
- Sufficient time and resources to do data collection – the effort spent in the construction of the Delphi panel and the time spent to design, gather, and analyze the surveys was considerable.
- Because audiences are receptive – the Delphi technique utilizes experts in the field who appreciate an expert approach to complex topics, where they can make their opinions known.
- Researcher as active learner – this is the consistent with the DPM program approach.

Creswell's definition of qualitative research says that (Pg. 15): "qualitative research is an inquiry process of understanding based on distinct methodological traditions of inquiry that explore a social or human problem. The researcher builds a complex, holistic picture, analyzes words, reports detailed views of informants, and conducts the study in a natural setting," seeking an answer to a what question. This definition seemed to fit both the exegetical research strategy, and a qualitative approach followed by a quantitative analysis perfectly.

The next question was how best to design a test protocol.

7.4 Strategy for Design of the Test

With such a broad multifaceted and multidisciplinary topic, the challenge for the research and testing was vigilance to boundary maintenance. Alternatively, to borrow a term from Project Management, *Scope Creep* (gradual growth of the size of a project). As the research progressed, I discovered a number of major research projects that explored cross-cultural issues and leadership. There were a significantly smaller number of cross-cultural leadership studies, and a yet smaller number of broad horizontal studies – due to the costs, logistics, and language challenges. I realized that the scope of this work demanded that I attempt to connect my work with a broad survey. By doing this, I hoped to leverage the work of others who had the resources to do detailed field surveys in-country.

The value that this work was intended to add to the literature, and to the profession of Project Management, was from practitioner/academic blend. The practitioner side was to be provided by professionals, self included, who had worked internationally and dealt with cross-cultural leadership issues real-time. My research was from a different perspective, and utilized different types of people for the testing. What I mean by this is to say that most of the major studies took the perspective of how, for example, a Chinese individual living and working in China would respond to a question regarding power distance or collectivism. The issue that needed to be addressed was the multicultural reality of having a Chinese-American looking at the issues of power distance or collectivism.

My first choice of studies was the GLOBE survey that was discussed in Chapter 2.6. The breadth, thoroughness, and currency of the study were exactly what I sought. In addition, the study addressed the issues of culture, and the issue of leadership. I made inquiries with one of the authors of the study and requested samples of the questions that they utilized in their surveys (they used a qualitative questionnaire and a quantitative analysis of the findings). Unfortunately, samples were not available to me. This caused me to design my own correlation method to tie the leadership dimensions back to the GLOBE cultural findings. Tying culture to both leadership and to the GLOBE survey would require that the people surveyed had a strong background in culture, leadership, and cross-cultural leadership.

The correlation and the multicultural issues described above confirmed the need for a Delphi panel of experts. The next question was how best to engage the members, and what metrics to use. Clearly, there was a need for a qualitative start to the testing to permit the panel members to opine. These opinions would have to be analyzed to see if there was consensus on the initial round by utilizing a quantitative approach. Then the subsequent rounds would repeat the process. Working with severe restrictions on budget and time, I had to consider the advantages and disadvantages of doing face-to-face interviews or on-line surveys to accumulate the opinions.

The panel members are located around the world, and as professionals have severe restrictions on their schedules, as did I. The advantages of using the on-line approach were that it provided ultimate flexibility, and thus a more robust range of experts. The disadvantages were that face-to-face interaction would yield a deeper context and thus better understanding of the nuances of opinions. The insurmountable disadvantage of the face-to-face interactions was the cost and the time. Of course the advantages of one approach are the disadvantages of the other approach.

The real question was what information I would give up by not sitting with each panel member. As part of the knowledge transfer process, reflection, internalization of information and externalization (feedback) are necessary steps. The feedback was the potentially missing step for the on-line survey. The Delphi approach filled this need, and offered the opportunity for a perhaps more thorough exchange of knowledge between the panel members.

The design of the testing process followed from the above criteria:
- Delphi panel of experts
- Initial On-line qualitative survey with optional comments
- Quantitative Analysis of initial survey
- Second On-line qualitative survey quantitative analysis, and optional comments
- Quantitative Analysis of second survey

7.5 Testing Evaluation Criteria

Dorfman, Hanges, et al. (Pg. 677) utilized a 7-point Likert scale for measuring Culturally Endorsed Implicit Leadership Theory (CLT). For their analysis, they considered the cultural endorsement of leadership dimensions proven if 95% of the averages exceeded a mean of 5 on the 7-point scale. I think that a 7-point scale provides for more latitude and nuance in a qualitative survey, so this approach was adopted for the survey utilized to test the hypothesis.

The next issue was to establish a level of confirmation or rejection of the hypothesis. Starting with the CLT concept, I constructed a scale for this work is shown in Table 10.

.

Table 10 - Hypothesis Confirmation Criteria

Average	Hypothesis Agreement Level	Control Limits
= 7.0	Absolute Confirmation	$\sigma/2$
>= 6.0	Strong Confirmation	Assume
>= 5.0	Confirmation	$\sigma/2$
>= 4.0	Weak Confirmation	
>= 3.0	Weak Rejection	
>= 2.0	Medium Rejection	
>= 1.0	Strong Rejection	

At a *Target* level of 6.0, the hypothesis would have strong confirmation from the Delphi panel. At a level of 5.0, the hypothesis would be confirmed, following the CLT format. At a level above 4.0, there would be weak confirmation, and at or below 4.0 the hypothesis would be rejected. The example shown assumes a score of 6.0, and $\sigma/2$ standard/deviation/(σ)/of/2.0/was/ selected as the control limit for identifying dimensions that displayed variability that needed confirmation on the second Delphi session.

On each session, the Delphi panel (described in the next Section of this work) was first asked to rank the questions on a scale of 1 to 7 for the leadership dimensions: 1 = strongly disagree, 2 = disagree, 3 = somewhat disagree, 4 = neutral, 5 = somewhat agree, 6 = agree, and 7 = strongly agree. A similar Likert scale of 1 to 7 was utilized for the cultural questions: 1 = very weak, 2 = weak, 3 = somewhat weak, 4 = neutral, 5 = somewhat strong, 6 = strong, and 7 = very strong.   The 7-point scale was selected to provide for fewer granularities in the results, so the panel members opinions could be more accurately captured.

7.6 The Delphi Technique

This section of the paper will describe one possible research trial that could be conducted to prove or disprove the dissertation hypothesis. Again, the hypothesis is that there are core leadership qualities that are universally effective regardless of the ethnicities, the culture, the

182

economic environment, or the complexity of a project or program. As noted in this work, this is a question that was posed by House and Javidan (2004)(Pg.9): "What principles and laws of leadership and organizational processes transcend cultures, and can such principles be discovered and empirically verified?" The first part of the question was answered by the hypothesis, and explored in this work.

For verification of the principles, there are a number of broad and thorough studies conducted on an international scale such as the GLOBE survey, Hofstede, and Trompenaars to mention but three. Originally, an attempt was made to obtain the survey questions from the GLOBE survey, and recast them to connect the five-point hypothesis of this work. The premise was to confirm the correlation of an empirical survey that explored the hypothesis of this work, back to the GLOBE survey. By this approach it was thought that a limited sampling of data could be connected to an international sampling, and thereby enhance the richness of this testing. Unfortunately, the GLOBE study questions proved not to be available so this option was abandoned.

Other survey testing methods were considered, but the nature of the hypothesis is global and resources and time are not available to undertake a survey on this scale. Consideration was given to selective testing of one aspect of the hypothesis, such as trust. This idea was likewise discarded as it suffered from the same global resource issues, and it would only provide insight into one aspect of the hypothesis.

After review of the literature on other testing methods available, it was decided to explore the use of the Delphi technique for testing. According to research in the nursing field, Kennedy (2004) indicates that the (Pg. 1): "Delphi technique has gained popularity across many scientific disciplines as a method of inquiry." The author notes that in her studies there has been little or no substantiation of the Delphi technique, by utilizing subsequent surveys or other testing methods. In the author's work, she utilized two groups of experts (one composed of nurses and one composed of the recipients of the care) and then correlated the findings. She found a congruence of 97%.

According to Buckley (1994) one advantage of the Delphi technique is when the problem does not lend itself to precise analytical techniques but can benefit from subjective judgments on a collective basis. While there has been significant research on cross-cultural leadership from a cultural perspective (like the GLOBE survey), and on leadership (like the Bass & Stogdill work) itself, there has been little or no research that starts to prove a model of cross-cultural leadership attributes that is based on the body of research.

Keeney (2001) provides a critique of the Delphi method in nursing, and concludes that (Pg. 199): "It is clear from reviewing the advantages and criticisms of the Delphi that the arguments are no stronger or no more valid on one side than the other. This technique must be evaluated against the proposed study and advantages over other methods for this purpose."

Czinkota and Ronkainen (2005) pointed to two other studies performed in the international business area relative to its useful accuracy and stated (no page number HTML document): " To evaluate the accuracy of the Delphi technique for forecasting in the international business arena, we scrutinized three major Delphi studies carried out in the field (Czinkota, 1986; Czinkota & Ronkainen, 1992, 1997). In the 1986 study, 17 key forecasts were made of which 14 were deemed accurate 5 years later. In spite of this 82% ''hit-rate,'' however, the panel did not foresee one key, world altering event, namely the collapse of the Iron Curtain."

It may well be, however, that this failure to foresee was a function of the fact that this particular study drew only on experts from one country. Input on a global level might at least have raised the possibility of such an event. In the 1992 study, which did use a global panel, 40 key predictions were made, with a 1997 accuracy of 32 dimensions or 80%. All the inaccuracies, however, were in the form of overstatements, i.e., the anticipation of more rapid transformations than actually took place, rather than in direction. Finally, the 1997 study offered 6 years later an accuracy level of 65% of its 69 predictions. Again, a major world-altering event and its consequences had not been predicted: the attacks of September 11, 2001. However, the imminence of these events was apparently missed even by the major intelligence agencies around the world. Overall, the average predictive accuracy in the three studies comes to 76%, which makes the Delphi method a powerful forecasting tool. Of course, the key aspect to the usefulness of this type of research will remain the selection of the participants, since their level of knowledge and degree of enthusiasm in participating in such a research venture will vitally affect the quality of the output."

Hasson, Keeney et al. (2000) proposed research guidelines from their experience in using the Delphi technique for medical research. They recommend that the following topics be addressed in designing a Delphi methodology:

Research Problem Identification

Turoff (1970) outlined four objectives that call for the use of the Delphi technique. One of those objectives was to correlate informed judgments on a topic that spans a wide range of disciplines. Reid (1988) contends that the decision to use the Delphi technique must center upon the appropriateness of the available alternatives. It is argued that the use of experts in the field is a technique perfectly suited to this hypothesis for two main reasons. First, the technique has not been utilized in the past, based upon the research performed. This provides the opportunity to cross verify the empirical data accumulated through the global research studies noted in this work. It also offers the opportunity to connect the research to this unified model of cross-cultural leadership. Second, it offers the opportunity to check the validity of the cross discipline (social, psychological, ethical, managerial, cultural, anthropological, etc.) nature of the hypothesis.

Understanding the Process

The Delphi technique is a multistage process designed to combine opinion into group consensus (McKenna 1994). The process being:

- Pilot Testing – small group
- Initial questionnaire – qualitative comments solicited
- Initial feedback – quantitative after statistical analysis of the initial opinions
- Subsequent questionnaire – qualitative comments solicited again
- Subsequent feedback – quantitative after statistical analysis. This provided participants the opportunity to change their opinions.

Selection of Experts

Selecting Panel members who had a balance between impartiality, and an interest in the topic. Some studies have over 60 experts, some as few as 15. Selection of people knowledgeable in the field, and their commitment to multiple rounds of questions on the same topic are essential.

Informing Experts

It is important to explain what is required of them, how much time it will require, what they will be required to provide, what the purpose of the study is to be, and what will be done with the information.

Data Analysis - Discovery of opinions

According to Green, Jones, et al. (1999) two or three rounds are preferred. The authors also suggested that an 80% consensus should be the goal. Others such as Crisp, Pelletier et al. (1997) suggest that percentages should not be used, but rather the process should stop when stability of the data occurs.

Data Analysis - Process of determining the most important issues

According to Duffield (1993) the study undertaken provided pre-existing information for ranking purposes. Duffield designed a Delphi technique to make use of two panels of experts. The questions (168 each subdivided into categories) provided to the experts on both panels were predetermined from a review of the literature. Initially the method was tested for validity with four nurses that did not serve on the panels.

Data Analysis - Managing opinions[21]

Analytical software is utilized to analyze the responses, and provide feedback to the participants on the central tendencies (means) and on the levels of dispersion (standard deviation). Based upon the work of Lincola and Guba (1985) the criteria for qualitative studies such as the Delphi technique should be credibility (truthfulness), fittingness (applicability), auditability (consistency), and confirmability. According to Duffield (1993) (Pg. 230), "the method of retaining competencies as outlined by Murphy (1983) was adopted rather than the 50% acceptance level set by Goodrich (1982) which was seen to be too low to discriminate adequately."

Therefore those competencies with a mean score of three ("agree" on the Likert scale) or above were retained as necessary for the role of first-line nurse managers and those below three were excluded. Consensus for the purpose of this study was defined as the point at which 10% or less of the competencies moved from above to below the mean of 3.00 (the point of acceptance or rejection of competencies) or the reverse, from below to above the mean of 3.00 on a round. Therefore, when 17 competencies or fewer moved from above or below the mean score of 3.00 on a round consensus was achieved and no further rounds were undertaken. Data was analyzed using SPSS". Consensus for panel 1 was achieved after the second round when only six competencies (3.57%) moved from above or below the mean of 3.00 between rounds 1 and 2. All the other competencies remained where they were on the first round, either above or below the predetermined mean score of 3.00." The results were then compared between panels, finding 89% of the attributes were the same on both panels.

Presentation and Interpretation

The author indicates that there are a number of methods for presenting the data two of which are graphical and statistical. Both of these techniques were utilized in the testing of this work.

---

[21] Software – Nud*ist, Ethnograph, SPSS, and Atlas.ti

Some of the arguments against the Delphi technique are that it is not rigorous scientific approach, and that it is subject to bias. There are an equal number of arguments that it is an appropriate method to use in circumstances where there is a crossing of disciplinary boundaries. Due to the nature of the topic, the Delphi technique offers a structured way to analyze the hypothesis by utilizing experts in the field.

The methodology for the study has been formulated based upon a review of Delphi techniques utilized in the nursing, agricultural, and librarian fields. Starting with the structure from Hasson, Keeney et al. (2000), the following outline has been established to structure the methodology:

Research Problem
Prove or disprove the validity of the hypothesis that trust, empathy, transformation, power, and communications are *etic*/globally accepted attributes/expectations for leaders.
Definition of Experts
For purposes of this testing, an expert is defined as: 1) a person that has at least 20 years of practical experience working in an international/multicultural environment, in any industry; or 2) a person that has an advanced degree in leadership or cross-cultural studies with over 20 years of research, teaching, publication experience, or a combination of all.
Selection of Experts
There is a schism between the academic community and the practicing community over leadership and cross-cultural issues. Both have perspectives that are not only valid, but also essential for consideration in research such as this. Therefore, the expert panel included both views of the research problem – theory and practice. In addition, the global nature of the cross-cultural issues argues that there should be people on the panel from different cultural backgrounds. Utilizing the work of Dorfman, Hanges, et al. (2004) the experts sought should represent as many regions as possible from Eastern Europe, Nordic Europe, Germanic Europe, Latin Europe, Latin America, Confucian Asia, Southern Asia, Anglo, Sub-Saharan Africa, Middle East (10 different regions).

There was an effort made to select experts from a diversity of business backgrounds (personal care products to power generation), and experts that had work experience outside of their mother country. Table 11 provides a summary view of the demographics for the panel. A number of panel members were not able to participate (sub-Saharan Africa for example), but as can be seen there was experience in every regional area. In

187

addition, there was a good balance of experience over all of the business areas with NGO's being the smallest.

Software

The participants are geographically dispersed, and actively engaged in business and academia. Thus, an electronic platform was sought to provide a minimal amount of disruption. As a member of the International Council for Research and Innovation in Building and Construction (CIB), I found the survey tool utilized by CIB to be effective and economical.

Table 11 - Delphi Panel Demographics

Panel Demographics

Cultures & Experience	Panel Culture	Panel Experience Years
Cultures		
Eastern Europe (Albania, Georgia, Greece, Hungary, Kazakhstan, Poland, Russia, Slovenia)	0	17
Nordic Europe (Denmark, Finland, Sweden)	0	11
Germanic Europe (Austria, Germany East, Germany West, Netherlands, Switzerland)	1	13
Latin Europe (France, Israel, Italy, Portugal, Spain)	2	59
Latin America (Argentina, Bolivia, Brazil, Colombia, Costa Rica, Ecuador, El Salvador, Guatemala, Mexico, Venezuela)	1	21
Confusian Asia (China, Hong Kong, Japan, South Korea, Singapore, Taiwan)	3	95
Southern Asia (India, Indonesia, Iran, Malaysia, Philippines, Thailand)	3	71
Sub Saharian Africa (Namibia, Nigeria, South Africa, Zambia, Zimbabwe)	0	14
Middle East (Egypt, Kuwait, Morocco, Qatar, Turkey)	1	49
Anglo (Australia, Canada, Ireland, New Zealand, South Africa, United Kingdom, United States)	13	349
English Carribean	1	
Years of Experience		
Academia - Number of Years		206
Business - Number of Years		376
Government - Number of Years		69
Non-Profit - Number of Years		9

The webpage can be located at www.SurveyMonkey.com. This tool enables researchers to create a customized survey with a wide range of question formats. The tool can be linked through email invitations or by direct notification from the site itself. In the direct notification, the respondents can be tracked individually without the other participants knowing who they are. The first round was conducted by the direct notification, but some of the panel members had the notifications blocked by SPAM screens. On the second round, email links were provided with the panel members having to provide their names to eliminate the blockers.

The SurveyMonkey tool enables downloads of the survey data in Excel® spreadsheet format. Unfortunately, the tool does not provide for the feedback of medians and standard deviations so a personal spreadsheet had to be constructed for each panel member that provided their response to the first session along with the median, average, and standard deviation of the scores for the entire Delphi panel.

First Round Questions

As with other previous work, (e.g. Duffield) there was an initial list of questions that was developed from the research. The first round provided the panels with a list of 45 questions with multiple parts, 156 total questions including the three on panel member demographics. The questions explored the leadership dimensions first, and then queried the connections between the leadership dimensions and the GLOBE cultural dimensions. The panel was asked to connect the hypothesis categories of truth, empathy, transformation, power, and communication, to the GLOBE survey dimensions of culture. The panel members were also provided the opportunity to provide a commentary on the dimensions.

Once the question bank was established the work supervisor, Dr. Derek Walker, tested it. Dr. Walker reviewed the questions with regard to clarity and applicability to the research hypothesis. He was able to spot ambiguities and areas where more definition was required and pilot the tuning of the survey. The survey questions were adjusted to include his comments, and then reviewed again before being finalized. The first round was left open for well over two months to enable members to reconcile schedules, and to enable those academics in the southern hemisphere to return from holiday.

First Round Analysis

The scores of the panel members were analyzed to find the statistical median of each question, the average, and the standard deviation. The results of the first round indicated a reasonably tight grouping of opinion on most of the questions, with a few outliers. The first round data was inspected to determine which leadership and cultural dimensions had a standard deviation greater than 2.0. As there were only four such points, I decided to narrow the control limits. By inspection, on all but 19 out of 153 questions, the standard deviation was less than 1.7 or 87.6% concurrence. I re-set the control limits so that half the standard deviation ($\sigma/2$) was less than 1.0, and then prepared scatter plots for each of these 19 dimensions.

Second Round Questions

The median, average, and standard deviation for each question was provided to each panel member. On the questions where the standard deviation was greater than 1.7 scatter graphs were also provided to enable the panel members to visualize the responses. In addition, each panel member was provided with their answers to the first round of questions. The panel members were then asked to reassess their first session answers, and to adjust them as they saw fit. The panel members were again provided the opportunity to provide a commentary on the dimensions. Of the 25 panelists who agreed to participate, only a portion were able to make time in their schedules to complete the survey. Fifteen panel members completed both session 1 and 2. The remainder completed either the first session or the second session.

Second Round Analysis

As with the first round, the scores were analyzed to find the median, average, and standard deviation of the responses. This is discussed in Section 8.2 of this work.

Feedback to Panel

The results of the analysis were provided back to the panel members for their information, and to show appreciation for their participation.

7.7 Chapter Summary

This Chapter described the testing method, the strategy for the design of the test, the test evaluation criteria, and a discussion of the Delphi panel technique and methodology. As with many of the cross-cultural surveys, the qualitative method was utilized to acquire the opinions, and a quantitative analysis was then performed on the data. The following Chapter provides the results of the testing

8. Results
8.1 Chapter Introduction

The results of the Delphi panel survey, and the confirmation or rejection of the hypotheses will be provided in this Chapter. The results will be compared to the acceptance criteria, analyzed, and discussed. The significance of the findings will be discussed in the summary of this Chapter

8.2 Interpretation of Results

The results of the two Delphi panel sessions are provided below, along with a discussion of the findings for each of the XLQ dimensions and aspects.

8.2.1   XLQ Aspect Leadership

Leadership is the first aspect of XLQ, with its dimensions being trust, empathy, transformation, power, and communications. This section will review the results of each leadership dimension in turn.

Trust

All of the Dimension Descriptors for trust were confirmed, though a few were weak confirmation. Trust itself was strongly confirmed with a mean score of 6.46. Table 12 provides the results of the Delphi survey for both sessions. As this format will be used for each of the XLQ Leadership Aspects, a brief review of the format is in order. The XLQ Aspects (leadership and culture), and the XLQ Dimensions are the basic divisions in this work. The Dimension Descriptors came from the exegetical research and are described in Appendix 1. These were the adjectives used to describe the Dimensions of, in this case, trust. The mean for Session 1 and Session 2 follow, and the column titled "Mean % Change" represents the change in the mean from Session 1 to Session 2.

The column titled "Mean Both Sessions" calculates the mean for all responses. Some of the panelists that participated in Session 1 were unable to participate in Session 2, and some in Session 2 were unable to participate in Session 1. There were also a few cases where panelists did not answer specific questions. Therefore, the "Mean Both Sessions" takes the mean of all responses to each question, as does the "Std Dev Both Sessions" column. The last column shows if the hypothesis was confirmed. Table 10 (shaded areas indicate weak confirmation) provides the criteria for confirmation.

Table 12 – XLQ Leadership/Trust

Hypothesis Testing Results

XLQ Aspect	XLQ Dimension	Dimension Descriptor	Mean Session 1	Mean Session 2	Mean Both Sessions	Std Dev Both Sessions	Mean % Change	Hypothesis Confirmation Strength
Leadership	Trust		6.33	6.59	6.46	0.82	4%	Strong Confirmation
		Care and Concern	5.58	5.47	5.53	1.36	-2%	Confirmation
		Esteem	5.95	6.18	6.06	1.01	4%	Strong Confirmation
		Face	5.47	5.71	5.58	1.38	4%	Confirmation
		Character	6.21	6.53	6.36	0.99	5%	Strong Confirmation
		Honesty & Integrity	6.37	6.53	6.44	0.81	2%	Strong Confirmation
		Duty & Loyalty	5.84	5.94	5.89	1.19	2%	Confirmation
		Admiration	4.63	4.65	4.64	1.66	0%	Weak Confirmation
		Competence	6.21	6.18	6.19	1.09	-1%	Strong Confirmation
		Technical	4.58	5.00	4.78	1.17	8%	Weak Confirmation
		Jugement	6.37	6.12	6.25	0.73	-4%	Strong Confirmation
		Dependability	6.00	6.18	6.08	1.23	3%	Strong Confirmation
		Predictability	4.95	5.24	5.08	1.36	5%	Confirmation
		Commitments	6.58	6.76	6.67	0.53	3%	Strong Confirmation
		Fearlessness	4.74	5.12	4.92	1.50	7%	Weak Confirmation
		Confidence	6.00	5.94	5.97	0.94	-1%	Confirmation
		Self-Sacrifice	4.16	4.76	4.44	1.58	13%	Weak Confirmation
		Humaneness	5.21	5.82	5.50	1.52	11%	Confirmation
		Tolerance	5.00	5.65	5.31	1.45	11%	Confirmation
		Respect	6.05	6.47	6.25	0.91	6%	Strong Confirmation
		Integrator	5.47	6.12	5.78	1.29	11%	Confirmation
		Goals	5.47	5.65	5.56	1.61	3%	Confirmation
		Cohesiveness	5.53	5.71	5.61	0.99	3%	Confirmation
		Integrity & Ethics	5.11	6.11	5.59	1.69	16%	Confirmation
		Values	5.89	6.22	6.05	1.08	5%	Strong Confirmation
		Ethics	5.89	5.61	5.76	1.36	-5%	Confirmation
		Truth & Justice	5.05	5.61	5.32	1.75	10%	Confirmation
		Fairness	6.00	6.50	6.24	0.80	8%	Strong Confirmation
		Candor	4.74	4.83	4.78	1.81	2%	Weak Confirmation

The Dimension Descriptors of admiration, technical competence, fearlessness, self-sacrifice, and candor all had results less than 5.0. The mean was stable for admiration and candor, whereas it increased significantly for technical competence, fearlessness, and self-sacrifice. Inspection of the panelist's data points indicates that the difference was not reconsideration, but rather the difference between the panelists who participated.

The weakest confirmation was for self-sacrifice at a mean score of 4.4.

In Figure 32, the x-axis is the rankings for the self-sacrifice and the y-axis the number of panelists choosing each score. As the figure indicates, while the panelists were divided on this topic the mean is above the neutral position of 4.0. One panelist, who scored this Dimension Descriptor at 2.0 on both sessions, noted, "in general where I 'disagree' with the statements I would say that the statements are strongly true for specific cultures." This was the only comment received and was, perhaps, a feeling shared by other panelists. In cultures with high Power Distance indices, it is certainly true that a leader would not need to display strong self-sacrifice, whereas in a Western culture, such as the USA, this would be more important.

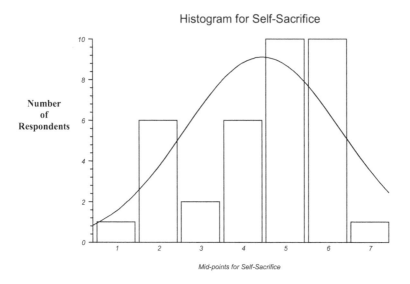

Figure 32 – Leadership/Trust/Self-Sacrifice

From experience, I was surprised to see that admiration (4.64) and candor (4.78) did not receive higher scores. The question for admiration was "Admiration - of others and self - is an essential ingredient of trust." I suspect that the self-admiration concept likely skewed this question for some of the panelists. The responses to the candor question are shown in Figure 33. Twenty-four scored candor at or above 5.0 with the mean skewed to the right. A lack of candor will either erase trust, or if subtle ultimately erode it. It is interesting that the panelists felt a weaker role for candor in trust relationships.

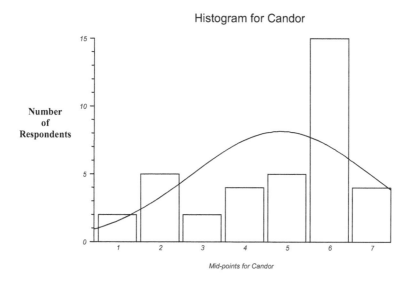

Figure 33 - Leadership/Trust/Candor

The opening question "Leadership requires the creation and maintenance of Trust, regardless of culture" confirmed the Trust Dimension hypothesis with a mean of 6.46. In addition, all of the main Dimension Descriptors (shown in bold in Table 12) were confirmed by the panelists, with fearlessness being the weakest at 4.92.

The hypothesis that the XLQ Dimension of Trust, and its Dimension Descriptors, is *emic* was confirmed by the Delphi panelists.

Empathy

All of the Dimension Descriptors for empathy were confirmed, though servant leadership was weak confirmation. Empathy itself was confirmed with a mean score of 5.68.

Table 13 (shaded areas indicate weak confirmation) provides the results of the Delphi survey for both sessions.

The results for servant leadership were somewhat surprising. One panelist provided the following comment: "in a country that utilizes servants (maids, cooks, etc.) leadership is by dictatorship without the master giving of oneself."

Table 13 – XLQ Leadership/Empathy

Hypothesis Testing Results

XLQ Aspect	XLQ Dimension	Dimension Descriptor	Mean Session 1	Mean Session 2	Mean Both Sessions	Std Dev Both Sessions	Mean % Change	Hypothesis Confirmation Strength
Leadership	Empathy		5.37	6.00	5.68	1.38	11%	Confirmation
		Cultural Intelligence	5.79	6.06	5.92	1.38	4%	Confirmation
		Metaphors	5.47	6.00	5.73	1.10	9%	Confirmation
		Customs	5.68	6.00	5.84	1.04	5%	Confirmation
		Humaneness	4.74	5.56	5.14	1.60	15%	Confirmation
		Compassion	5.79	5.83	5.81	0.84	1%	Confirmation
		Consideration	6.32	6.50	6.41	0.55	3%	Strong Confirmation
		Servant Leadership	4.42	4.83	4.62	1.78	9%	Weak Confirmation
		Self Sacrifice	5.06	4.94	5.00	1.55	-2%	Confirmation
		Empowerment	5.72	6.00	5.86	1.33	5%	Confirmation

Figure 34 shows that the results are skewed to the right, with a number of scores at 6.0, and 2.0. As the quote from the panelist illustrates, the concept of servant leadership will potentially conflict with authoritarian (large Power Distance) cultures, and I suspect that other panelists had a similar view.

The hypothesis that the XLQ Dimension of Empathy, and its Dimension Descriptors, is *emic* was confirmed by the Delphi panelists.

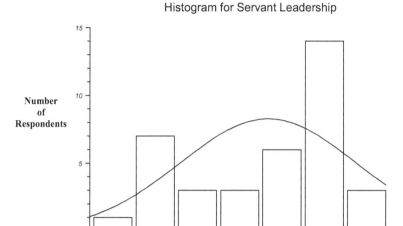

Histogram for Servant Leadership

Number of Respondents

Mid-points for Servant Leadership

Figure 34 - Leadership/Empathy/Servant Leadership

Transformation

All of the Dimension Descriptors for transformation were confirmed, though uniqueness was weak confirmation. Transformation itself was confirmed with a mean score of 5.61. Table 14 (shaded areas indicate weak confirmation) provides the results of the Delphi survey for both sessions.

The question posed for uniqueness was "uniqueness is an essential ingredient of Charisma." The mean increased on this item mostly due to the panelists who participated in Session 2. Figure 35 shows the distribution of scores. Uniqueness was thought to be a good descriptor of that unusual quality that facilitates the perception of a leader as charismatic. Judging on the number of 4.0 scores, some the panelists were indifferent on this dimension.

Table 14 – XLQ Leadership/Transformation

Hypothesis Testing Results

XLQ Aspect	XLQ Dimension	Dimension Descriptor	Mean Session 1	Mean Session 2	Mean Both Sessions	Std Dev Both Sessions	Mean % Change	Hypothesis Confirmation Strength
Leadership	Transformation		5.50	5.72	5.61	1.25	4%	Confirmation
		Inspiration	5.74	5.89	5.81	1.29	3%	Confirmation
		Expectations	6.11	5.67	5.89	0.99	-8%	Confirmation
		Mentoring	6.11	6.00	6.05	1.00	-2%	Strong Confirmation
		Charisma	5.74	5.89	5.81	1.00	3%	Confirmation
		Decisive	5.42	5.33	5.38	1.21	-2%	Confirmation
		Uniqueness	4.74	5.11	4.92	1.28	7%	Weak Confirmation
		Risk Change	5.53	5.11	5.32	1.58	-8%	Confirmation
		Desire to change	6.11	6.06	6.08	1.26	-1%	Strong Confirmation
		Security	5.63	5.50	5.57	1.17	-2%	Confirmation
		Vision	6.32	6.72	6.51	1.10	6%	Strong Confirmation
		Foresight	6.05	6.06	6.05	0.85	0%	Strong Confirmation
		Goals	6.32	6.50	6.41	0.64	3%	Strong Confirmation

Figure 35 - Leadership/Transformation/Uniqueness

The hypothesis that the XLQ Dimension of Transformation, and its Dimension Descriptors, is *emic* was confirmed by the Delphi panelists.

Power

All of the Dimension Descriptors for power were confirmed, except for coercive power, which showed weak rejection. The Dimension Descriptors of position, political, warmth, and reward showed weak confirmation. Power itself was confirmed with a mean score of 5.46. The panelists provided an interesting set of scores for power. First on coercive power, I thought that the panelists would strongly disagree. In fact, they saw a weak rejection as shown in Figure 50. I suspect that panelists were again focused on cultures with large Power Distance indices when answering this question.

Bass and Stogdill (1990) believe that referent power is a strong force, though not a well tested form of power. I believe that it is perhaps the form of power that is most desirable for a leader, for it is power bestowed upon the leader by the follower, voluntarily. The panelists also shared this opinion as is shown in Table 15 (shaded areas indicate weak confirmation).

Table 15 – XLQ Leadership/Power

| | | | | | | Mean | Std Dev | | |
| | | | Mean | Mean | Both | Both | Mean % | Hypothesis |
XLQ Aspect	XLQ Dimension	Dimension Descriptor	Session 1	Session 2	Sessions	Sessions	Change	Confirmation Strength
Leadership	Power		5.32	5.61	5.46	1.41	5%	Confirmation
		Knowledge Power	5.37	5.72	5.54	1.45	6%	Confirmation
		Sharing knowledge	5.00	5.00	5.00	1.62	0%	Confirmation
		Mentor	5.05	5.41	5.22	1.64	7%	Confirmation
		Position Power	4.53	4.50	4.51	1.80	-1%	Weak Confirmation
		Legitimate	5.00	5.28	5.14	1.80	5%	Confirmation
		Political	4.42	3.89	4.16	1.66	-14%	Weak Confirmation
		Power Distance	5.32	5.50	5.41	1.57	3%	Confirmation
		Locust	6.16	6.17	6.16	0.69	0%	Strong Confirmation
		Communitinarism	5.58	5.83	5.70	1.13	4%	Confirmation
		Referent Power	5.79	5.50	5.65	1.64	-5%	Confirmation
		Bravery	5.37	5.17	5.27	1.28	-4%	Confirmation
		Warmth	4.68	4.72	4.70	1.65	1%	Weak Confirmation
		Reward & Punishment Power	5.21	4.78	5.00	1.76	-9%	Confirmation
		Coersive	3.63	3.78	3.70	2.00	4%	Weak Rejection
		Reward	4.53	4.28	4.41	1.76	-6%	Weak Confirmation

Hypothesis Testing Results

198

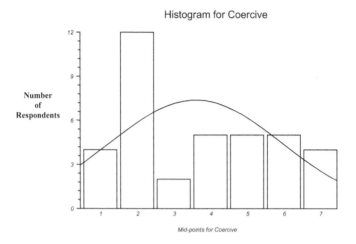

Histogram for Coercive

Figure 36 - Leadership/Power/Coercive

The weak confirmation by the panelists of political power and position power seem to support the referent power score as well. I suspect the reason to be that generally people perceive political power and position power in a negative way, and in a way that would diminish rather than enhance the power of a leader. I had also expected knowledge power to be a bit stronger than it was. While the panelists confirmed it with a score of 5.54, I had thought that it would be of greater importance. Often, knowledge power helps to build referent power.

The hypothesis that the XLQ Dimension of Power, and its Dimension Descriptors, is *emic* was confirmed by the Delphi panelists. The one exception was that the panelists did not confirm coercive power.

Communication

All of the Dimension Descriptors for communication were confirmed. The Dimension Descriptor of storytelling was the only weak confirmation at 4.89. Communication itself was strongly confirmed with a mean score of 6.41 as shown in Table 16 (shaded areas indicate weak confirmation). The panelists considered communication an important aspect of leadership.

Table 16 – XLQ Leadership/Communication

Hypothesis Testing Results

XLQ Aspect	XLQ Dimension	Dimension Descriptor	Mean Session 1	Mean Session 2	Mean Both Sessions	Std Dev Both Sessions	Mean % Change	Hypothesis Confirmation Strength
Leadership	Communication		6.47	6.33	6.41	1.07	-2%	Strong Confirmation
		Adaptability	5.95	6.06	6.00	1.37	2%	Strong Confirmation
		Understanding	5.63	6.11	5.86	1.36	8%	Confirmation
		Communication	6.21	6.50	6.35	0.95	4%	Strong Confirmation
		Competence	6.26	6.17	6.22	1.00	-2%	Strong Confirmation
		Cultural	5.58	5.67	5.62	1.38	2%	Confirmation
		Communication	5.74	5.78	5.76	1.12	1%	Confirmation
		Listening	5.95	6.06	6.00	1.27	2%	Strong Confirmation
		Creativity	5.63	6.00	5.81	1.20	6%	Confirmation
		Storytelling	4.95	4.83	4.89	1.45	-2%	Weak Confirmation
		Metaphor	5.68	5.35	5.53	1.23	-6%	Confirmation
		Patience	5.63	5.44	5.54	1.57	-3%	Confirmation
		Time	6.00	5.94	5.97	1.21	-1%	Confirmation
		Repetition	5.00	5.06	5.03	1.55	1%	Confirmation
		Sensitivity	5.74	5.81	5.77	1.26	1%	Confirmation
		Facework	5.00	5.22	5.11	1.71	4%	Confirmation
		Wisdom	6.16	6.33	6.24	0.83	3%	Strong Confirmation
		Accuracy	6.05	6.35	6.19	0.92	5%	Strong Confirmation
		Culture	5.79	6.00	5.89	0.88	4%	Confirmation
		Conflict Management	6.53	6.67	6.59	0.90	2%	Strong Confirmation
		Knowledge	6.63	6.56	6.59	0.64	-1%	Strong Confirmation
		Listening	6.32	6.22	6.27	1.15	-2%	Strong Confirmation
		Preparation	5.95	5.72	5.84	1.26	-4%	Confirmation

The panelists also scored conflict resolution as very important with a mean score of 6.59. The literature indicates that conflict is either born or nurtured by a lack of communications, and knowledge. Followers pay particular heed to how a leader handles conflict, regardless of culture. In my experience as an arbitrator, mediator, and subject matter expert a leader must be able to manage conflict gracefully. Chapter 5 discussed conflict management in detail, as it is such an important part of any interpersonal interaction. The panelists confirmed that this was their opinion as well.

I was interested to see that the panelists scored storytelling as a weak confirmation. As I have described in this work, and in a recent paper (Grisham 2006), storytelling has been utilized since mankind evolved. Storytelling, poetry and metaphors provide a vehicle for people to relate complex ideas and emotions effectively. Leaders often display the ability to tell engaging stories, and to inspire people to seek more knowledge. Figure 37 shows that there was a group of panelists whose experience caused them to score storytelling as a weak contributor to communication.

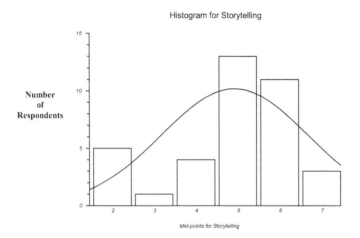

Histogram for Storytelling

Figure 37 - Leadership/Communication/Storytelling

I hope that future research explores this topic in more detail, for I believe it is an essential tool for a leader.

The hypothesis that the XLQ Dimension of Communication, and its Dimension Descriptors, is *emic* was confirmed by the Delphi panelists.

Summary

The XLQ Aspect Leadership and its Dimensions and Dimension Descriptors were confirmed, except for the Dimension Descriptor coercive power. Figure 38 provides a graphical overview of the findings from the Leadership Dimensions.

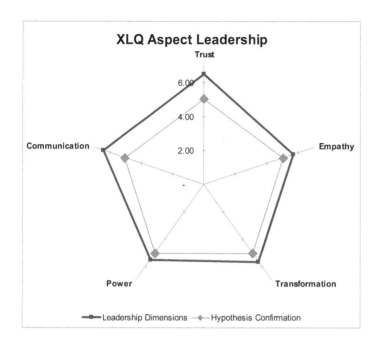

XLQ Aspect Leadership

Trust

6.00

4.00

Communication

2.00

Empathy

-

Power

Transformation

━■━Leadership Dimensions ━◆━Hypothesis Confirmation

Figure 38 - XLQ Aspect Leadership

8.2.2   XLQ Aspect Culture

Culture is the second Aspect of XLQ. As shown in Figure 14, the nine dimensions of culture utilized in this work were taken from the GLOBE survey: Uncertainty Avoidance, Power Distance, Institutional Collectivism, Group Collectivism, Gender Egalitarianism, Assertiveness, Future Orientation, Performance Orientation, and Humane Orientation.   As discussed in Section 6.7, the hypothesis is that the XLQ Leadership Dimensions are connected to the GLOBE survey dimensions of culture.

To test the hypothesis the Delphi panelists were asked to score the strength of the connection between the XLQ Leadership Dimensions and the GLOBE cultural dimensions. This section will review the results of each leadership dimension in turn.

In the following sections, I have used XLQ Leadership dimensions to illustrate the connections between the data and the application of the theory to practice. Each XLQ Cultural Aspect below would rely on all of the XQL Leadership Aspects to some degree obviously. Therefore, I have not expanded the narrative to include a complete mapping of XLQ Leadership Aspects onto XLQ Culture Aspects, but rather taken specific examples to illustrate the connection and application.

Uncertainty Avoidance

Uncertainty Avoidance is the extent that people strive to avoid uncertainty by relying upon social norms, rituals, and bureaucratic practices. The panelists confirmed the hypothesis for all of the Leadership Dimensions, with empathy and transformation being weakly confirmed as shown in Table 17 (shaded areas indicate weak confirmation). Only one of the panelists commented on this XLQ Aspect by saying that "if leadership is about change then all attributes of leadership are dealing with the ability to take people outside of their known - (except where leadership is conservation orientated)." His scoring of all dimensions was accordingly 7.0. Leaders must be able to lead change, thus I agree with the panelist's comment.

Table 17 - XLQ Culture/Uncertainty Avoidance

					Mean	Std Dev		
			Mean	Mean	Both	Both	Mean %	Hypothesis
XLQ Aspect	XLQ Dimension	Dimension Descriptor	Session 1	Session 2	Sessions	Sessions	Change	Confirmation Strength
Culture	Uncertainty Avoidance	Trust	5.59	5.72	5.66	1.63	2%	Confirmation
		Empathy	4.53	4.83	4.69	1.45	6%	Weak Confirmation
		Transformation	4.12	4.72	4.43	1.50	13%	Weak Confirmation
		Power	5.76	6.00	5.89	0.99	4%	Confirmation
		Communication	5.76	6.00	5.89	0.93	4%	Confirmation

Hypothesis Testing Results

The Uncertainty Avoidance dimension of the GLOBE survey (Luque and Javidan 2004) asked the respondents to score this dimension from both a practice (how things are actually done – "as-is"), and a values (how things should be done – "should-be") perspective. The GLOBE survey asked questions about both the societal and organizational opinions of the people surveyed. As international organizations vary widely, I have chosen to focus on the GLOBE societal questions in this work. Two of the questions were (Pg. 619):

- For *as-is* – "In this society, orderliness and consistency are stressed, even at the expense of experimentation and innovation (reverse scored)." As noted by the authors (Pg. 619): "the items were coded so that strong agreement with the statements resulted in a high Uncertainty Avoidance scale of scores." Reverse score means that a rank of 1 assigned by the person being interviewed was translated into a score of 7 by the GLOBE team.

- For *should-be* – "I believe that orderliness and consistency should be stressed, even at the expense of experimentation and innovation (reverse scored)."

For Russia the a*s-is* score was 2.88 which was the lowest score recorded (society does not stress orderliness), and the *should-be* score was 5.07 (that it should stress orderliness more). For Switzerland the *as-is* score was 5.37 which was the highest score recorded (society stresses orderliness), and the *should-be* score was 3.16 that orderliness should be given less stress. Consider the leadership potential for the XLQ Empathy dimension in both cases. To understand that people feel there should be more orderliness in Russia and less in Switzerland enables a leader to increase his or her stature in the eyes of the followers by simply understanding that this dichotomy exists.

Then using the XLQ Transformation dimension, a leader has the option to nurture more orderliness with Russian team members, and nurture more empowerment and volition with the Swiss. In all such transactions extreme care must be exercised to understand the personal views of the individuals themselves, as each Russian or Swiss person will have different views of orderliness, depending upon their values and upbringing.

The panelists' scores for Trust, Power, and Communication confirm the hypothesis. Using the same examples as above the XLQ Trust dimension would empower the Swiss individual to take on more responsibility, or power, and would provide the Russian individual with the added security or stability being sought. Clearly, on the empowerment side, a leader would need to adjust the approach to power with both of these people. Communication of goals and objectives would likewise need to be adjusted to fit the two individuals, the Swiss generally needing less specific direction, the Russian individual needing more.

If both were on the same team, the leader must be aware of the way that each individual perceives this different approach by the leader. If they are trained to understand the cultural differences between the members of the team, they will be more likely to accept the dichotomy. In fact, if educated about the differences, the Swiss individual will often offer to provide the added guidance to the Russian individual. It can become a symbiotic relationship.

The hypothesis, that each of the XLQ Leadership Dimensions is correlated with the GLOBE dimension of Uncertainty Avoidance, was confirmed by the Delphi panelists.

Power Distance

Power Distance is the degree that people expect and agree that power would be stratified and concentrated at high levels of organizations. The panelists confirmed the hypothesis for all of the Leadership Dimensions, with empathy and transformation being weakly confirmed as shown in Table 18 (shaded areas indicate weak confirmation).

Table 18 - XLQ Culture/Power Distance

Hypothesis Testing Results

XLQ Aspect	XLQ Dimension	Dimension Descriptor	Mean Session 1	Mean Session 2	Mean Both Sessions	Std Dev Both Sessions	Mean % Change	Hypothesis Confirmation Strength
Culture	Power Distance	Trust	5.29	5.06	5.17	1.46	-5%	Confirmation
		Empathy	4.35	4.78	4.57	1.58	9%	Weak Confirmation
		Transformation	5.06	4.59	4.82	1.31	-10%	Weak Confirmation
		Power	5.88	6.00	5.94	1.06	2%	Confirmation
		Communication	5.35	5.39	5.37	1.44	1%	Confirmation

One of the panelists commented on this XLQ Aspect by saying that "The strength of the dimensions of leadership are based on a culture that does not accept authority. If the country accepts authority, then my experience indicates that the leadership can function with fewer skills." This concept was mirrored in the GLOBE survey as well.

The Power Distance dimension of the GLOBE survey (Carl, Gupta et al. 2004) asked the respondents to score this dimension from both a practice (how things are actually done – "as-is"), and a values (how things should be done – "should-be") perspective.   Two of the questions were (Pg. 537):

- For *as-is* – "In this society, followers are expected to (reverse scored):" Obey their leaders without question = 1, Question their leaders when in disagreement = 2. Reverse score means that a rank of 1 assigned by the person being interviewed was translated into a score of 7 by the GLOBE team.
- For *should-be* – "I believe that followers should (reverse scored):" Obey their leaders without question = 1, Question their leaders when in disagreement = 2. Reverse score means that a rank of 1 assigned by the person being interviewed was translated into a score of 7 by the GLOBE team.

The extreme examples are worth mentioning. For Morocco a*s-is* score was 5.80 which was the highest score recorded (authority is accepted), and the s*hould-be* score was 3.11 (it should not be to the same extent). Therefore, the perspective of the Moroccans surveyed was that while the society stresses the acceptance of authority, it should not to the same extent. For Denmark the *as-is* score was 3.89 which was the lowest score recorded (authority can be questioned), and the *should-be* score was 2.76 (authority should be questioned even more than it is). The use of the XLQ Power dimension in both cases means that for a Moroccan there should be questioning of authority and more regard for a person's abilities. In Denmark, there is more questioning of authority, and there should be more. A leader should realize that both groups want to question authority more than they do, and be prepared to empower the team and facilitate the natural growth that will occur.

In this example, a leader could team the Moroccan with the Dane and facilitate a joint exploration of ideas to occur. Using the XLQ Trust dimension, a leader would accomplish this by providing both individuals the security to explore their *should-be* be values. As with all of the XQL Cultural Aspects, knowledge of the cultures is essential, and sensitivity to the diversity (one size does not fit all) of the individuals is critical.

The hypothesis, that each of the XLQ Leadership Dimensions is correlated with the GLOBE dimension of Power Distance, was confirmed by the Delphi panelists.

Institutional Collectivism
Institutional Collectivism is the degree to which society and organizations encourage and reward collective distribution of resources. The panelists confirmed the hypothesis, with weak confirmation of transformation as shown in Table 19 (shaded areas indicate weak confirmation).

The Institutional Collectivism dimension of the GLOBE survey (Gelfand, Bhawuk et al. 2004) asked the respondents to score this dimension from both a practice (how things are actually done – "as-is"), and a values (how things should be done – "should-be") perspective. The authors distinguish between Institutional practices and values, the subject of this section, and that of In-Group practices and values, which is the subject of the next section. Two of the questions were (Pg. 464):

- For *as-is* – "In this society, leaders encourage group loyalty even if individual goals

206

suffer (reverse scored)." Reverse score means that a rank of 1 assigned by the person being interviewed was translated into a score of 7 by the GLOBE team.

- For *should-be* – "I believe that, in general leaders should encourage group loyalty even if individual goals suffer (reverse scored):"

Table 19 - XLQ Culture/Institutional Collectivism

						Std Dev		
					Mean	Both		
			Mean	Mean	Both	Both	Mean %	Hypothesis
XLQ Aspect	XLQ Dimension	Dimension Descriptor	Session 1	Session 2	Sessions	Sessions	Change	Confirmation Strength
Culture	Institutional Collectivism	Trust	5.94	5.67	5.80	1.16	-5%	Confirmation
		Empathy	5.88	5.47	5.68	0.94	-8%	Confirmation
		Transformation	5.47	4.33	4.89	1.37	-26%	Weak Confirmation
		Power	5.29	5.00	5.14	1.44	-6%	Confirmation
		Communication	5.65	5.56	5.60	1.01	-2%	Confirmation

Hypothesis Testing Results

At the extremes, for Sweden the a*s-is* score was 5.22 which was the highest score recorded (where group loyalty is encouraged), and the *should-be* score was 3.94 (individual goals should be more encouraged). The perspective of Swedish individuals surveyed was that while society stresses the importance of group loyalty, it should do so to a lesser degree. For Greece the *as-is* score was 3.25 which was the lowest score recorded (individual goals are encouraged), and the *should-be* score was 5.4, that group loyalty should be more strongly encouraged. Therefore, the Greeks wanted more focus on group goals, while the Swedes wanted a bit less focus.

In this example, a leader could team the Greek with the Swede and facilitate a natural balancing or normalization to occur. By using the XLQ Leadership dimension of Trust a leader could facilitate this by providing both individuals the security to explore their *should-be* values. The XLQ Communication dimension would facilitate their learning for one another. On the XLQ Power dimension, a leader could create an opportunity by encouraging the Greek to lead the way. As with all of the XQL Cultural Aspects, knowledge of the cultures is essential, and sensitivity to the diversity (one size does not fit all) of the individuals is critical.

The hypothesis, that each of the XLQ Leadership Dimensions is correlated with the GLOBE dimension of Institutional Collectivism, was confirmed by the Delphi panelists.

Group Collectivism

Group Collectivism is the degree to which individuals express pride, loyalty and cohesiveness in their organizations and families. The panelists confirmed the hypothesis, with weak confirmation of transformation as shown in Table 20 (shaded areas indicate weak confirmation).

For the Philippines the a*s-is* score was 6.36 which was the highest score recorded (family loyalty is strongly encouraged), and the *should-be* score was 6.18 (family loyalty is about where it should be). In the Philippines the a*s-is* and the *should-be* scores showed a remarkable convergence of values and practice. In New Zealand the *as-is* score was 3.67, which was one of the lowest scores recorded (family loyalty is not stressed), and the *should-be* score was 6.21, family loyalty should be strongly encouraged. Therefore, both groups felt that family loyalty should be emphasized, but the New Zealanders said that in practice family loyalty should be emphasized more than it is. Figure 12 shows that there is little deviation between the *as-is* and *should-be* scores disparity regarding the concept of group collectivism.

The Group Collectivism dimension of the GLOBE survey (Gelfand, Bhawuk et al. 2004) asked the respondents to score this dimension from both a practice (how things are actually done – "as-is"), and a values (how things should be done – "should-be") perspective. Two of the questions were (Pg. 464):

- For *as-is* – "In this society, parents take pride in the individual accomplishments of their children (reverse scored)." Reverse score means that a rank of 1 assigned by the person being interviewed was translated into a score of 7 by the GLOBE team.
- For *should-be* – "In this society, parents should take pride in the individual accomplishments of their children (reverse scored)."

For the Philippines the a*s-is* score was 6.36 which was the highest score recorded (family loyalty is strongly encouraged), and the *should-be* score was 6.18 (family loyalty is about where it should be). In the Philippines the a*s-is* and the *should-be* scores showed a remarkable convergence of values and practice. In New Zealand the *as-is* score was 3.67, which was one of the lowest scores recorded (family loyalty is not stressed), and the *should-be* score was 6.21, family loyalty should be strongly encouraged. Therefore, both groups felt that family loyalty should be emphasized, but the New Zealanders said that in practice family loyalty should be emphasized more than it is. Figure 12 shows that there is little deviation between the *as-is* and *should-be* scores disparity regarding the concept of group collectivism.

Table 20 - XLQ Culture/Group Collectivism

XLQ Aspect	XLQ Dimension	Dimension Descriptor	Mean Session 1	Mean Session 2	Mean Both Sessions	Std Dev Both Sessions	Mean % Change	Hypothesis Confirmation Strength
Culture	Group Collectivism	Trust	6.13	6.06	6.09	1.06	-1%	Strong Confirmation
		Empathy	5.87	5.61	5.73	1.10	-5%	Confirmation
		Transformation	4.75	4.89	4.82	1.34	3%	Weak Confirmation
		Power	4.88	5.11	5.00	1.39	5%	Confirmation
		Communication	5.31	5.61	5.47	1.05	5%	Confirmation

The XLQ Empathy and Trust dimensions would be an important considerations for the New Zealanders, as they would be encouraged to work in their *should-be* world. A leader could provide the security for the New Zealander to bond with the team, extended family, and the understanding that this is what his/her *should-be world* looks like. For the people from the Philippines, they could help provide a sense of balance for this team, as they are accustomed to being a part of a family, and could facilitate the work of the leader in showing the New Zealander by example.

The hypothesis, that each of the XLQ Leadership Dimensions is correlated with the GLOBE dimension of Group Collectivism, was confirmed by the Delphi panelists.

Gender Egalitarianism

Gender Egalitarianism is the degree to which societies and organizations promote gender equality. The panelists confirmed the hypothesis on all dimensions as shown in Table 21 (shaded areas indicate weak confirmation).

The Gender Egalitarianism dimension of the GLOBE survey (Emrich, Denmark et al. 2004) asked the respondents to score this dimension from both a practice (how things are actually done – "as-is"), and a values (how things should be done – "should-be") perspective. Two of the questions were (Pg. 360):

- For *as-is* – "In this society, who is more likely to serve in a position of high office:" men = 1, and women = 7.
- For *should-be* – "I believe that opportunities for leadership positions should be:" 1 = more available for men than for women, 7 = more available for women that for men.

Table 21 - XLQ culture/Gender Egalitarianism

XLQ Aspect	XLQ Dimension	Dimension Descriptor	Mean Session 1	Mean Session 2	Mean Both Sessions	Std Dev Both Sessions	Mean % Change	Hypothesis Confirmation Strength
Culture	Gender Egalitarianism	Trust	5.38	5.61	5.50	1.33	4%	Confirmation
		Empathy	5.44	5.11	5.26	1.54	-6%	Confirmation
		Transformation	4.94	5.06	5.00	1.23	2%	Confirmation
		Power	5.31	4.94	5.12	1.43	-7%	Confirmation
		Communication	5.31	5.33	5.32	1.41	0%	Confirmation

For Hungary the a*s-is* score was 4.08 which was the highest score recorded (women are slightly more likely to have a position of power), and the *should-be* score was a more robust 4.63 indicating that women should be in positions of power. In South Korea, the lowest score recorded, the a*s-is* score was 2.5 (men frequently hold positions of power), and the *should-be* score was 4.22. The mean *as-is* score for the survey was 3.35, and the *should-be* score for the survey was 4.58. The *should-be* score was close to that of the Hungarians *should-be* score. Therefore, both groups felt that there should be more equity in gender, but that there is far less in practice. In Sweden the scores were reversed, with the *as-is* score being 3.84 and *should-be* score 1.15. In Qatar the scores were also reversed but by less of a margin, with an *as-is* score of 3.63 and a *should-be* score of 3.38.

Consider the XLQ Empathy dimension first. Many people, not all, want to have more gender equality in their societies, and many firms are pushing hard to make men and women more equal in the workplace. Countries like Egypt with two low scores (*as-is* 2.81, *should-be* 3.18) are exceptions. In my international experience with a multi-national firm, we had a global gender equality policy that we attempted to apply in every country in which we did business. Training sessions were obligatory, and the policy was initiated by the CEO. However, thousands of years of societal practice cannot be overcome in a few years. A leader must empathize with the values and aspirations of the firm and of the individual in striving for gender equality, but must balance these against social customs and taboos. If followers trust the leader to support them in their endeavors, they will be more inclined to adjust to an environment in which gender diversity is celebrated.

The hypothesis, that each of the XLQ Leadership Dimensions is correlated with the GLOBE dimension of Gender Egalitarianism, was confirmed by the Delphi panelists.

210

Assertiveness

Assertiveness is the degree that an individual expresses assertive, confrontational or aggressive behavior in organizations and society. The panelists confirmed the hypothesis with weak confirmation on Trust and Empathy, as shown in Table 22 (shaded areas indicate weak confirmation).

The Assertiveness dimension of the GLOBE survey (Den Hartog 2004) asked the respondents to score this dimension from both a practice (how things are actually done – "as-is"), and a values (how things should be done – "should-be") perspective. Two of the questions were (Pg. 407):

- For *as-is* – "In this society, people are generally (reverse scored):" Assertive = 1, Nonassertive = 7. Reverse score means that a rank of 1 assigned by the person being interviewed was translated into a score of 7 by the GLOBE team.
- For *should-be* –"In this society, people should be encouraged to be (reverse scored):" Assertive = 1, Nonassertive = 7.

Table 22 - XLQ Culture/Assertiveness

XLQ Aspect	XLQ Dimension	Dimension Descriptor	Mean Session 1	Mean Session 2	Mean Both Sessions	Std Dev Both Sessions	Mean % Change	Hypothesis Confirmation Strength
Culture	Assertiveness	Trust	4.71	4.44	4.57	1.48	-6%	Weak Confirmation
		Empathy	4.24	4.35	4.29	1.27	3%	Weak Confirmation
		Transformation	5.06	5.28	5.17	1.10	4%	Confirmation
		Power	5.88	5.83	5.86	1.29	-1%	Confirmation
		Communication	5.35	5.06	5.20	1.08	-6%	Confirmation

For Albania the a*s-is* score was 4.89 which was the highest score recorded (people tend to be assertive), and the *should-be* score was a 4.41 indicating that people should be even less assertive. In Thailand, one of the lowest scores recorded, the a*s-is* score was 3.64 (people are non assertive), and the *should-be* score was 3.48, indicating that people felt they should be even more nonassertive. This is an interesting set of scores for Thailand. I lived in Thailand for about a year, and found that Thai's prefer to avoid confrontation. They are however very strong in their beliefs, and while they do not avoid explaining themselves, it is often done in delicate manner.

211

If a leader has a team made up of Albanians and Thai's, the Albanians would have a tendency not to follow the ideas of others, and the Thai's generally not to put forward their ideas, based on the scores. Using the XLQ Power dimension, a leader could empower the Thai's to take the lead in decisions, and the Albanians to support them. Using the XLQ Transformation and Communication dimensions, the leader could inspire the Albanians to use their natural assertiveness to inspire the Thai's, and the Thai's natural courtesy to balance the Albanian's potential assertiveness. If the team included Turks (*as-is* 4.53, *should-be* 2.66), and Malays (*as-is* 3.87, *should-be* 4.81), the picture becomes even more interesting. The Turks believing that people should be far less assertive and the Malays believe that they should be more assertive.

If a Leader empowers people to share their opinions in a non-aggressive manner, then everyone would be comfortable sharing their ideas – trust and security. I lived in Istanbul for about nine months and found that Turks have very strong beliefs, like the Thai's, but often they do not share them because of the Power Distance considerations in their culture. They do tend to share them when supported and encouraged to do so though. Using the XQL Communication dimensions would provide the example for the team to follow so that everyone was calibrated. The XLQ dimension of Trust would provide a stable foundation for those not inclined to share their ideas. The key here is that assertiveness should not be confused with aggressiveness.

The hypothesis, that each of the XLQ Leadership Dimensions is correlated with the GLOBE dimension of Assertiveness, was confirmed by the Delphi panelists.

Future Orientation

Future Orientation is the degree to which individuals engage in future activities such as planning, and postponing collective gratification. The panelists confirmed the hypothesis with weak confirmation on Trust and Empathy, as shown in Table 23 (shaded areas indicate weak confirmation).

The Future Orientation dimension of the GLOBE survey (Ashkanasy, Gupta et al. 2004) asked the respondents to score this dimension from both a practice (how things are actually done – "as-is"), and a values (how things should be done – "should-be") perspective. Two of the questions were (Pg. 302):

212

- For *as-is* – "In this society, the accepted norm is to (reverse scored):" Plan for the future = 1, Accept the status quo = 7. Reverse score means that a rank of 1 assigned by the person being interviewed was translated into a score of 7 by the GLOBE team.
- For *should-be* –"I believe that the accepted norm in this society should be (reverse scored)." Plan for the future = 1, Accept the status quo = 7.

For Singapore the a*s-is* score was 5.07 which was the highest score recorded (people plan for the future), and the s*hould-be* score was a 5.51 indicating that people should plan for the future even more. In Russia, the lowest score recorded, the a*s-is* score was 2.88 (people accept the status quo), and the *should-be* score was 5.48, indicating that people should plan. This is an interesting set of scores for Russia considering that they are what Gannon (2004) calls a "Torn Culture." The soviet era concepts and beliefs still linger in the society, and from my travel there, it was clear that the Russians were in a quandary between the old days and the new era. Everyone knows the story of Singapore and of Lee Kuan Yew its patriarchical leader. Planning is a bedrock principle for many Singaporeans, and the scores bear this out.

Table 23 - XLQ Culture/Future Orientation

XLQ Aspect	XLQ Dimension	Dimension Descriptor	Mean Session 1	Mean Session 2	Mean Both Sessions	Std Dev Both Sessions	Mean % Change	Hypothesis Confirmation Strength
Culture	Future Orientation	Trust	5.56	5.82	5.70	1.02	4%	Confirmation
		Empathy	4.75	4.94	4.85	1.28	4%	Weak Confirmation
		Transformation	5.38	5.71	5.55	1.37	6%	Confirmation
		Power	4.69	4.76	4.73	1.46	2%	Weak Confirmation
		Communication	5.19	5.82	5.52	1.37	11%	Confirmation

Using the XLQ Transformation and Communication dimensions, a leader make a team and have the Singaporeans take the lead in planning. The Russians could learn the mindset and how to plan, which is what they would want anyway according to the GLOBE scores. If people feel comfortable taking risks, moving away from the status quo, then they will be more inclined to accept change and to look toward the future with anticipation. The XQL Trust dimension will serve well in such circumstances to help provide a stable platform for the team members to experiment.

The hypothesis, that each of the XLQ Leadership Dimensions is correlated with the GLOBE dimension of Future Orientation, was confirmed by the Delphi panelists.

Performance Orientation

Performance Orientation is the degree to which society or organization rewards performance and excellence. The panelists confirmed the hypothesis as shown in Table 24.

The Performance Orientation dimension of the GLOBE survey (Javidan 2004) asked the respondents to score this dimension from both a practice (how things are actually done – "as-is"), and a values (how things should be done – "should-be") perspective. Two of the questions were (Pg. 246):

* For *as-is* – "In this society, students are encouraged to strive for continuously improved performance (reverse scored):" Strongly agree = 1. Reverse score means that a rank of 1 assigned by the person being interviewed was translated into a score of 7 by the GLOBE team.

* For *should-be* – "In this society, students should be encouraged to strive for continuously improved performance (reverse scored):" Strongly agree = 1.

Table 24 - XLQ Culture/Performance Orientation

XLQ Aspect	XLQ Dimension	Dimension Descriptor	Mean Session 1	Mean Session 2	Mean Both Sessions	Std Dev Both Sessions	Mean % Change	Hypothesis Confirmation Strength
Culture	Performance Orientation	Trust	5.38	5.50	5.44	0.96	2%	Confirmation
		Empathy	5.00	5.00	5.00	0.95	0%	Confirmation
		Transformation	5.81	5.89	5.85	1.08	1%	Confirmation
		Power	5.56	5.47	5.52	1.23	-2%	Confirmation
		Communication	5.38	5.50	5.44	1.33	2%	Confirmation

For Switzerland the a*s-is* score was 4.94 which was the highest score recorded (people indicated that students are encouraged to strive for improved performance), and the s*hould-be* score was a 5.82 indicating that people should be more encouraged to improve performance. In Venezuela, one of the lowest scores recorded, the a*s-is* score was 3.32 (people are not encouraged to strive for more performance), and the s*hould-be* score was 6.35, indicating that people should be significantly encouraged to strive for improved performance.

For the leader, using the XLQ dimensions of Transformation and Communication, if the Swiss lead the way in setting the standards, the people from Venezuela will readily accept the opportunity, since the scores indicate that there is a hunger for performance improvement in that country. For the Venezuelans, the XLQ Trust and Empathy dimensions will also be important so that they feel secure.

If a leader has a team made up of Singaporeans and Russians, the Russians could take the lead in planning for the future, despite their inclinations to revert to the older ways. Singaporeans would not be inclined to forgo the status quo, so the issue for a leader would be one of showing the way – XQL Transformation dimension.

The hypothesis, that each of the XLQ Leadership Dimensions is correlated with the GLOBE dimension of Performance Orientation, was confirmed by the Delphi panelists.

Humane Orientation

Humane Orientation is the degree that societies and organizations reward fair, altruistic, friendly, generous, and caring for others. The panelists confirmed the hypothesis, with weak confirmation of Transformation and Power, as shown in Table 25 (shaded areas indicate weak confirmation).

The Humane Orientation dimension of the GLOBE survey (Kabasakal and Bodur 2004) asked the respondents to score this dimension from both a practice (how things are actually done – "as-is"), and a values (how things should be done – "should-be") perspective. Two of the questions were (Pg. 571):

- For *as-is* – "In this society, people are generally (reverse scored):" Very concerned about others = 1. Not at all concerned about others = 7. Reverse score means that a rank of 1 assigned by the person being interviewed was translated into a score of 7 by the GLOBE team.
- For *should-be* – "In this society, people should be encouraged to be (reverse scored):" Very concerned about others = 1. Not at all concerned about others = 7.

Table 25 - XLQ Culture/Humane Orientation

XLQ Aspect	XLQ Dimension	Dimension Descriptor	Mean Session 1	Mean Session 2	Mean Both Sessions	Std Dev Both Sessions	Mean % Change	Hypothesis Confirmation Strength
Culture	Humane Orientation	Trust	5.69	5.94	5.82	1.17	4%	Confirmation
		Empathy	6.00	5.65	5.82	1.33	-6%	Confirmation
		Transformation	4.13	5.11	4.65	1.74	19%	Weak Confirmation
		Power	4.38	4.22	4.29	1.57	-4%	Weak Confirmation
		Communication	5.63	5.67	5.65	1.04	1%	Confirmation

For Zambia the *as-is* score was 5.23 which was the highest score recorded (people are very concerned about others), and the *should-be* score was a 5.53 indicating that people should be even more concerned about others. In West Germany, the lowest score recorded, the *as-is* score was 3.18 (people are not very concerned about others), and the *should-be* score was 5.44, indicating that people should be significantly more concerned about others.

The XLQ dimensions of Trust and Transformation are obvious choices for the leader in this circumstance. As with most of the other GLOBE dimensions in this section of the work, the two groups will compliment one another naturally. The Zambian team can demonstrate the very attributes that the West Germans desire, and this will create an opportunity to develop Communications pathways that will be strong and efficient.

The hypothesis, that each of the XLQ Leadership Dimensions is correlated with the GLOBE dimension of Humane Orientation, was confirmed by the Delphi panelists.

Summary

The XLQ Aspect Culture and its Dimensions and Dimension Descriptors were confirmed except for the Dimension Assertiveness, which was weakly confirmed. Figure 39 provides a graphical overview of the findings form the Culture Dimensions.

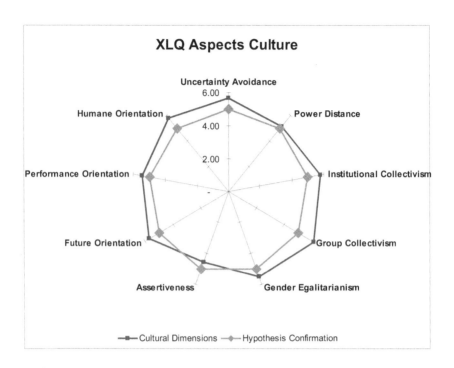

Figure 39 – XLQ Aspect Culture

8.3 Chapter Summary

The results of the Delphi panel survey have demonstrated that the hypotheses were confirmed with Assertiveness being weakly confirmed, and with the Leadership Dimension Descriptor coercive power being rejected.

The significance of the results is that the XQL model can provide a framework for cross-cultural leadership. Whether a leader is working in their home country at one extreme, or working as an expat with teams in multiple countries at the other extreme, the same skills can by utilized to lead. The XLQ model also provides a framework for teaching leadership skills, and thus improving the effectiveness of leaders.

For the Project Management discipline, there has been a call by the community for a multi disciplinary approach to the study of leadership, and of cross-cultural leadership as has been noted in this work (Turner and Mueller 2005). This work is an attempt to fill in that gap in the knowledge base. In addition, this work provides a model that can be utilized to improve the effectiveness of Project Management Leadership.

9. Conclusion

9.1 Introduction

As discussed in Chapter 1, the initial goal was to discover a Quibla compass for cross-cultural leadership. The research topics shown in Figure 3 have served as the basic structure for this work: culture, leadership, conflict, and knowledge. The hypothesis set forth in Figure 4 that the XLQ Leadership Dimensions are trust, empathy, transformation, power, and communication. Chapters 4, 5, and 6 explored leadership, conflict, and the hypothesis in detail.

This work has also explored the connection between the leadership hypothesis and culture, by exploring the relationship of the hypothesis to the GLOBE survey results. I have called this the XLQ Culture Dimension. Chapters 2 and 3 explored culture and cultural knowledge in detail.

In Chapters 7 and 8, the XLQ Leadership Dimension and the XLQ Culture Dimension are merged into the design and testing of the hypotheses. The design and testing of knowledge was included under the XLQ Empathy Dimension as shown in Table 20 and in Table 22. The design and testing of conflict was included in the XLQ Communication Dimension as shown in Table 23.

9.2 Discussion

The goal of this work was to develop a model for cross-cultural leadership. The methodology was discussed in Chapter 1 of this work. To meet this goal the first step was to explore the existing literature on cross-cultural leadership, knowledge transfer through metaphor, and conflict management in a multi-cultural environment. This was done in Chapter 2, 3, 4, and 5 of this work. The review included multi-disciplinary sources, and utilized an exegetical approach in the evaluation of the literature. The hypothesis was defined in Chapter 6, and tested utilizing the Delphi technique described in Chapter 7. The results of the testing were then provided and discussed in Chapter 8.

In concluding this work, I would first like to present the XLQ Leadership Model using a simple graphical metaphor as shown in Figure 40.

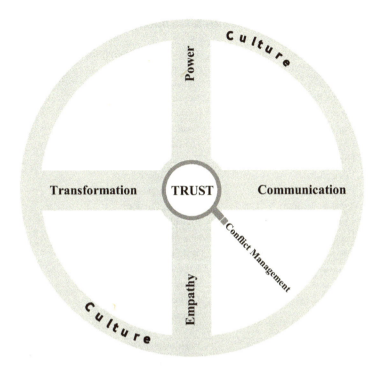

Figure 40 - XLQ Model

The hub of the steering wheel is Trust, without it, leadership cannot function. The spokes of the wheel are Transformation, Communication, Power, and Empathy. The rim of the wheel is culture, for without it, the wheel would in fact not be a wheel, and would be ineffective. The lubricant for the wheel is Conflict Management. Conflict can be used to stimulate creativity, but if not managed can cause enough friction so that the wheel cannot turn. The wheel also assumes that the leader has knowledge of each component of the wheel, and an understanding of the goal. A weakness in any component will reduce the effectiveness of the leader, and will potentially lead to a non-sustainable business model.

The XLQ Model was constructed from the XLQ Aspects of Leadership and Culture. The XLQ Leadership Dimensions (Trust, Empathy, Transformation, Power, and Communications) are made up of Descriptors and Sub-descriptors as shown in Table 26 (also, see Table 19 through Table 23):

Table 26 - XLQ Leadership Descriptors & Sub-Descriptors

XLQ Dimension	Descriptors	Sub-Descriptors
Trust	Care and Concern	Esteem, Face
	Character	Honesty & Integrity, Duty & Loyalty, Admiration
	Competence	Technical, Jugement
	Dependability	Predictability, Commitments
	Fearlessness	Confidence, Self-Sacrifice
	Humaneness	Tolerance, Respect
	Integrator	Goals, Cohesiveness
	Integrity & Ethics	Values, Ethics
	Truth & Justice	Fairness, Candor
Empathy	Cultural Intelligence	Metaphors, Customs
	Humaneness	Compassion, Consideration
	Servant Leadership	Self Sacrifice, Empowerment
Transformation	Inspiration	Expectations, Mentoring
	Charisma	Decisive, Uniqueness
	Risk Change	Desire to change, Security
	Vision	Foresight, Goals
Power	Knowledge Power	Sharing knowledge, Mentor
	Position Power	Legitimate, Political
	Power Distance	Locus, Communitinarism
	Referent Power	Bravery, Warmth
	Reward & Punishment Power	Coercive, Reward
Communication	Adaptability	Understanding, Communication
	Competence	Cultural, Communication, Listening
	Creativity	Storytelling, Metaphor
	Patience	Time, Repetition
	Sensitivity	Facework
	Wisdom	Accuracy, Culture
	Conflict Management	Knowledge, Listening, Preparation

I also want to reemphasize that the cultural issues raised in this work must be used in the manner in which they are intended, as has been noted in this work (Gibson and Zellmer-Bruhn 2001). Adler has argued that it is legitimate to use stereotypes in cross-cultural contexts if they are (Pg. 297): "descriptive rather than evaluative, substantiated, and subject to change." According to Webster's Ninth New College Edition Dictionary, stereotype means "a standardized mental picture that is held in common by members of a group and that represents an oversimplified common, affective attitude, or uncritical judgment." The use of metaphors, the research done by many renowned authors like Hofstede, and the GLOBE survey, only provide a sort of Quibla compass – a general direction.

I argue, strongly, that general patterns of social attitudes and beliefs can greatly enhance the sensitivity of a leader to the diversity of our societies. However, each individual has a different way of defining themselves, and their values. For leaders it is critical to spend the time necessary every day to check on the location, physical and emotional, of the team and also to provide just the right level of guidance, mentoring, and coaching needed. The XLQ Model hopes to provide a structured way to provide effective cross-cultural leadership in an infinitely diverse world.

I began the work with the hope of finding a Quibla compass for cross-cultural leadership, or a general guide for Project Managers working internationally. As the research progressed, and the patterns of knowledge formed, I discovered that a more tangible metaphor would be a better model. I decided that the steering wheel metaphor, shown in Figure 40, was a more useful way of describing the model in a more simple and understandable way.

9.3   Implications for Project Management

International Project Management, and business management, has suffered from a lack of a codified approach to the training of people to work in multi-cultural environments. There are no shortages of cultural training programs in existence, and certainly no shortage of leadership and cultural theories. What this work has attempted to do is to provide a simple model for cross-cultural leadership that can be used for evaluating and improving leadership skills, resulting in improved performance.

The model provides a simple outline of leadership attributes that can be utilized to structure assessment and training for Project Managers in a consistent and systematized manner. For the model, it does not matter if the Project Manager was born in China and raised in the USA, or born in the USA and raised in Japan since it is a universal *etic* template. So training for leadership skills in Malaysia or Botswana can be structured in the same way, with the emphasis on the XLQ Leadership Dimensions.

The model also provides a structure for future research and testing. For example, if testing a group of executives from three countries for the importance of face, the relationship of face to

XLQ Leadership can be linked. Future research can be connected back to XLQ Model to further amplify and confirm/reject the Descriptors and Sub-descriptors. Also, research on metrics for evaluation and training can utilize the Delphi panel scores as a benchmarking system.

For the field of Project Management, the XLQ Model can easily be included in the PMBOK structure. As noted in this work, there is effectively nothing in the PMBOK at this time for leadership or culture. The XLQ Model could be appended into the Human Resource Management knowledge area, or the Integration Management knowledge area readily. As more people work on cross-cultural teams, they will need to have these skills to compete effectively and assure successful projects.

What I found in undertaking the literature review of this work was a significant body of very useful research that was focused on specific detailed aspects of leadership and/or culture. The difficulty, described by numerous authors, is in knowing how to connect the detailed research back to a systematic model. It is my hope that this work provides such a model for the benefit of others.

9.4   Limitations and Future Research

Limitations

As with any work, time and resources must be limited, and that was the case with this work. The literature on culture and leadership is near limitless. A search for the word leadership at www.amazon.com for books yielded over 16,000 references, and for culture over 55,000 references. A search conducted in the electronic EBSCO database for articles at RMIT University yielded over 57,000 articles relating to leadership, and over 62,000 articles relating to culture. The first challenge was to find as many views as possible from different disciplines (philosophy, literature, warfare, anthropology, psychology, sociology, art, knowledge management, conflict, Project Management, business management, religion, etc.). The second challenge was to attempt to focus on the pivotal works to the extent possible. I can only hope that my efforts in this regards were adequate. There is a wealth of significant work in culture and leadership and I attempted to highlight those authors who seemed to change the course of the dialogue.

The third challenge was that the early research literature was undertaken, almost completely, from a Western perspective. Fortunately, in the last ten years there has been a rapid increase in research from other perspectives – like Turkish or Chinese. This has added a needed depth, but has also added even more complexity to an already complex debate. The fourth challenge was to codify the research. I found that the exegetical approach was a useful one for the complexity of these topics.

The fifth, and certainly not the last challenge, was how to test the hypothesis. Hofstede's initial survey of IBM personnel, and the GLOBE survey, had the benefit of access to multiple managers and researchers in multiple countries. Both also had the benefit of significant financial and researcher resources. For my work, I had far more restrictive financial considerations than did these two surveys. The use of the Delphi panel to leverage the knowledge of a few individuals was my approach to overcome the resource limitations.

Future Research

As I was writing the work, I left footnotes in earlier versions for future research topics. I found about two on almost every page of the document, so they are too numerous to recap here. However, it is important to point to three topics that I believe deserve immediate attention.

The first research topic needs to be focused on metrics for evaluating and training on XLQ Leadership skills. There is a wealth of information on evaluation and training in the literature, but it needs to be related back to the XLQ Model. A research paper to investigate how to connect the previous work to the XLQ Model would enable a training program to be developed and tested in multiple cultures. To be useful, the model needs metrics that can provide a way of measuring the knowledge transfer.

Another topic that would help to calibrate leaders is to research the characteristics of leadership as perceived by people from different cultures. If I ask a Project Management training group in Trinidad and Tobago who they believe a leader to be, the immediate answers are Fidel Castro and Hugo Chavez. If I ask my Chinese friends, they say Sun Yat-Sen. If I ask an American Project Management group, they might say George Bush or Colin Powell. If I ask my friends in Turkey, they say Ataturk. When I tell the Americans about the views of the Trinidadians, they scoff and immediately reject their views. The exploration of who people consider leaders has been done in previous research, but usually from a Western perspective. A systematic review of leaders from different cultural perspectives, that could be evaluated using the XLQ model, would help to bridge some of the cultural gaps and improve the leadership training.

Lastly, research into virtual team trust and communications is needed. Many people work in a virtual environment, and the e-sociality dimension of leadership needs to be explored in far more detail than it has been to date. There is some interesting research on the topic, but once again, it needs to be connected to XLQ Leadership.

9.5 Summary

The work set out to test the hypothesis that there are *etic,* or globally viable, cross-cultural leadership skills. Those skills are Trust, Empathy, Transformation, Power, and Communication. The exegetical research further defined each dimension, and the hypothesis was then confirmed by the Delphi panel. The results were used to create the XLQ Model.

The research attempted to provide a broad survey of the thinking on culture and leadership over the past half century, from as many cultural perspectives as possible. The blessing was that there is an enormous wealth of research, and the curse was that there is an enormous amount of research. As shown in Figure 2, the process has taken me from the initial course work through introspection, retrospection, testing, evaluation, and sensemaking. I have also applied my 35 years of experience in giving a *sanity check* to the results. I have published a number of articles (Grisham 2006), (Grisham and Walker 2005), (Hudson, Grisham et al. 2005) that have evolved from this work and have presented a number of papers in Project Management conferences including the Project Management Institute Southern Caribbean Chapter (It's About Time, Cultural Knowledge Transfer, and Cross-Cultural Conflict). As one of the keynote speakers at the PMICC I spoke on the considerations for global virtual teams, which also came from the research for this work.

In addition, this work has served as the basis for a *Managing Cultural Diversity* course in an International Business program at St. Petersburg College. I teach for a number of institutions, and have been testing the hypotheses of this work in my courses, and building in the comments that I receive. Appendix 8 provides a listing of the companies that the students have represented.

My goal was to highlight the capstones and trendsetters to the best of my ability within the time available. I apologize to any authors that I did not have time to include, and to those that I have not given more consideration to in completing this work. I am humbled by the depth of the knowledge on culture and leadership, and did my best to respect those researchers that have gone before me.

The work is limited by the context and confines of the DPM course, and resources available, and is not intended as a panacea for solving all of the issues related to cross-cultural leadership. What the Cross-Cultural Leadership Intelligence (XLQ) model offers is a codified structure for helping Project Managers and business managers, working in multi-cultural environments, to assess their cross-cultural leadership skills and improve their performance. I hope that in the future it will provide a tool for establishing metrics that can be used for evaluation and training.

10.   References

Adams, S. M. (1999). "Settling Cross-Cultural Disagreements Begins with 'Where' Not 'How'." Academy of Management Executive **13**(1): 109.

Adler, N. (1997). International Dimensions of Organizational Behavior. Cincinnati, South-Western College.

Adler, N. J. (1983). "Cross-Cultural Management Research: The Ostrich and the Trend." Academy of Management Review **8**(2): 226.

Adler, N. J. (1991). Onternational Dimensions of Organizational Behavior. Boston, PWS-Kent Publishing.

Adler, N. J. (2002). From Boston to Beijing: Managing with a World View. Cincinnati, Ohio, South-Western/Thomson Learning.

Adler, N. J. and S. Bartholomew (1992). "Academic and Professional Communities of Disclosure: Generating Knowledge on Transnational Human Resource Management." Journal of International Business Studies **23**(3): 551.

Adler, N. J. and J. L. Graham (1989). "Cross-Cultured Interaction: The International Comparison Fallacy?" Journal of International Business Studies **20**(3): 515.

Adler, P. S. and S.-W. Kwon (2002). "Social Capital: Prospects for a New Concept." Academy of Management Review **27**(1): 17.

Agee, M. L. and H. E. Kabasakal (1993). "Exploring Conflict Resolution Styles: A Study of Turkish and American University Business Students." International Journal of Social Economics **20**(9): 3.

Ali, A. (1987). "The Arab Executive: A Study in Values and Work Orientation." American-Arab Affairs **winter**.

Ali, A. J. (1990). "Management Theory in a Transitional Society: The Arab's Experience." International Studies of Management and Organization **20**(3): 7-35.

Apte, M. L. (1985). Humor and Laughter: An Anthropological Approach. New York, Cornell University Press.

Arrien, A. (1993). The Four-Fold Way - Walking the Paths of the Warrior, Teacher, Healer, and Visionary. San Francisco, Harper.

Arrow, K. J. (1974). The Limits of Organization. New York, WW Norton & Company.

Arruda, C. A. and D. J. Hickson (1996). Sensitivity to Societal Culture in Managerial Decision-Making: An Anglo-Brazilian Comparison. Managing Across Cultures: Issues and Perspectives. P. Joynt and F. Warner. London, International Thomson Business Press.

Ashkanasy, N., V. Gupta, et al. (2004). Future Orientation. Culture, Leadership, and Organizations - The GLOBE Study of 62 Societies. R. J. House, P. J. Hanges, M. Javidan, P. W. Dorfman and V. Gupta. Thousand Oaks, Sage.

Ashkanasy, N. M. and C. O'Connor (1997). "Value Congruence in Leader-Member Exchange." Journal of Social Psychology **137**(5): 647-662.

Atwater, L. and D. Waldman (1998). "360 Degree Feedback and Leadership Development." Leadership Quarterly **9**(4): 423.

Augsburger, D. W. (1992). Conflict Mediation Across Cultures - Pathways & Patterns. Louisville, Westminster John Knox Press.

Avolio, B. J. and B. M. Bass (1999). "Re-examining the Components of Transformational and Transactional Leadership Using the Multifactor Leadership Questionnaire." Journal of Occupational & Organizational Psychology **72**(4): 441.

Avruch, K. (1998). Culture & Conflict Resolution. Washington, United States Institute of Peace Press.

228

Avruch, K. (1998). "Interactive Conflict Resolution: The Last 30 Years and Beyond." Peace & Conflict 4(2): 187.

Avruch, K. (1998). Introduction: Culture and Conflict Resolution. Conflict Resolution - Cross-cultural Perspectives. K. Avruch, P. W. Black and J. A. Scimecca. Westport, Praeger.

Avruch, K. and P. W. Black (1991). "The Culture Question and Conflict Resolution." Peace & Change 16(1): 22.

Ayoko, O. B., C. E. J. Härtel, et al. (2002). "Resolving the Puzzle of Productive and Destructive Conflict in Culturally Heterogeneous Workgroups: A Communication Accommodation Theory Approach." International Journal of Conflict Management 13(2): 165.

Bachmann, R. (2001). "Trust, Power and Control in Trans-Organizational Relations." Organization Studies (Walter de Gruyter GmbH & Co. KG.) 22(2): 337.

Badawy, M. R. (1979). Managerial Attitudes and Need Orientations of Mid-Eastern Executives: An Empirical Cross-Cultural Analysis. Annual Meeting of the Academy of Management Review, Atlanta, GA.

Bailey, F. G. (1998). Tertius Luctans: Idiocosm, Caricature, and Mask. Conflict Resolution - Cross-cultural Perspectives. K. Avruch, P. W. Black and J. A. Scimecca. Westport, Praeger.

Baldoni, J. (2003). Great Communication Secrets of Great Leaders. New York, McGraw-Hill.

Barber, B. (1984). Strong Democracy. Berkley, University of California Press.

Baron, D. and L. Padwa (1999). Moses on Management. New York, Pocket Books.

Bartholomew, S. and N. Adler (1996). Managing Across Cultures: Issues and Perspectives. P. Joynt and F. Warner. London, International Thomson Business Press.

Bartlett, C. A. and S. Ghoshal (1998). Managing Across Borders - The Transnational Solution. Boston, Harvard Business School Press.

Bass, B. M. (1985). Leadership and Performance Beyond Expectations. New York, Free Press.

Bass, B. M. (1985). "Leadership: Good, Better, Best." Organizational Dynamics 13(3): 26.

Bass, B. M. (1990). "From Transactional to Transformational Leadership: Learning to Share the Vision." Organizational Dynamics 18(3): 19.

Bass, B. M. (1997). "Does the Transactional-Transformational Leadership Paradigm Transcend Organizational and National Boundaries." American Psychologist 52(2): 130.

Bass, B. M. and R. M. Stogdill (1990). Bass & Stogdill's Handbook of Leadership: Theory, Research, and Managerial Applications. New York, Free Press; Collier Macmillan.

Baum, D. (2000). Lightning in a Bottle - Proven Lessons for Leading Change. Chicago, Dearborn.

Benedict, R. (1946). The Chrysanthemum and the Sword. Boston, Houghton Mifflin.

Bennis, W. (1989). On Becoming a Leader. San Francisco, Peresus Publishing.

Bennis, W. (1999). "Five Competencies of New Leaders." Executive Excellence 16(7): 4.

Bennis, W. (2002). "Leaders in Transition." Executive Excellence 19(4): 13.

Bennis, W. and P. W. Biederman (1997). Organizing Genius the Secrets of Creative Collaboration. Reading, Addison-Wesley.

Bennis, W. and B. Nanus (1985). Leaders The Strategies for Taking Charge. New York, Harper Business.

Bennis, W. G. (2004). The Seven Ages of the Leader. Harvard Business Review, Harvard Business School Publication Corp. 82: 46-53.

Berger, J. and J. Mohr (1982). Another Way of Telling. Cambridge, Granta Books.

Bibo, I. (1986). The Misery of the Eastern European Small States. Selected Studies. I. Bibo. Unknown, Magveto Publishing House.

Black, J. S., A. J. Morrison, et al. (1999). Global Explorers - The Next Generation. New York, Routledge.

Black, M. (1954-55). Metaphor. Proceedings of the Aristotelian Society.

Blair, I. V. and M. R. Banaji (1996). "Automatic and Controlled Processes in Stereotype Priming." Journal of Personality and Social Psychology 70(6): 1142-1163.

Blake, R. R. and J. S. Mouton (1964). The Managerial Grid. Houston, Gulf Publishing.

Boal, K. B. and J. M. Bryson (1988). Charismatic Leadership: A Phenomenological and Structural Approach. Emerging Leadership Vistas. J. G. Hunt, B. R. Baglia, H. P. Dachler and C. A. Schriesheim. Lexington, MA, Lexington Books: 5-28.

Boers, F. (2003). "Applied Linguistics Perspectives on Cross-Cultural Variation in Conceptual Metaphor." Metaphor & Symbol 18(4): 231-238.

Bonthous, J. (1993). "Understanding Intelligence Across Cultures." Competitive Intelligence Review 4(2/3): 12-19.

Bonthous, J. M. (1994). "Culture - The Missing Intelligence Variable." The Strategic Planning Society News (none)(March).

Bordon, G. A. (1991). Cultural Orientation: An Approach to Understanding Intercultural Communications. Upper Saddle River, Prentice Hall.

Bourdieu, P. (1980). Le Sens Pratique. Paris, Editions de Minuit.

Brake, T. (2002). Managing Globally. New York, Dorling Kindersley.

Brassington, F. and S. Pettit (2000). Principles of Marketing. London, Prentice Hall.

Brett, J. M. (2001). <u>Negotiating Globally: How to Negotiate Deals, Resolve Disputes, and Make Decisions Across Cultural Boundaries</u>. San Francisco, Jossey-Bass.

Brislin, R. W. and J. F. Liu (2004). Intercultural Communication, Contact, and International Business Assignments. <u>The Psychology of Ethnic and Cultural Conflict:</u>
<u>Psychological Dimensions to War and Peace</u>. Y.-T. Lee. Westport, Conn, Greenwood Publishing Group.

Brown, J. S. and S. G. Estee. (1995). "The People Are the Company." from http: www.fastcompany.com/online/01/people.html.

Brown, P. and S. Levinson (1987). <u>Politeness: Some Universals in Language Usage</u>. Cambridge, Cambridge University Press.

Buckley, C. (1994). "Delphi Technique Supplies the Classic Result." <u>The Australian Library Journal</u> **August**.

Burbank, V. (1987). "Female Agression in Cross-Cultural Perspective." <u>Behavior Science Review</u> **21**: 70-100.

Burbles, N. C. and S. Rice (1991). "Dialogue across differences: continuing the conversation." <u>Harvard Educational Review</u> **61**.

Burbules, N. C. (1993). <u>Dialogue in Teaching. Theory And Practice</u>. New York, Teachers College, Columbia University.

Burbules, N. C. and S. Rice (1991). "Dialogue Across Differences: Continuing the Conversation." <u>Harvard Educational Review</u> **61**(4): 393.

Burke, M. J. and R. Russell (1986). "A Cumulative Study of the Effectiveness of Managerial Training." <u>Journal of Applied Psychology</u> **71**(2): 232.

Burley-Allen, M. (1982). <u>Listening: The Forgotten Skill</u>. New York, John Wiley & Sons.

Burns, J. M. (1978). <u>Leadership</u>. New York, Harper & Row.

Buskens, V. (2002). Social Networks and Trust. New York, Kluwer Academic Publishers.

Campbell, J. (1986). The Inner Reaches of Outer Space - Metaphor as Myth and Religion. Novato, New World Library.

Carl, D., V. Gupta, et al. (2004). Power Distance. Culture, Leadership, and Organizations - The GLOBE Study of 62 Societies. R. J. House, P. J. Hanges, M. Javidan, P. W. Dorfman and V. Gupta. Thousand Oaks, Sage.

Carlson, P. and M. S. Blodgett (1997). "International Ethics Standards for Business: NAFTA, CAUX Principles and Corporate Codes of Ethics." Review of Business 18(3): 20.

Carte, P. and C. Fox (2004). Bridging the Culture Gap: A Practical Guide to International Business Communication. London, Sterling, VA Kogan Page.

Chaiken, S. L., D. H. Gruenfeld, et al. (2000). Persuasion in Negotiations and Conflict Situations. The Handbook of Conflict Resolution - Theory and Practice. M. Deutsch and P. T. Coleman. San Francisco, Jossey-Bass.

Chang, H. C. and G. R. Holt (1994). A Chinese Perspective on Face as Inter-Relational Concern. The Challenge of Facework: Cross-Cultural and Interpersonal Issues. S. Ting-Toomey. Albany, State University of New York.

Chanock, M. (1987). Lae Custom, and Social Order: The Colonial Experience in Malawi and Zambnia. Cambridge, Cambridge University Press.

Chase, S. (1938). The Tyranny of Words. New York, Harcourt, Brace & Company.

Chemers, M. M. (1997). An Integrative Theory of Leadership. London, Lawrence Erlbaum.

Chen, M. (2001). Inside Chinese Business. Boston, Harvard Business School Press.

Chew, P. K. (2001). Notes and Ideas Chapters. The Conflict and Culture Reader. P. K. Chew. New York, New York University Press.

Child, J., M. Boisot, et al. (1990). The Management of Equity Joint Ventures in China. Beijing, China-EC Management Institute.

Christenson, D. and D. H. T. Walker (2004). "Understanding the Role of "Vision" in Project Success." Project Management Journal **35**(3): 39-52.

Cicmil, S. and D. Hodgson (2005). "New Possibilities for Project Management Theory: A Critical Engagement." Project Management Institute **Unknown**(Unknown).

Clark, M. S. and J. Mills (1979). "Interpersonal Attraction in Exchange and Communal Relationships." Journal of Personality and Social Psychology **37**(1): 643.

Clarke, C. C. and G. D. Lipp (1998). "Conflict Resolution for Contrasting Cultures. (Cover story)." Training & Development **52**(2): 20.

Cleary, T. (1989). Zen Lessons: The Art of Leadership. Boston, Shambala.

Cleland, D. I. (1995). "Leadership and the Project Management Body of Knowledge." International Journal of Project Management **13**(2): 82-88.

Cohen, A. (1990). "A Cross-Cultural Study of the Effects of Environmental Unpredictability on Agression in Folktales." American Anthropologist **92**(2): 474-480.

Cohen, R. (1986). Negotiating Across Cultures: Common Obstacles in International Diplomacy. Washington, Institute of Peace Press.

Cohen, R. (1990). Culture and Conflict in Egyptian-Israeli Relations: A Dialogue of the Deaf. Newbury Park, Sage.

Cohen, T. (1979). Metaphor and the Cultivation of Intimacy. On Metaphor. S. Scaks. Chicago, University of Chicago Press.

Cohen, W. A. (1990). The Art of the Leader. Englewood Cliffs, Prentice Hall.

234

Coleman, H. K. L. (1995). "Strategies for Coping with Cultural Diversity." The Counseling Psychologist **23**.

Coleman, H. L. K. (1997). "Conflict in Multicultural Counseling Relationships: Source and Resolution." Journal of Multicultural Counseling & Development **25**(3): 195-200.

Coleman, P. T. (2000). Power and Conflict. The Handbook of Conflict Resolution - Theory and Practice. M. Deutsch and P. T. Coleman. San Francisco, Jossey-Bass.

Conger, J. A. and R. N. Kanungo (1987). "Toward a Behavioral Theory of Charismatic Leadership in Organizational Settings." Academy of Management Review **12**(4): 637.

Conger, J. A. and R. N. Kanungo (1998). Charismatic Leadership in Organizations. Thousand Oaks, Sage.

Connection, C. C. (1987). "Chinese Values and the Search for Culture-Free Dimensions of Culture." Journal of Cross-Cultural Psychology **18**.

Connors, K. E. (1998). "Conflict Resolution & Recognition of Diversity via an Art Experience." Journal of Art & Design Education **17**(3): 275.

Corne, P. W. (1992). "The Complex Art of Negotiation Between Different Cultures." Arbitration Journal **47**(4): 46-50.

Cornelissen, J. P. (2002). "On the Organizational Identity™ Metaphor." British Journal of Management **13**(4): 259-268.

Cottle, T. (1967). "The Circles Test: An Investigation of Perceptions of Temporal Relatedness and Dominance." Journal of Projective Technique and Personality Assessments **31**(None): 58-71.

Creswell, J. W. (1998). Qualitative Inquiry and Research Design: Choosing Among Five Traditions. Thousand Oaks, Sage.

Crisp, J., D. Pelletier, et al. (1997). "The Delphi Method?" Nursing Research **46**: 116-118.

Csikszentmihalyi, M. (2001). The Context of Creativity. <u>The Future of Leadership - Today's Top Leadership Thinkers Speak to Tomorrow's Leaders</u>. W. Bennis, G. M. Spreitzer and T. G. Cummings. San Francisco, Jossey-Bass: 14-25.

Cummings, L. L. and P. Bromiley, & Cummings, L. L (1996). The Organizational Trust Inventory (OTI): Development and Validation. <u>Trust in Organizations: Frontiers of Theory and Research</u>. R. Kramer and T. Tyler. Thousand Oaks, Sage.

Curtin, L. L. (1996). "The Caux Round Table Principles for Business." <u>Nursing Management</u> **27**(2): 54-57.

Cusher, K. and R. Brislin (1997). Key Concepts in the Field of Cross-Cultural Training: An Introduction. <u>Improving Intercultural Interactions</u>. K. Cusher and R. Brislin. Thousand Oaks, Sage.

Czinkota, M. R. and I. A. Ronkainen (2005). "International Business and Trade in the Next Decade: Report from a Delphi Study." <u>Journal of World Business</u> **40**(4): 111-123.

Dalton, M., C. Ernst, et al. (2002). <u>Success for the New Global Leader</u>. San Francisco, Jossey-Bass.

Darlington, G. (1996). Culture: A Theoretical Review. <u>Managing Across Cultures: Issues and Perspectives</u>. P. Joynt and F. Warner. London, International Thomson Business Press.

Dawson, R. (1995). <u>Secrets of Power Negotiating</u>. Hawthorne, NJ, Career Press.

Day, D. V. (2000). "Leadership Development: A Reveiw in Context." <u>Leadership Quarterly</u> **11**(4): 581.

de Vries, K. and F. R. Manfred (2005). "Leadership Group Coaching in Action: The Zen of Creating High Performance Teams." <u>Academy of Management Executive</u> **19**(1): 61-76.

Deignan, A. (2003). "Metaphorical Expressions and Culture: An Indirect Link." <u>Metaphor & Symbol</u> **18**(4): 255-271.

Den Hartog, D. N. (2004). Assertiveness. <u>Culture, Leadership, and Organizations - The GLOBE Study of 62 Societies</u>. R. J. House, P. J. Hanges, M. Javidan, P. W. Dorfman and V. Gupta. Thousand Oaks, Sage.

Den Hartog, D. N., R. J. House, et al. (1999). "Culture Specific and Cross-Culturally Generalizable Implicit Leadership Theories: Are Attributes of Charismatic/Transformational Leadership Universally Endorsed?[1]." <u>Leadership Quarterly</u> **10**(2): 219.

Denison, D. R., R. Hooijberg, et al. (1995). "Paradox and Performance: Toward a Theory of Behavioral Complexity in Managerial Leadership." <u>Organization Science</u> **6**(5): 524-540.

Denning, S. (2004). <u>Squirrel Inc: A Fable of Leadership Through Storytelling</u>. San Francisco, John Wiley & Sons.

Deutsch, M. (1958). "Trust and Suspicion." <u>Conflict Resolution</u> **2**.

Deutsch, M. (1973). <u>The Resolution of Conflict: Constructive and Destructive Processes</u>. New Haven, Yale University Press.

Deutsch, M. (2000). A Framework for Thinking About Research on Conflict Resolution Training. <u>The Handbook of Conflict Resolution - Theory and Practice</u>. M. Deutsch and P. T. Coleman. San Francisco, Jossey-Bass.

Dimmock, C. A. J. (2000). <u>Designing the Learning-Centered School: A Cross-Cultural Perspective</u>. London; New York, Falmer Press.

DiStefano, J. J. (1992). <u>International Management Behavior</u>. Boston, PWS Kent.

Donaldson, T. (2001). Values in Tension - Ethics Away from Home. <u>The Conflict and Culture Reader</u>. P. K. Chew. New York, New York University Press.

Dorfman, P. (2004). International and Cross-Cultural Leadership Research. <u>Handbook for International Management Research</u>. B. J. Punnett and O. Shenkar. Ann Arbor, University of Michigan Press.

Dorfman, P. W., P. L. Hanges, et al. (2004). Leadership and Cultural Variation. Culture, Leadership, and Organizations - The GLOBE Study of 62 Societies. R. J. House, P. J. Hanges, M. Javidan, P. W. Dorfman and V. Gupta. Thousand Oaks, Sage.

Dorfman, P. W. and R. J. House (2004). Cultural Influences on Organizational Leadership. Culture, Leadership, and Organizations - The GLOBE Study of 62 Societies. R. J. House, P. J. Hanges, M. Javidan, P. W. Dorfman and V. Gupta. Thousand Oaks, Sage.

Dorfman, P. W. and J. P. Howell (1997). "Leadership in Western and Asian Countries: Commonalities and Differences in Effective Leadership Processes Across Cultures." Leadership Quarterly 8(3): 233.

Downton, J. V. (1973). Rebel Leadership: Commitment and Charisma in the Revolutionary Process. New York, Free Press.

Drath, W. H. (1998). Approaching the Future of Leadership Development. The Center for Creative Leadership Handbook of Leadership Development. C. D. McCauley, R. S. Moxley and E. Van Velsor. San Francisco, Jossey-Bass.

Drucker, P. F. (1973). Management: Tasks, Responsibilities, Practices. New York, Harper Business.

Drucker, P. F. (1988). "The Coming of the New Organization." Harvard Business Review 66(2): 132.

Drucker, P. F. (2000). The Age of Discontinuity: Guidelines to our Changing Society. New Brunswick (USA), Transaction Publishing.

Duffield, C. (1993). "The Delphi Technique: A Comparison of Results Obtained Using Two Expert Panels." International Journal of Nursing Studies 30(3): 227-237.

Earle, T. C. (2004). "Thinking Aloud About Trust: A Protocol Analysis of Trust in Risk Management." Risk Analysis: An International Journal 24(1): 169-183.

Earley, C. P. and S. Ang (2003). Cultural Intelligence, Individual Interactions Across Cultures. Stanford, Stanford University Press.

Earley, C. P. and M. Erez (1997). Introduction. New Perspectives on International Industrial/Organizational Psychology. C. P. Earley and M. Erez. San Francisco, The New Lexington Press.

Earley, P. C. and H. Singh (2000). New Approaches to International and Cross-Cultural Management Research. Innovations in International and Cross-Cultural Management. P. C. Earley and H. Singh. Thousand Oaks, Sage Publications: viii, 374.

Eden, D. and U. Levitan (1975). "Implicit Leadership Theory as a Determinant of the Factor Structure Underlying Supervisory Behavior Scales." Journal of Applied Psychology 60((none)): 736-741.

Eisenberg, N. (2002). Empathy-Related Emotional Responses, Altruism, and Their Socialization. Visions of Compassion: Western Scientists and Tibetan Buddhists Examine Human Nature. R. J. Davidson and A. Harrington. Oxford, Oxford University Press.

Ekman, P. (2003). Emotions Revealed: Recognizing Faces and Feelings to Improve Communication and Emotional Life. New York, Times Books.

Elashmawi, F. (2001). Competing Globally: Mastering Multicultural Management and Negotiation. Boston, Butterworth-Heinemann.

Elkington, J. (1997). Cannibals with Forks. London, Capstone Publishing.

Emrich, C. G., F. L. Denmark, et al. (2004). Cross-Cultural Differences in Gender Egalitarianism. Culture, Leadership, and Organizations - The GLOBE Study of 62 Societies. R. J. House, P. J. Hanges, M. Javidan, P. W. Dorfman and V. Gupta. Thousand Oaks, Sage.

Enshassi, A. and R. Burgess (1990). "Training for Construction Site Managers Involved with Multicultural Work Teams." International Journal of Project Management 8(2): 95-101.

239

Erez, M. (1997). A Cultural Based Model of Work Motivation. New Perspectives on International Industrial/Organizational Psychology. C. P. Earley and M. Erez. San Francisco, The New Lexington Press.

Etheridge, L. (1987). Can Governments Learn? New York, Pergamon Press.

Fang, T. (1999). Chinese Business Negotiating Style. Thousand Oaks, Sage.

Farris, G., E. Senner, et al. (1973). "Trust, Culture and Organizational Behavior." Industrial Relations 12(2): 144-157.

Feldman, R. and C. A. Voelke (1992). A World Treasury of Folk Wisdom. San Francisco, Harper.

Fernandez, J., Ed. (1991). The Theory of Tropes in Anthropology. Stanford, Stanford University Press.

Fiedler, F. E. (1996). "Research on Leadership Selection and Training: One View of the Future." Administrative Science Quarterly 41(2): 241-250.

Fieg, J. (1976). A Common Core: Thais and Americans. Yarmouth, Intercultural Press.

Filley, A. C. (1978). "Some Normative Issues in Conflict Management." California Management Review 21(2): 61.

Fischer, R. (1997). Interactive Conflict Resolution, Syracuse University Press.

Fisher, R. and W. Ury (1983). Getting to Yes: Negotiating an Agreement Without Giving in. London, Penguin Books.

Fisher, W. P. and C. C. Muller (2005). Four-Dimensional Leadership. Upper Saddle River, Pearson-Prentice Hall.

Fiske, A. (1991). Structures of social life. New York, Free Press.

Flyvbjerg, B. (2001). Making Social Science Matter. Cambridge, UK, Cambridge University Press.

French, J. and B. H. Raven (1959). The Basis of Social Power. Studies of Social Power. D. Cartwright. Ann Arbor, Institute for Social Research.

Frost, T., D. V. Simpson, et al. (1978). "Some Correlates of Trust." Journal of Psychology **99**(1): 103.

Gannon, M. (2002). Cultural Metaphors: Their Use in Management Practice and as a Method for Understanding Cultures. Online Readings in Psychology and Culture. W. J. Lonner, D. L. Dinnel, S. A. Hayes and D. N. Sattler. Bellingham, Center for Cross-Cultural Research, Western Washington University.

Gannon, M. (2004). Understanding Global Cultures - Metaphorical Journeys Through 28 Nations, Clusters of Nations, and Continents. Thousand Oaks, Sage.

Gannon, M. J. (2001). Understanding Global Cultures - Metaphorical Journeys Through 23 Nations. Thousand Oaks, Sage.

Gao, G. (1998). "An Initial Analysis of the Effects of Face and Concern for "Other" in Chinese Interpersonal Communication." International Journal of Intercultural Relations **22**(4): 467-482.

Garlow, J. L. (2002). The 21 Irrefutable Laws of Leadership Tested by Time - Those Who Followed Them and Those Who Didn't. Nashville, Thomas Nelson.

Geertz, C. (1973). The interpretation of culture. New York, Basic Books.

Gelfand, M., D. P. S. Bhawuk, et al. (2004). Individualism and Collectivism. Culture, Leadership, and Organizations - The GLOBE Study of 62 Societies. R. J. House, P. J. Hanges, M. Javidan, P. W. Dorfman and V. Gupta. Thousand Oaks, Sage.

Gelfand, M. and C. McHusker (2002). Negotiation and Conflict Management. Handbook of Cross Cultural Management. M. J. Gannon and K. Newman. London, Blackwell.

George, B. (2003). Authentic Leadership: Rediscovering the Secrets to Creating Lasting Value. San Francisco, Jossey-Bass.

Gesteland, R. R. (2002). Cross-Cultural Business Behavior. Copenhagen, Copenhagen Business School.

Ghoshal, S. and C. A. Bartlett (1990). "The Multinational Corporation as an Interorganizational Network." Academy of Management Review **15**(4): 626.

Gibson, C. B. (1997). Do You Hear What I Hear? A Framework for Reconciling Intercultural Communication Difficulties Arising from Cognitive Styles and Cultural Values. New Perspectives on International Industrial/Organizational Psychology. C. P. Earley and M. Erez. San Francisco, The New Lexington Press.

Gibson, C. B. and M. E. Zellmer-Bruhn (2001). "Metaphors and Meaning: An Intercultural Analysis of the Concept of Teamwork." Administrative Science Quarterly **46**(2): 274-303.

Giles, H. (1973). "Communication Effectiveness as a Function of Accented Speech." Speech Monographs **40**(4): 330-333.

Gillian, C. (1998). Remapping the Moral Domain: New Images of Self in Relationship. Mapping the Moral Domain. C. Gilligan, J. Ward and J. Taylor. Cambridge, Harvard University Press.

Gioia, D. A. and P. P. Poole (1984). "Scripts in Organizational Behavior." Academy of Management Review **9**(3): 449.

Glenn, E. S., D. Witmeyer, et al. (1977). "Cultural Styles of Persuasion." International Journal of Intercultural Relations **1**(3): 52-66.

Goldsmith, M., C. L. Greenberg, et al. (2003). Global Leadership - The Next Generation. Upper Saddle River, Prentice Hall.

Goleman, D. (1995). Emotional Intelligence. New York, Bantam.

Goleman, D. (1998). "The Emotionally Competent Leader." Healthcare Forum Journal **41**(2): 36.

Goleman, D., R. Boyatzis, et al. (2002). <u>Primal Leadership: Realizing the Power of Emotional Intelligence</u>. Boston, Harvard University Press.

Goltz, T., Ed. (1990). <u>Turkey</u>. Singapore, Hofer Press.

Goold, M. (1990). <u>Strategic Control</u>. London, The Economist Books.

Graen, G. B. and G. Hui (1996). "Managing Changes in Globalizing Business: How to Manage Cross-Cultural Business Partners." <u>Journal of Organizational Change Management</u> **9**(3): 62.

Graen, G. B. and M. Uhl-Bien (1995). "Relationship-Based Approach to Leadership: Development of Leader-Member Exchange (LMX) Theory of Leadership Over 25 Years: Applying a Multi-Level Multi-Domain Perspective." <u>Leadership Quarterly</u> **6**(2): 219-247.

Green, B., M. Jones, et al. (1999). "Applying the Delphi Technique in a Study of GP's Information Requirements." <u>Health and Social Care in the Community</u> **17**(3): 198-205.

Greenberg, J. (2001). "Studying Organization Justice Cross-Culturally: Fundamental Challenges." <u>International Journal of Conflict Management</u> **12**(4): 365.

Greenleaf, R. (1997). <u>Servant Leadership</u>. New York, Paulist Press.

Griffeth, R. W., P. W. Hom, et al. (1980). <u>A Multivariate, Multinational Comparison of Managerial Attitudes</u>. Annual Meeting of the Academy of Management, Detroit.

Grisham, T. (2006). "Metaphor, Poetry, Storytelling, & Cross-Cultural Leadership." <u>Management Decision</u> **44**(4).

Grisham, T. and D. H. T. Walker (2005). "Nurturing a Knowledge Environment for International Construction Organizations Through Communities of Practice." <u>Construction Innovation Journal</u> **(pending)**.

Gross, T. (1996). <u>The Last Word on Power: Executive Reinvention for Leaders Who Must Make the Impossible Happen</u>. New York, Doubleday Dell.

Gudykunst, W. B. and Y. Matsumoto (1996). "The Influence of Cultural Individualism-Collectivism, Self Construals, and Individual Values on Communication Styles Across Cultures." Human Communication Research **22**: 510.

Gurevitch, Z. D. (2001). The Power of Not Understanding - The meeting of Conflicting Identities. The Conflict and Culture Reader. P. K. Chew. New York, New York University Press.

Habib, G. M. (1987). "Measures of Manifest Conflict in International Joint Ventures." Academy of Management Journal **30**(4): 808.

Hagan, C. M. (1995). Comparative Management: Africa, Middle East, and India. Boca Raton, Florida Atlantic University.

Haire, M., E. E. Ghiselli, et al. (1966). Managerial Thinking: An International Study. New York, Wiley.

Hall, E. T. (1960). The Silent Language. Garden City, New York, Anchor Press.

Hall, E. T. (1966). The Hidden Dimension. Garden City, New York, Doubleday.

Hall, E. T. (1976). Beyond Culture. New York, Anchor.

Hall, E. T. (1983). The Dance of Life - The Other Dimension of Time. Garden City, Anchor Press/Doubleday.

Hall, E. T. and M. R. Hall (1987). Hidden Differences: Doing Business with the japanese. Garden City, New York, Anchor Press/Doubleday.

Hall, E. T. and M. R. Hall (1990). Understanding Cultural Differences. Yarmouth, ME, Intercultural Press.

Hamel, G., Y. L. Doz, et al. (1989). "Collaborate With Your Competitors - And Win." Harvard Business Review **67**(1): 133-139.

Hamel, G. and C. K. Prahalad (1994). Competing for the Future. Boston, Harvard Business School Press.

Hamill, J. F. (1990). Ethno-Logic: The Anthropology of Human Reasoning. Urbana, University of Illinois Press.

Hampden-Turner, C. and F. Trompenaars (1993). The Seven Cultures of Capitalism: Value Systems for Creating Wealth in the United States, Britain, Japan, France, Sweden and the Netherlands. New York, Doubleday.

Hampden-Turner, C. and F. Trompenaars (1996). A World Turned Upside Down: Doing Business in Asia. Managing Across Cultures: Issues and Perspectives. P. Joynt and F. Warner. London, International Thomson Business Press.

Hanges, P. L. and M. W. Dickson (2004). The Development and Validation of the GLOBE Culture and Leadership Scales. Culture, Leadership, and Organizations - The GLOBE Study of 62 Societies. R. J. House, P. J. Hanges, M. Javidan, P. W. Dorfman and V. Gupta. Thousand Oaks, Sage.

Harkins, P. J. (1999). Powerful Conversations: How High Impact Leaders Communicate. New York, McGraw-Hill Professional.

Harrington, A. (1995). "Metaphoric Connections: Holistic Science in the Shadow of the Third Reich." Social Research 62(2): 357-385.

Harrington, A. (2002). A Science of Compassion or a Compassionate Science? What Do We Expect from a Cross-Cultural Dialogue with Buddhism? Visions of Compassion: Western Scientists and Tibetan Buddhists Examine Human Nature. R. J. Davidson and A. Harrington. Oxford, Oxford University Press.

Harris, P. R., R. T. Moran, et al. (2004). Managing Cultural Differences - Global Leadership Strategies for the 21st Century. 6th edition. Boston, Elsevier.

Hasson, F., S. Keeney, et al. (2000). "Research Guidelines for the Delphi Survey Technique." Journal of Advanced Nursing 32(4): 1008-1015.

Haviland, J. B. (1977). Gossip, Reputation, and Knowledge in Zinacantan. Chicago, University of Chicago Press.

Hawkes, T. (1972). Metaphor. Bristol, Methuen & Company.

Heifetz, R. A. (1994). Leadership Without Easy Answers. London, Harvard Business Press.

Heifetz, R. A. and M. Linsky (2002). Leadership on the Line - Staying Alive Through the Dangers of Leading. Boston, Harvard University Press.

Heil, G., W. Bennis, et al. (2000). Douglas McGregor, Revisited. New York, John Wiley & Sons.

Heller, F. A. and B. Wilpert (1981). Competence and Power in Managerial Decision Making. Chichester, Wiley.

Henderson, W. (1986). Metaphor in Economics. Talking about Text. M. Coulthard. Birmingham, England, University of Birmingham.

Hendricks, R. G. (1989). Lao-Tzu Te-Tao Ching. Toronto, Random House.

Henrie, M. and A. Sousa-Poza (2005). "Project Management: A Cultural Literary Review." Project Management Journal 36(2): 5-14.

Hetland, H. and G. M. Sandal (2003). "Transformational Leadership in Norway: Outcomes and Personality Correlates." European Journal of Work & Organizational Psychology 12(2): 147.

Hickson, L. (1986). "The Social Context of Apology on Dispute Settlement: A Cross-Cultural Study." Ethnology 25: 283-294.

Highwater, J. (1994). The Language of Vision - Meditations on Myth and Metaphor. New York, Grove Press.

Hildreth, P., C. Kimble, et al. (2000). "Communities of Practice in the Distributed International Environment." Journal of Knowledge Management 4(1): 27-38.

Hinken, T. R. and C. A. Schriesheim (1986). Influence Tactics Used by Subordinates: A Theoretical and Empirical Analysis and Refinement of the Kipnis, Schmidt, and Wilkinson Scales. Chicago, Academy of Management.

Hodgetts, R. M. and F. Luthans (1994). "New Paradigm Organizations: From Total Quality to Learning to World-Class." Organizational Dynamics **22**(3): 4.

Hofstede, G. (1980). Culture's Consequences: International Differences in Work Related Values. Beverly Hills, Sage.

Hofstede, G. (1982). "Intercultural Cooperation in Organizations." Management Decision **20**: 53-67.

Hofstede, G. (1984). Culture's Consequences: International Differences in Work-Related Values. Beverly Hills, Sage.

Hofstede, G. (1991). Culture and Organizations: Software of the Mind. New York, McGraw-Hill.

Hofstede, G. (1996). Images of Europe: Past, Present and Future. Managing Across Cultures: Issues and Perspectives. P. Joynt and F. Warner. London, International Thomson Business Press.

Hofstede, G. (2001). Culture's Consequence. Thousand Oaks, Sage.

Hofstede, G. and M. H. Bond (1988). "The Confucius Connection: From Cultural Roots to Economic Growth." Organizational Dynamics **16**(4): 5-21.

Hooijberg, R., J. G. Hunt, et al. (1997). "Leadership Complexity and Development of the Leaderplex Model." Journal of Management **23**(3): 375-408.

Hoppe, M. (1993). "The Effects of National Culture on the Theory and Practice of Managing R&D Professionals Abroad." R&D Management **23**(4): 313-325.

Hoppe, M. H. (1990). A Comparative Study of Country Elites: International Differences in Work-Related Values and Learning and Their Implications for Management Training and Development. Chapel Hill, University of North Carolina.

Horowitz, D. L. (1985). Ethnic Groups in Conflict. Berkley, University of California Press.

House, R. J. and M. Javidan (2004). Overview of GLOBE. Culture, Leadership, and Organizations - The GLOBE Study of 62 Societies. R. J. House, P. J. Hanges, M. Javidan, P. W. Dorfman and V. Gupta. Thousand Oaks, Sage.

House, R. J., N. S. Wright, et al. (1997). Cross-Cultural Research on Organizational Leadership: A Critical Analysis and Proposed Theory. New Perspectives on International Industrial/Organizational Psychology. C. P. Earley and M. Erez. San Francisco, The New Lexington Press.

Hudson, K., T. Grisham, et al. (2005). "Conflict Management, Negotiation, and Effective Communication: Essential Skills for Project Managers." Australian Project Manager 25(4): 25-27.

Hui, C. and G. Graen (1997). "Gunanxi and Professional Leadership in Contemporary Sino-American Joint Ventures in Mainland China." Leadership Quarterly 8(4): 451-465.

Hunter, J. C. (2004). The World's Most Powerful Leadership Prinicple: How to become a Servant Leader. New York, Crown Business.

Huntington, S. (1996). The Clash of Civilizations and Remaking of the New World Order. New York, Simon & Schuster.

Inglehart, R. (1997). Modernization and Postmodernization. Princeton, Princeton University Press.

Inglehart, R., M. Basanez, et al. (1998). Human Values and Beliefs: A Cross-Cultural Sourcebook. Ann Arbor, University of Michigan.

Jakel, O. (1995). The Metaphorical Conception of Mind: "Mental Activity is Manipulation". Language and the Cognitive Construal of the World. J. R. Taylor and R. E. MacLaury. Berlin, Mouton de Gruyter.

Jarvenpaa, S. L., K. Knoll, et al. (1998). "Is Anybody Out There? Antecedents of Trust in Global Virtual Teams." Journal of Management Information Systems 14(4): 29.

Javidan, M. (2004). Performance Orientation. Culture, Leadership, and Organizations - The GLOBE Study of 62 Societies. R. J. House, P. J. Hanges, M. Javidan, P. W. Dorfman and V. Gupta. Thousand Oaks, Sage.

Javidan, M. and M. Hauser (2004). The Linkage Between GLOBE Findings and Other Cross-Cultural Information. Culture, Leadership, and Organizations - The GLOBE Study of 62 Societies. R. J. House, P. J. Hanges, M. Javidan, P. W. Dorfman and V. Gupta. Thousand Oaks, Sage.

Jehn, K. A. (1995). "A Multimethod Examination of the Benefits and Detriments of Intragroup Conflict." Administrative Science Quarterly 40(2): 256-282.

Jehn, K. A. (1997). "A Qualitative Analysis of Conflict Types and Dimensions in Organizational Groups." Administrative Science Quarterly 42(3): 530-557.

Johnston, A. (1995). "Thinking About Strategic Culture." International Security 19(4).

Jolley, R. P., Z. Zhi, et al. (1998). "How Focus of Interest in Pictures Changes with Age: A Cross-Cultural Comparison." International Journal of Behavioral Development 22(1): 127-149.

Jomini, B. D. (1862). Art of War. Westport, Greenwood Press.

Jones, L. B. (1994). Jesus CEO. New York, Hyperion.

Journal, I. (1944). Psychology for the Fighting Man. Washington, Penguin.

Joynt, P. and F. Warner, Eds. (1996). Managing Across Cultures: Issues and Perspectives. London, International Thomson Business Press.

Kabasakal, H. and M. Bodur (2004). Humane Orientation in Societies, Organizations, and Leader Attributes. Culture, Leadership, and Organizations - The GLOBE Study of 62 Societies. R. J. House, P. J. Hanges, M. Javidan, P. W. Dorfman and V. Gupta. Thousand Oaks, Sage.

Kagitcibasi, C. (1990). Family and Home Based Intervention. <u>Applied Cross Cultural Psychology</u>. R. Brislin. Newbury Park, Sage.

Kashima, Y. and V. Callan, Eds. (1994). <u>The Japanese Work Group</u>. Handbook of Industrial and Organizational Psychology. Palo Alto, Consulting Psychologist Press.

Kasper-Fuehrer, E. C. and N. M. Ashkanasy (2001). "Communicating Trustworthiness and Building Trust in Interorganizational Virtual Organizations." <u>Journal of Management</u> **27**(3): 235.

Kaufman, J. (1999). Why Doesn't Business, Like Baseball, Create Improbable Heroes? <u>Wall Street Journal</u>. **October:** A1.

Keeney, S., F. Hasson, et al. (2001). "A Critical Review of the Delphi Technique as a Research Methodology for Nursing." <u>International Journal of Nursing Studies</u> **38**(2): 195-200.

Keller, T. (1999). "Images of the Familiar: Individual Differences and Implicit Leadership Theories." <u>Leadership Quarterly</u> **10**(4): 589.

Kennedy, H. P. (2004). "Methodological Issues in Nursing Research / Enhancing Delphi Research: Methods and Results." <u>Journal of Advanced Nursing</u> **45**(5): 504-511.

Kilcourse, T. (1985). "A Framework for Training Influential Managers." <u>Journal of European Industrial Training</u> **9**(4): 23-26.

Kilmann, R. H. and K. W. Thomas (1978). "Four Perspectives on Conflict Management: An Attributional Framework for Organizing Descriptive and Normative Theory." <u>Academy of Management Review</u>
<u>Academy of Management Review</u> J1 - Academy of Management Review **3**(1): 59.

Kim, M.-S., H.-R. Lee, et al. (2004). "A Test of a Cultural Model of Conflict Styles." <u>Journal of Asian Pacific Communication</u> **14**(2): 197-222.

Kim, M.-S. and T. Leung (2000). "Multicultural View of Conflict Management Styles: Review and Critical Synthesis." <u>Communication Yearbook</u> **23**(None): 227-269.

Kimmel, P. R. (1995). Facilitating the Contrast-Culture Method. Intercultural Sourcebook: Cross-Cultural Training Methodologies, Vol. 1. S. M. Fowler and M. Mumford. Yarmouth, Intercultural Press.

Kimmel, P. R. (2000). Culture and Conflict. The Handbook of Conflict Resolution - Theory and Practice. M. Deutsch and P. T. Coleman. San Francisco, Jossey-Bass.

King, A. (1991). "Guanxi and Network Building: A Socielogical Interpretation." Daedalus 10(2): 63.

Klapp, O. E. (1954). "Heros, Villians and Fools, as Agents of Social Control." American Sociological Review 19(1): 56-62.

Kluckhohn, F. R. (1967). Values and Value-Orientations in the Theory of Action: An Exploration in Definition and Classification. Toward a General Theory of Action. T. Parsons and E. A. Shils. Cambridge, Harvard University Press.

Kluckhohn, F. R. and F. L. Strodtbeck (1961). Variations in Value Orientations. New York, Harper Collins.

Kociatkiewicz, J. (2000). "Dreams of Time, Times of Dreams: Stories of Creation from Roleplaying Game Sessions." Studies in Cultures, Organizations & Societies 6(1): 71.

Korsbybski, A. (1933). Science and Sanity, Institute of General Semantics.

Kovecses, Z. (2003). "Language, Figurative Thought, and Cross-Cultural Comparison." Metaphor & Symbol 18(4): 311-320.

Kovecses, Z. (2005). Metaphor in culture - Universality and Variation. Cambridge, Cambridge University Press.

Kozan, K. (2000). Interpersonal Conflict Management Styles of Jordanian Managers. The Handbook of Conflict Resolution - Theory and Practice. M. Deutsch and P. T. Coleman. San Francisco, Jossey-Bass.

Kozan, M. K. (1989). "Cultural Influences on Styles of Handling Interpersonal Conflicts: Comparisons Among Jordanian, Turkish, and U.S. Managers." Human Relations **42**(9): 787-999.

Kozlowski, S. W. J. and K. J. Klein (2000). A Multi-Level Approach to Theory and Research in Organizations: Contextual, Temporal, and Emergent Processes. Multilevel Theory, Research, and Methods in Organizations: Foundation, Extensions, and New Directions. S. W. J. Kozlowski and K. J. Klein. San Francisco, Jossey-Bass.

Kramer, L. (2004). "Music, Metaphor and Metaphysics." Musical Times **145**(1888): 5-18.

Kramer, R. and T. R. Tyler (1996). Trust in Organizations: Frontiers of Theory and Research. Trust in Organizations: Frontiers of Theory and Research. R. Kramer and T. R. Tyler. Thousand Oaks, Sage.

Kras, E. S. (1995). Management in Two Cultures: Bridging the Gap Between U.S. and Mexican Managers. Yarmouth, ME, Intercultural Press.

Krauss, R. M. and M. Deutsch (1966). "Communication in Interpersonal Bargaining." Journal of Personality and Social Psychology **4**: 572-577.

Krauss, R. M. and E. Morsella (2000). Communication and Conflict. The Handbook of Conflict Resolution - Theory and Practice. M. Deutsch and P. T. Coleman. San Francisco, Jossey-Bass.

Krishnamurti, J. (1996). The Essential Krishnamurti. San Francisco, Harper.

Kroeber, A. and C. Kluckhohn (1985). Culture: A Critical Review of Concepts and Definitions. New York, Random House.

Kubler-Ross, E. and D. Kessler (2005). On Grief and Grieving. New York, Scribner.

Lachman, R., A. Nedd, et al. (1994). "Analyzing Cross-National Management and Organizations: A Theoretical Framework." Management Science **40**(1): 40.

LaFromboise, T. M., H. L. K. Coleman, et al. (1993). "Psychological Impact of Biculturalism." Psychological Bulletin **114**(3): 395.

Lakoff, G. (1995). "Metaphor, Morality, and Politics, or, Why Conservatives Have Left Liberals in the Dusk." Social Research **62**(2): 177.

Lakoff, G. and M. Johnson (1980). Methphors We Live By. Chicago, University of Chicago Press.

Lakoff, G. and M. Johnson (1999). Philosophy in the Flesh: The Embodied Mind and its Challenge to Western Thought. New York, Basic Books.

Lama, D. (1995). The World of Tibetan Buddhism. Boston, Wisdom Publications.

Laurent, A. (1983). "The Cultural Diversity of Western Management Conceptions." International Studies of Management and Organization **8**: 75-76.

Lave, J. and E. C. Wenger (1991). Situated Learning - Legitimate Peropheral Participation. Cambridge, Cambridge University Press.

Lawler III, E. E. (2001). The Era of Human Capital Has Finally Arrived. The Future of Leadership - Today's Top Leadership Thinkers Speak to Tomorrow's Leaders. W. Bennis, G. M. Spreitzer and T. G. Cummings. San Francisco, Jossey-Bass**:** 14-25.

LeBaron, M. (2003). Bridging cultural Conflicts - A New Approach for a Changing World. San Francisco, Jossey-Bass.

Ledeen, M. A. (1999). Machiavelli on Modern Leadership. New York, St. Martin's Press.

Lederach, J. P. (2000). Of Nets, Nails, and Problems: The Folk Language of Conflict Resolution in a Central American Setting. The Handbook of Conflict Resolution - Theory and Practice. M. Deutsch and P. T. Coleman. San Francisco, Jossey-Bass.

Lederach, J. P. (2001). Preparing for Peace - Conflict Transformation Across Cultures. The Conflict and Culture Reader. P. K. Chew. New York, New York University Press.

Lee, C. H. and K. J. Templer (2003). Cultural Intelligence Assessment and Measurement. <u>Cultural Intelligence Individual Interactions Across Cultures</u>. P. C. Earley and S. Ang. Stanford, Stanford Business Books.

Leeds, C. (1996). Pragmatic and Holistic Approaches to Management in Emerging and Newly Emergent Democracies. <u>Managing Across Cultures: Issues and Perspectives</u>. P. Joynt and F. Warner. London, International Thomson Business Press.

Lennie, I. (1999). "Managing Metaphorically." <u>Studies in Cultures, Organizations & Societies</u> **5**(1): 43.

Leslie, J. B. and J. W. Fleenor (1998). <u>Feedback to Managers: A Review and Comparison of Multi-Rater Instruments for Managerial Development</u>. Greensboro, Center for Creative Leadership.

Lessem, R. and F. Neubauer (1994). <u>European Management Systems: Towards Unity out of Cultural Diversity</u>. London, McGraw-Hill.

Leung, K. (1987). "Some Determinants of Reactions to Procedural Models of Conflict Resolution - A Cross-National Study." <u>Journal of Personality and Social Psychology</u> **53**(5): 898-908.

Leung, K. (1997). Negotiation and Reward Allocations Across Cultures. <u>New Perspectives on International Industrial/Organizational Psychology</u>. C. P. Earley and M. Erez. San Francisco, The New Lexington Press.

Levine, S. (1998). <u>Getting to Resolution - Turning Conflict into Collaboration</u>. San Francisco, Berrett-Koehler.

Levinson, D. (1994). <u>Aggression and Conflict - A Cross-Cultural Encyclopedia of the Human Experience</u>. Santa Barbara, ABC-CLIO.

Lewicki, R. J. and B. B. Bunker (1995). Trust in Relationships: A Model of Development and Decline. <u>Conflict, Cooperation, and Justice: Essays Inspired by the Work of Morton Deutsch</u>. B. B. Bunker and J. Z. Rubin. San Francisco, Jossey-Bass.

Lewicki, R. J., D. J. Mcallister, et al. (1998). "Trust and Distrust: New Relationships and Realities." Academy of Management Review **23**(3): 438-458.

Lewicki, R. J. and C. Wiethoff (2000). Trust, trust development, and trust repair. The handbook of conflict resolution. M. Deutsch and P. T. Coleman. San Francisco, Jossey-Bass.

Lewicki, R. J. and C. Wiethoff (2000). Trust, Trust Development, and Trust Repair. The Handbook of Conflict Resolution - Theory and Practice. M. Deutsch and P. T. Coleman. San Francisco, Jossey-Bass.

Lewin, K. (1936). Some Social-Psychological Differences Between the US and Germany. Principles of Topological Psychology. K. Lewin. Unknown, Unknown.

Lewis, H. S. (1974). Leaders and Followers: Some Anthropological Perspectives. Reading, MA, Addison-Wesley.

Lewis, J. D. and A. Weigert (1985). "Trust as a Social Reality." Social Forces **63**(4): 967.

Lientz, B. P. and K. P. Rea (2003). International Project Management. San Diego, Elsevier.

Lincola, Y. S. and E. G. Guba (1985). Naturalistic Inquiry. London, Sage.

Ling, W. Q. and L. Fang (2003). The Chinese Leadership Theory. Advances in Global Leadership. W. H. Mobley and P. W. Dorfman. Oxford, JAI.

Lipman-Blumen (2001). Why Do We Tolerate Bad Leaders? Magnificent Uncertitude, Anxiety, and Meaning. The Future of Leadership - Today's Top Leadership Thinkers Speak to Tomorrow's Leaders. W. Bennis, G. M. Spreitzer and T. G. Cummings. San Francisco, Jossey-Bass: 14-25.

Liu, Y. (1999). "Justifying My Position in Your Terms: Cross-Cultural Argumentation in a Globalized World." Argumentation **13**(3): 297-315.

Loosemore, M. and H. S. A. Muslmani (1999). "Construction Project Management in the Persian Gulf: Inter-Cultural Communication." International Journal of Project Management **17**(2): 95-100.

Lord, R. G. (2001). "Thinking Outside the Box by Looking Inside the Box: Extending the Cognitive Revolution in Leadership Research." Leadership Quarterly 11(4): 551.

Lord, R. G., R. J. Foti, et al. (1984). "A Test of Leadership Categorization Theory: Internal Structure, Information Processing, and Leadership Theories." Organizational Behavior and Human Performance 34(3): 343.

Lord, R. G. and K. J. Maher (1991). Leaership and Information Processing: Linking Perceptions and Performance. New York, Routledge.

Luhmann, N. (1988). Familiarity, Confidence, Trust: Problems and Alternatives. Trust: Making and Breaking Cooperative Relations. D. Gambetta. Oxford, Blackwell: 94-107.

Luque, M. S. and M. Javidan (2004). Uncertainty Avoidance. Culture, Leadership, and Organizations - The GLOBE Study of 62 Societies. R. J. House, P. J. Hanges, M. Javidan, P. W. Dorfman and V. Gupta. Thousand Oaks, Sage.

Luthans, F. and R. M. Hodgetts (1996). Managing in America: Recreating a Competitive Culture. Managing Across Cultures: Issues and Perspectives. P. Joynt and F. Warner. London, International Thomson Business Press.

Maasen, S. and P. Weingart (2003). Metaphors and the Dynamics of Knowledge. London, Routledge.

Mac Cormac, E. R. (1990). A Cognitive Theory of Metaphor. Cambridge, Massachusetts, MIT Press.

Machiavelli, N. (1961). The Prince. Bungay, Penguin.

Machiavelli, N. (1983). Discorsi Sopra la Prima Decca di Tito Livio. Torino, Unknown.

Makilouko, M. (2004). "Coping with Multicultural Projects: The Leadership Styles of Finnish Project Managers." International Journal of Project Management 22(5): 387-396.

Manz, C. C. and H. P. Sims Jr. (1991). "SuperLeadership: Beyond the Myth of Heroic Leadership." Organizational Dynamics **19**(4): 18.

Marquardt, M. J. and N. O. Berger (2000). Global Leaders for the Twenty-First Century. Albany, State University of New York Press.

Matthews, A. M., R. G. Lord, et al. (1990). The Development of Leadership Perception in Children. Akron, University of Akron.

Mayer, R., J. H. Davis, et al. (1995). "An Integrative Model of Organizational Trust." Academy of Management Review **20**(3): 709-734.

Mayo, A. J. and N. Nohria (2005). In Their Time: The Greatest Business Leaders of the Twentieth Century. Boston, Harvard Business School Press.

Maznevski, M. (1994). Synergy and Performance in Multi-Cultural Teams. Ontario, University of Western Ontario.

McAllister, D. (1995). "Affect and Cognition-Based Trust as Foundations for Interpersonal Cooperation in Organizations." Academy of Management Journal **38**(1): 24.

McCarthy, B. and C. Keene (1996). About Learning. Old Barrington, Excel.

McCauley, C. D. (2000). A Systemic Approach to Leadership Development. 15th Annual Conference of the Society for Industrial and Organizational Psychology, New Orleans.

McCauley, C. D. and E. Van Velsor (2004). Center for Creative Leadership Handbook of Leadership Development. San Francisco, Jossey-Bass.

McClelland, D. (1961). The Achieving Society. Princeton, Van Nostrand.

McKenna, H. P. (1994). "The Delphi Technique: A Worthwhile Approach to Nursing?" Journal of Advanced Nursing **19**(6): 1221-1225.

McLuhan, M. (1964). Understanding Media: The Extensions of Man. New York, The New American Library.

Mead, M., Ed. (1955). Cultural Patterns and Technical Change. New York, UNESCO.

Mintzberg, H. (1998). "Covert Leadership: Notes on Managing Professionals." Harvard Business Review 76(6): 140.

Misumi, J. (1985). The Behavioral Science of Leadership: An Interdisciplinary Japanese Research Program. Ann Arbor, University of Michigan Press.

Misztal, B. A. (1996). Trust in Modern Societies. Cambridge, Polity Press.

Mobley, W. H., M. J. Gessner, et al. (1999). Introduction. Advances in Global Leadership. W. H. Mobley, M. J. Gessner and V. Arnold. Stamford, JAI Press.

Montuschi, E. (1995). What is Wrong with Talking of Metaphors in Science. From a Metaphorical Point of View: A Multidiciplinary Approach to the Cognitive Content of Metaphor. Z. Radman. Berlin, DeGruyer.

Morgan, G. (1986). Images of Organization. Beverly Hills, Sage.

Morisaki, S. and W. B. Gudykunst (1994). Face in Japan and the United States. The Challenge of Facework: Cross-Cultural and Interpersonal Issues. S. Ting-Toomey. Albany, State University of New York.

Morris, M. W., J. M. Podolny, et al. (2000). Incorporating Relational Constructs Into Models of Culture. Innovations in International and Cross-Cultural Management. P. C. Earley and H. Singh. Thousand Oaks, Sage: viii, 374.

Morrison, T., W. A. Conaway, et al. (1994). Kiss, Bow, or Shake Hands - How To Do Business in Sixty Countries. Holbrook, Bob Adams.

Mullavey-O'Brien, C. (1997). Empathy in Cross-Cultural Communications. Improving Intercultural Interactions. K. Cusher and R. Brislin. Thousand Oaks, Sage.

Mumford, M. D., S. J. Zaccaro, et al. (2000). "Leadership Skills for a Changing World: Solving Complex Social Problems." Leadership Quarterly **11**(1): 11.

Munroe, R. H., R. L. Munroe, et al. (1981). Handbook of Cross-Cultural Human Development. London, Taylor & Francis.

Nader, L. (1998). Harmony Models and the Construction of Law. Conflict Resolution - Cross-cultural Perspectives. K. Avruch, P. W. Black and J. A. Scimecca. Westport, Praeger.

Naroll, R., G. L. Michik, et al. (1980). Holocultural Research Methods. Handbook of Cross-Cultural Psychology: Methodology. H. C. Triandis and J. W. Berry. Boston, Allyn-B Acon. **2**.

Nemetz, P. L. and S. L. Christensen (1996). "The Challenge of Cultural Diversity: Harnessing a Diversity of Views to Understand Multi-Culturalism." Academy of Management Review **21**(2): 434.

Neumann, C. (2001). "Is Metaphor Universal? Cross-Language Evidence from German and Japanese." Metaphor and Symbol **16**(1/2): 123-142.

Newman, K. (1983). Law and Economic Organization: A Comparative Study of Preindustrial Societies.

Nicholson, L. and A. R. Anderson (2005). "News and Nuances of the Entrepreneurial Myth and Metaphor: Linguistic Games in Entrepreneurial Sense-Making and Sense-Giving." Entrepreneurship: Theory & Practice **29**(2): 153-172.

Nisan, M. and L. Kohlberg (1982). "Universality and Variation in Moral Judgment: A Longitudinal and Cross-Sectional Study in Turkey." Child Development **53**(4): 865.

Niven, P. R. (2002). Balanced Scorecard Step by Step: Maximizing Performance and Maintaining Results. New York, Wiley.

Novinger, T. (2001). Intercultural Communications: A Practical Guide. Austin, University of Texas Press.

259

Nudler, O. (1990). On Conflicts and Metaphors: Towards an Extended Rationality. Conflict: Human Needs Theory. J. Burton. New York, St. Martin's.

Oetzel, J., S. Ting-Toomey, et al. (2001). "Face and Facework in Conflict: A Cross-Cultural Comparison of China, Germany, Japan, and the United States." Communication Monograph **68**(3): 235-258.

Oetzel, J. G. (1998). "The Effects of Self-Construals and Ethnicity on Self-Reported Conflict Styles." Communication Reports **11**(2): 133.

Ogden, C. K. and I. A. Richards (1936). The Meaning of Meaning: A Study of the Influence of Language Upon Thought and the Science of Symbolism. New York, Harcourt Brace.

Osland, J. (1995). The Adventure of Working Abroad: Hero Tales from the Global Frontier. San Francisco, Jossey-Bass Publishers.

Osland, J. S. and A. Bird (2000). "Beyond Sophisticated Stereotyping: Cultural Sensemaking in Context." Academy of Management Executive **14**(1): 65.

Özçaliskan, S. (2003). "In a Caravanserai With Two Doors I Am Walking Day and Night: Metaphors of Death and Life in Turkish." Cognitive Linguistics **14**(4): 281.

Palmer, H. (1990). The Enneagram: Understanding Yourself and Others in Your Life. San Francisco, Harper San Francisco.

Parsons, T. (1951). The Social System. New York, Free Press.

Pearce, T. (2003). Leading Out Loud: Inspiring Change Through Authentic Communication. San Francisco, John Wiley & Sons.

Perkins, J. (2004). Confessions of an Economic Hit Man. San Francisco, Berrett-Koehler.

Peters, T. (1992). Liberation Management. London, Macmillan.

Peterson, M. F. and J. G. Hunt (1997). "International Perspectives on International Leadership." Leadership Quarterly **8**(3): 203.

Pettigrew, T. (1998). "Intergroup Contact Theory." Annual Review of Psychology **49**(1): 65-85.

Pfeffer, J. (1977). "The Ambiguity of Leadership." Academy of Management Review **2**(1): 104.

Pheng, L. S. and C. H. Y. Leong (2000). "Cross-Cultural Project Management for International Construction in China." International Journal of Project Management **18**(5): 307.

Pike, K. L. (1967). Language in Relation to a Unified Theory of the Structure of Human Behavior. The Hague, Mouton.

Pitt, L., P. Berthon, et al. (1996). As the World Spins: Short-Term Changes in International Clusters. Managing Across Cultures: Issues and Perspectives. P. Joynt and F. Warner. London, International Thomson Business Press.

PMBOK (2004). A Guide to the Project Management Body of Knowledge, 3rd Edition. Newtown Square, PA, Project Management Institute.

Podsakoff, P. M., S. B. MacKenzie, et al. (1995). "Searching for a Needle in a Haystack: Trying to Identify the Illusive Moderators of Leadership Behaviors." Journal of Management **21**(3): 422.

Podsakoff, P. M., S. B. MacKenzie, et al. (1996). "Transformational Leader Behaviors and Substitutes for Leadership as Determinants of Employee Satisfaction, Commitment, Trust, and Organizational Citizenship Behaviors." Journal of Management **22**(2): 259.

Podsakoff, P. M. and C. A. Schriesheim (1985). "Field Studies of French and Raven's Bases of Power. Critique, Reanalysis, and Suggestions for Future Research." Psychological Bulletin **97**(Unknown): 387-411.

Pondy, L. R. (1967). "Organizational Conflict: Concepts and Models." Administrative Science Quarterly **12**(2): 296.

Popkewitz, T. S. (2000). Educational Knowledge: Changing Relationships Between the State, Civil Society, and the Educational Community. Albany, State University of New York Press.

Post, W. (2005). Alert to Bad Vibrations, Animals Felt the Tsunami Coming. St. Petersburg Times. St. Petersburg, FL: 7A.

Powell, W. W. (1990). "Neither Market nor Hierarchy: Network Forms of Organization." Research in Organizational Behavior 12: 295.

Putnam, L. L. and M. S. Poole (1987). Putnam, L. L., & Poole, M. S. Handbook of Organizational Communication. F. M. Jablin, L. L. Putnam, K. H. Roberts and L. W. Porter. Newbury Park, Sage.

Radden, G. (1996). Motion Metaphorized: The Case of Coming and Going. Cognitive Linguistics in the Redwoods: The Expansion of a New Paradigm in Linguistics. E. H. Casad. Berlin, Mouton de Gruyter.

Rahim, M. A. (1983). "A Measure of Styles of Handling Interpersonal Conflict." Academy of Management Journal 26(2): 368.

Rahim, M. A. (2002). "Toward a Theory of Managing Organizational Conflict." International Journal of Conflict Management 13(3): 206.

Rahim, M. A. and T. V. Bonoma (1997). "Managing Organizational Conflict: A Model for Diagnosis and Intervention." Psychological Reports 44.

Ralston, D. A., D. J. Gustafson, et al. (1992). "Eastern Values: A Comparison of Managers in the United States, Hong Kong, and the Peoples Republic of China." Journal of Applied Psychology 77(5): 664-671.

Ravlin, E., D. Thomas, et al. (2000). Beliefs About Values, Status, and Legitimacy in Multicultural Groups. Innovations in International and Cross-Cultural Management. P. C. Earley and H. Singh. Thousand Oaks, Sage: viii, 374.

Ray, B. (1989). The Relationship of Job Satisfaction, Individual Characteristics, and Leadership Behaviors to Corporate Cultural Beliefs and Climate for Change. Commerce, TX, East Texas State University.

Reed, M. (1990). "From Paradigms to Images: The Paradigm Warrior Turns Post-Modern Guru." Personnel Review **19**.

Reid, N. G. (1988). The Delphi Technique, Its Contributions to the Evaluation of Professional Practice. Professional Competence and Quality Assurance in the Caring Professional. R. Ellis. Beckenham, Croon-Helm: 230-262.

Reidenbach, R. E. and D. P. Robin (1990). "Toward the Development of a Multidimensional Scale for Improving Evaluations of Business Ethics." Journal of Business Ethics **9**(8): 639.

Renard, M. and K. Eastwood (2003). "Cultural Masks: Giving Voice to the Margins." Administrative Theory & Praxis **25**(4): 499-512.

Richards, I. (1965). The Philosophy of Rhetoric. New York, Oxford University Press USA.

Ricoeur, P. (1977). The Rule of Metaphor. London, Routledge and Kegan Paul.

Riggio, R., J. Maessamer, et al. (1991). "Social and Academic Intelligence: Conceptually Distinct But Overlapping Constructs." Personality and Individual Differences **12**(7): 695-702.

Rinpoche, S. (1994). The Tibetan Book of Living and Dying. San Francisco, Harper.

Roberts, W. (1989). Leadership Secrets of Attila the Hun. New York, Warner Books.

Ronen, S. (1986). Comparative and Multinational Management. New York, Wiley.

Ronen, S. and A. I. Kraut (1977). "Similarities Among Countries Based on Employee Work Values and Attitudes." Columbia Journal of World Business **12**(2): 89-96.

Rosen, R., P. Digh, et al. (2000). Global Literacies - Lessons on Business Leadership and National Cultures. New York, Simon & Schuster.

Rosnow, R. L. and G. A. Fine (1976). Rumor and Gossip: The Psychology of Hearsay. Unknown, Elsevier Science Ltd.

Roth, A. E., V. Prasnikar, et al. (1991). "Bargaining and Market Behavior in Jerusalem, Ljubljana, Pittsburgh, and Tokyo: An Experimental Study." American Economic Review **81**(5): 1068-1095.

Rousseau, D. M., S. B. Sitkin, et al. (1998). "Not So Different After All: A Cross-Discipline View of Trust." Academy of Management Review **23**(3): 393-404.

Ruble, T. L. and K. W. Thomas (1976). "Support for a Two Dimensional Model of Conflict Behavior." Organizational Behavior and Human Behavior **16**.

Russell, B. (1938). Power. London, Allen and Unwin.

Russell, B. (1938). Power: A New Social Analysis. New York, Norton.

Ryan, R. (2003). "Towards a Geography of the Symbolic." Pretexts **12**(2): 211-221.

Sagiv, L. and V. Gupta (2002). Schwartz Theory of Cultural Dimensions of Values. Reconciling the Findings of Five Cross-Cultural Research Programs: Hofstede, Trompenaars, World Values Survey, Schwartz, and GLOBE. Academy of Management Meeting, Denver CO.

Sagiv, L. and S. H. Schwartz (2000). A New Look at National Culture: Illustrative Applications to Role Stress and Managerial Behavior. The Handbook of Organizational Culture and Climate. N. N. Ashkanasy, C. Wilderom and M. F. Peterson. Newbury Park, Sage.

Said, E. W. (1991). Orientalism. London, Penguin.

Said, E. W. (1994). Culture and Imperialism. London, Vintage.

Saint-Exupery, A. D. (1950). The Wisdom of the Sands. Orlando, FL, Harcourt Brace.

Salem, P. E. (2001). A Critique of Western Conflict Resolution from a Non-Western Perspective. The Conflict and Culture Reader. P. K. Chew. New York, New York University Press.

Scandura, T. A., G. B. Graen, et al. (1986). "When Managers Decide Not to Decide Autocratically: An Investigation of Leader-Member Exchange and Decision Influence." Academy of Management Proceedings: 203-207.

Scandura, T. A., M. A. Von Glinow, et al. (2003). When East Meets West: Leadership "Best Practices" in the United States and the Middle East. Advances in Global Leadership. W. H. Mobley and P. W. Dorfman. Oxford, JAI.

Schein, E. H. (1985). Organizational Culture and Leadership. San Francisco, Jossey-Bass.

Schmincke, D. (2000). The Code of the Executive. New York, Plume.

Schneider, S. C. and J.-L. Barsoux (2003). Managing Across Cultures. London, Prentice Hall Financial Times.

Schon, D. (1987). Educating the Reflective Practitioner. San Francisco, Jossey-Bass.

Schwartz, S. H. (1992). Universals in the Content and Structure of Values: Theoretical Advances and Empirical Tests in 20 Countries. Advances in Experimental Social Psychology. M. Zanna. San Diego, Academic Press.

Schwartz, S. H. (1994). Cultural Dimensions of Values: Towards an Understanding of National Differences. Individualism and Collectivism: Theory, Methods, and Applications. U. Kim, H. C. Traiandis, C. Kagitcibasi, S. C. Choi and G. Yoon. Thousand Oaks, Sage.

Schwartz, S. H. (1999). "A Theory of Cultural Values and Some Implications for Work." Applied Psychology: An International Review 48(1): 23-47.

Scimecca, J. A. (1998). Conflict Resolution in the United States: The Emergence of a Profession? Conflict Resolution - Cross-Cultural Perspectives. K. Avruch, P. W. Black and J. A. Scimecca. Westport, Praeger.

Scott, C. L. (1980). "Interpersonal Trust: A Comparison of Attitudinal and Situational Factors." Human Relations 33(11): 805.

265

Sekaran, U. (1983). "Methodological and Theoretical Issues and Advancements in Cross-Cultural Research." Journal of International Business Studies **14**(2): 61.

Senge, P. M. (1990). The Fifth Discipline - The Art & Practice of the Learning Organization. Sydney, Australia, Random House.

Service, U. A. (1944). Psychology for the Fighting Man. Washington, Penguin.

Shakespeare, W. (2005). The Tragedy of Hamlet, Prince of Denmark. Unknown, EBook, Filiquarian Publishing, LLC.

Shamir, B. and J. M. Howell (1999). "Organizational and Contextual Influences on the Emergence and Effectiveness of Charismatic Leadership." Leadership Quarterly **10**(2): 257.

Shirer, W. L. (1979). Gandhi, A Memoir. New York, Simon & Schuster.

Shore, B. and B. J. Cross (2005). "Exploring the Role of National Culture in the Management of Large-Scale International Science Projects." International Journal of Project Management **23**(1): 55-64.

Singelis, T. M. and W. J. Brown (1995). "Culture, Self, and Collectivist Communication." Human Communication Research **21**(3): 354.

Singelis, T. M. and P. Pedersen (1997). Conflict and Mediation Across Cultures. Improving Intercultural Interactions. K. Cusher and R. Brislin. Thousand Oaks, Sage.

Sinha, J. B. P. (1984). "A Model of Effective Leadership Styles in India." International Studies of Management and Organization **14**(2/3): 86-98.

Sinha, J. B. P. and R. N. Kanungo (1997). "Context Sensitivity and Balancing in Indian Organizational Behaviour." International Journal of Psychology **32**(2): 93-106.

Sirota, D. and J. M. Greenwood (1971). "Understanding Your Overseas Workforce." Harvard Business Review **49**(1): 53-60.

Sitkin, S. B. and N. L. Roth (1993). "Explaining the Limited Effectiveness of Legalistic "Remedies" for Trust/Distrust." Organisational Science 4(3): 367.

Skapinker, M. (1989). American CEO's Take a Parochial View of Competition. Financial Times. 16.

Slate, W. K. I. (2004). Paying Attention to "CULTURE" in International Commercial Arbitration. ICCA conference, Beijing, China.

Smith, H. L. and L. M. Krueger (1933). A Brief Summary of Literature on Leadership. Bloomington, Indiana University, School of Education Bulletin.

Smith, K. K. and V. M. Simmons (1983). "A Rumpelstiltskin Organization: Metaphors on Metaphors in Field Research." Administrative Science Quarterly 28(3): 377.

Smith, P. A. C. (2001). "Action Learning and Reflective Practice in Project Environments That are Related to Leadership Development." Management Learning 32(1): 31.

Smith, P. B. and M. F. Peterson (1994). Leadership as Event Management: A Cross-Cultural Survey Based Upon Middle Managers from 25 Nations. International Congress of Applied Psychology, Madrid.

Smith, P. B. and S. H. Schwartz (1997). Values. Handbook of Cross-Cultural Psychology. J. W. Berry, M. Segall and C. Kagitçibasi. Boston, Allyn & Bacon.

Spears, L., Ed. (1995). Reflections on Leadership. New York, Wiley.

Spence, G. (1995). How to Argue and Win Every Time - At Home, At Work, In Court, Everywhere, Every Day. New York, St. Martins Press.

Spencer, L. M. ((undated)). The Navy Leadership and Management Education and Training Program. Unpublished Manuscript.

Spicer, A. (1997). "Cultural and Knowledge Transfer: Conflict in Russian Multi-National Settings." Academy of Management Proceedings: 194.

Spitzberg, B. and W. Cupach (1984). Interpersonal Communication Competence. Beverly Hills, Sage.

Stewart, T. A. (2001). Trust Me on This - Organizational Support for Trust in a World Without Hierarchies. The Future of Leadership - Today's Top Leadership Thinkers Speak to Tomorrow's Leaders. W. Bennis, G. M. Spreitzer and T. G. Cummings. San Francisco, Jossey-Bass: 14-25.

Streufert, S., R. M. Pogdash, et al. (1988). "Simulation Based Assessment of Managerial Competence Reliability and Validity." Personnel Psychology 41(3): 537-555.

Sullivan, J., R. B. Peterson, et al. (1981). "The Relationship Between Conflict Resolution Approaches and Trust - A Cross Cultural Study." Academy of Management Journal 24(4): 803.

Sweet, R. B. (1995). "Creatures of the Metaphor." Humanist 55(6): 26.

Szulanski, G. and R. J. Jensen (2004). "Overcoming Stickiness: An Empirical Investigation of the Role of the Template in the Replication of Organizational Routines." Managerial & Decision Economics 25(6/7): 347-363.

Tayeb, M. (1987). "Contingency Theory and Culture: A Study of Matched English and the Indian Manufacturing Firms." Organization Studies (Walter de Gruyter GmbH & Co. KG.) 8(3): 241.

Tayeb, M. (1988). Organizationa and National Culture. London, Sage.

Tayeb, M. (1994). "Organizations and National Culture: Methodology Considered." Organization Studies (Walter de Gruyter GmbH & Co. KG.) 15(3): 429.

Thamhain, H. J. (2004). "Team Leadership Effectiveness in Technology-Based Project Environments." Project Management Journal 35(4): 35-46.

Thomas, D. C. and K. Inkson (2004). Cultural Intelligence - People Skills for Global Business. San Francisco, Berrett-Koehler.

Thompson, L. (1998). The Mind and Heart of the Negotiator. London, Prentice Hall International.

Tichy, N. and M. A. Devanna (1986). The Transformational Leader. New York, John Wiley & Sons.

Ting-Toomey, S., G. Gao, et al. (1991). "Culture, Face Maintenance, and Styles of Handling Interpersonal Conflict: A Study in Five Cultures." International Journal of Conflict Management 2(None): 275-296.

Ting-Toomey, S. and A. Kurogi (1998). "Facework Competence in Intercultural Conflict: An Updated Face-Negotiation Theory." International Journal of Intercultural Relations 22(2): 187.

Ting-Toomey, S., J. G. Oetzel, et al. (2001). "Self-Construal Types and Conflict Management Styles." Communication Reports 14(2): 87.

Tinsley, C. (1998). "Models of Conflict Resolution in Japanese, German, and American Cultures." Journal of Applied Psychology 83(None): 316-323.

Tinsley, C. H. and J. M. Brett (1997). "Managing Work Place Conflict: A Comparison of Conflict Frames and Resolutions in the U.S. and Hong Kong." Academy of Management Proceedings 97(None): 87-91.

Tollgerdt-Anderson, I. (1996). Attitudes, Values and Demands on Leadership - A Cultural Comparison Among Some European Countries. Managing Across Cultures: Issues and Perspectives. P. Joynt and F. Warner. London, International Thomson Business Press.

Triandis, H. and M. Gelfand (1998). "Convergent Measurement of Horizontal and Vertical Individualism and Collectivism." Journal of Personality and Social Psychology 74(1): 118-128.

Triandis, H. C. (1995). Individualism and Collectivism. Boulder, CO, Westview Press.

Triandis, H. C. (2003). "The Future of Workforce Diversity in International Organisations: A Commentary." Applied Psychology: An International Review 52(3): 486-495.

Triandis, H. C. (2004). "The Many Dimensions of Culture." Academy of Management Executive 18(1): 88-93.

Trice, H. M. and J. M. Beyer (1991). "Cultural Leadership in Organizations." Organization Science: A Journal of the Institute of Management Sciences 2(2): 149.

Trompenaars, A. (1993). Riding the Waves of Culture: Understanding Cultural Diversity in Business. London, The Economist Books.

Trompenaars, A. and C. Hampden-Turner (1998). Riding the Waves of Culture: Understanding Cultural Diversity in Global Business. New York, McGraw-Hill.

Trompenaars, F. (1984). The Organization of Meaning and the Meaning of Organization - A Comparitive Study on the Conceptions and Organizational Structure in Different Cultures, University of Pennsylvania.

Tse, D. K. and J. Francis (1994). "Cultural Differences in Conducting Intra- and Inter-Cultural Negotiations: A Sino-Canadian Comparison." Journal of International Business Studies 25(3): 537.

Tucker, M. F. (1999). Self-Awareness and Development Using the Overseas Assignment Inventory. Intercultural Sourcebook. Vol. 2: Cross-Cultural Training Methods. S. M. Fowleer. Yarmouth, Intercultural Press.

Tung, R. (1996). Managing in Asia: Cross-Cultural Dimensions. Managing Across Cultures: Issues and Perspectives. P. Joynt and F. Warner. London, International Thomson Business Press.

Turbayne, C. M. (1962). The Myth of Metaphor. New Haven, Yale University Press.

Turner, I. and I. Henry (1996). In Search of the Transnational: A Study of Structural Choice in International Companies. Managing Across Cultures: Issues and Perspectives. P. Joynt and F. Warner. London, International Thomson Business Press.

Turner, J. R. and R. Mueller (2005). "The Project Manager's Leadership Style as a Success Factor on Projects: A Literature Review." Project Management Journal 36(2): 49-61.

Turoff, M. (1970). "The Design of a Policy Delphi." Technological Forecasting and Social Change 2(2): 140-171.

Tzu, S. (1963). The Art of War. London, Oxford University Press.

Wagner, R. K. and R. J. Sternberg (1985). "Practical Intelligence in Real-World Pursuits: The Role of Tacit Knowledge." Journal of Personality and Social Psychology 49(None): 436-458.

Wang, E., H.-W. Chou, et al. (2005). "The Impacts of Charismatic Leadership Style on Team Cohesiveness and Overall Performance During ERP Implementation." International Journal of Project Management 23(3): 173-180.

Watts, A. and A. C. Huang (1975). Tao: The Watercourse Way. New York, Pantheon.

Wayzata (1993). Wayzata World Factbook. Grand Rapids, Wayzata Technology Inc.

Weisbord, M. and S. Janoff (2000). Future Search: An Action guide to Finding Common Ground in Organizations and Communities. San Francisco, Berrett-Koehler.

Wheatley, M. (2005). Finding Our Way. San Francisco, Berrett-Koehler.

Wheelwright, P. (1967). Metaphor & Reality. Bloomington, Indiana University Press.

Whitener, E. M. (2000). The Processes of Building Social Capital in Organizations: The Integrating Role of Trust. Paper presented at the Academy of Management Annual Meeting, Toronto Canada.

Wiener, N. (1950). The Human Use of Human Beings - Cybernetics and Society. New York, Avon.

Wilson, J. Q. (1993). The Moral Sense. New York, The Free Press.

Wilson, M., W. H. Hoppe, et al. (1996). Managing Across Cultures: A Learning Framework. Greensboro, Center for Creative Leadership.

Wofford, J. C. (1982). "An Integrative Theory of Leadership." Journal of Management 8(1): 27.

Wofford, J. C. (1999). "Laboratory Research on Charismatic Leadership: Fruitful or Futile?" Leadership Quarterly **10**(4): 523.

Worchel, S. (1974). "Societal Restrictiveness and the Presence of Outlets for the Release of Aggression." Journal of Cross-Cultural Psychology **5**: 109-123.

Xie, J., X. M. Song, et al. (1998). "Interfunctional Conflict, Conflict Resolution Styles, and New Product Success: A Four-Culture Comparison." Management Science **44**(12): S192.

Yang, K. S. (1988). Will Societal Modernization Eventually Eliminate Cross Cultural Psychological Differences? The Cross-Culutral Challenge to Social Psychology. M. H. Bond. Newbury Park, Sage.

Yeung, A. K. and D. A. Ready (1995). "Developing Leadership Capabilities of Global Corporations: A Comparative Study in Eight Nations." Human Resource Management **34**(4): 529-547.

Yin, R. (1994). Case Study Research. Thousand Oaks, California, Sage.

Yu, N. (2003). "Chinese Metaphors of Thinking." Cognitive Linguistics **14**(2/3): 141.

Yu, N. (2003). "Metaphor, Body, and Culture: The Chinese Understanding of Gallbladder and Courage." Metaphor & Symbol **18**(1): 13-31.

Yukl, G. (1989). Leadership in Organizations. Englewood Cliffs, Prentice Hall.

Yukl, G. (1998). Leadership in Organisations. Sydney, Prentice-Hall.

Yukl, G. and C. M. Flabe (1991). "The Importance of Different Power Structures in Downward and Lateral Relations." Journal of Applied Psychology **76**(3): 416-423.

11. Glossary

Term	Meaning
Barong	Barong is a fictional character in the Mythology of Bali. He is the king of the spirits, leader of the hosts of good, and enemy of Rangda in the mythological traditions of Bali. Banas Pati Rajah is the fourth "brother" or spirit child that accompanies a child throughout life. Banas Pati Rajah is the sprit which animates Barong. A protector spirit, he is often represented by a lion, and traditional performances of his struggles against Rangda are popular parts of Balinese culture with tourists. http://en.wikipedia.org/wiki/Barong_%28mythology%29
CQ	Cultural Intelligence
Diaphor	Juxtaposition of experience and movement
DPM	Doctor of Project Management program
Emic & Etic	Emic and etic are terms used by some in the social sciences and the behavioral sciences to refer to two different kinds of data concerning human behavior. An "emic" account of behavior is a description of behavior in terms meaningful (consciously or unconsciously) to the actor. An "etic" account is a description of a behavior in terms familiar to the observer. Scientists interested in the local construction of meaning, and local rules for behavior, will rely on emic accounts; scientists interested in facilitating comparative research and making universal claims will rely on etic accounts.
Epiphor	Describe similarity between a thing that is relatively well known and a thing that is more obscurely known
EQ	Emotional Intelligence
Ethnocentrism	The tendency to look at the world primarily from the perspective of one's own ethnic culture
Exegesis/Exegetical	Means "to draw the meaning out of" a given text. Traditional exegesis requires the following: analysis of significant words in the text in regard to translation; examination of the general historical and cultural context, confirmation of the limits of the passage, and lastly, examination of the context within the text.
GLOBE research program	Global Leadership and Organizational Behavior Effectiveness
Guanxi	Connections
Hermeneutics	Hermeneutics may be described as the theory of interpretation and understanding of a text through empirical means. It should not be confused with the concrete practice of interpretation called exegesis.
Idiocosm	An individualistic view of the world
Kinesics	body language
Metaphor	The use of a word or phrase to refer to something that it isn't, implying a similarity between the word or phrase used and the thing described, and without the words "like" or "as". http://en.wiktionary.org/wiki/Metaphor
Metonymy	The use of a single characteristic to identify a more complex entity. The phrase "the White House said" is a metonymy, using "the White House" to stand for the presidential administration. http://en.wiktionary.org/wiki/Metonymy
Object-language	Transmittal of messages through clothing and physical appearance.
Paralanguage	How something is said, intonation, pauses.
Parochialism	selfishness, narrowness, pettiness
PMBOK	Project Management Body of Knowledge
PMI	Project Mangement Institute
Proxemics	Territorial proximity
Scope Creep	The gradual, possibly imperceptable, increase in the boundaries of a project. The boundaries being defined by the scope of the work.
Sine quo non	Used to denote something that is an essential part of the whole
Synecdoche	A metaphor by which an inclusive term stands for something included, or vice versa; A metaphor in which a part is spoken of as the whole (hand for laborer) or vice-versa (the court for the judge). http://en.wiktionary.org/wiki/Synecdoche
Tacit Knowledge	Understanding. Explicit knowledge is information. Tacit knowledge represents the reception, internalization, consideration, and externalization feedback loop.
Trope	The use of a word or expression in a different sense from that which properly belongs to it; the use of a word or expression as changed from the original signification to another, for the sake of giving life or emphasis to an idea; a figure of speech. http://en.wiktionary.org/wiki/Trope
Typology	The systematic classification of the types of something according to their common characteristics. http://en.wiktionary.org/wiki/typology
Wayang	Wayang is an Indonesian word for theater. When the term is used to refer to kinds of puppet theater, sometimes the puppet itself is referred to as wayang. "Bayang", the Javanese word for shadow or imagination, also connotes "spirit." Performances of shadow puppet theater are accompanied by gamelan in Java, and by "gender wayang" in Bali. http://en.wikipedia.org/wiki/Wayang
XLQ	Cross-cultural Leadership Intelligence

12.   Appendices

Appendix 1 - Exegetical Cross Reference Example

TRUST CORRELATION

Trust Synonyms	GLOBE	Thesis	Question
Community (Acknowledgement of community)	Collaborative Team Orientation	Care & Concern	
Affection	Integrity	Care & Concern	
Care (Emotional)	Integrity	Care & Concern	yes
Caring	Integrity	Care & Concern	
Compliance with norms (Diffuse/Specific)	Integrity	Care & Concern	
Concern (Emotional)	Integrity	Care & Concern	yes
Esteem	Integrity	Care & Concern	
Face	Self-sacrifice	Care & Concern	
Face	Self-sacrifice	Care & Concern	yes
Ascription (conflict between cultures)	Team Integrator	Care & Concern	
Conviction	Integrity	Character	
Duty (fulfill commitment)	Integrity	Character	yes
Duty to Family (Social responsibility)	Integrity	Character	
Faithfulness	Integrity	Character	
Honesty	Integrity	Character	yes
Honorable	Integrity	Character	
Idealized influence	Integrity	Character	
Integrity (Identification based trust)	Integrity	Character	yes
Admiration	Integrity	Character	
Believe in	Integrity	Character	
Character	Integrity	Character	
Choose who we trust (Cognitive)	Integrity	Character	
Guardianship	Integrity	Character	
Loyalty	Integrity	Character	yes
Loyalty (Group Collectivism)	Integrity	Character	
Authenticity	Integrity	Character	yes
Achievement (conflict between cultures)	Administratively Competent	Competence	
Competence	Administratively Competent	Competence	yes
Judgment	Decisive	Competence	yes
Meaning (Interpret of meaning)	Decisive	Competence	
Optimism	Diplomatic	Competence	
Patience	Diplomatic	Competence	yes
Social Literacy (pragmatic trust)	Integrity	Competence	
Intellectual communication		Competence	
Accountability	Integrity	Dependablity	
Commitments (Deliver on commitments)	Integrity	Dependablity	yes
Consistency (personal and emotional control)	Integrity	Dependablity	
Constancy	Integrity	Dependablity	
Depend on	Integrity	Dependablity	
Devoted	Integrity	Dependablity	
Predictability	Integrity	Dependablity	yes
Reliability / Dependability	Integrity	Dependablity	yes
Sincerity	Integrity	Dependablity	
Expectation	Integrity	Dependablity	
Reciprocal	Self-sacrifice	Dependablity	
Hope	Integrity	Fearless	
Avoidance (Fear of the unknown)	Self-sacrifice	Fearless	
Comfortable (Uncertainty Avoidance)	Self-sacrifice	Fearless	
Confidence	Self-sacrifice	Fearless	yes
Conflict	Self-sacrifice	Fearless	
Confront danger	Self-sacrifice	Fearless	yes
Loss of anxiety	Self-sacrifice	Fearless	
Reduction of threats	Self-sacrifice	Fearless	
Risk Taking (encourages)	Self-sacrifice	Fearless	
Security	Self-sacrifice	Fearless	
Humaneness	Humane Orientation	Humane	yes
Parents love	Humane Orientation	Humane	
Tolerance	Humane Orientation	Humane	yes
Respect	Integrity	Humane	yes
Intimacy	Modesty	Humane	
Shame (Social responsibility)		Humane	
Group Identity (Strengthen identity of group)	Collaborative Team Orientation	Integrator	
Pride Group Collectivism)	Collaborative Team Orientation	Integrator	
Goals & Objectives (Identification based trust)	Performance Oriented	Integrator	yes
Cohesiveness (Group Collectivism)	Team Integrator	Integrator	yes
Strength of relationship		Integrator	
Synchronize actions		Integrator	yes
Synchronize expectations		Integrator	
Synchronize interpretations		Integrator	
Moral duty	Integrity	Integrity & Ethics	
Moral Judgment	Integrity	Integrity & Ethics	
Morality	Integrity	Integrity & Ethics	yes
Religiousness	Integrity	Integrity & Ethics	
Faith	Self-sacrifice	Integrity & Ethics	yes
Interests (Identification based trust)		Integrity & Ethics	
Perspective (Way of seeing)		Integrity & Ethics	yes
Similar Reactions (Identification based trust)		Integrity & Ethics	
Persuasion	Diplomatic	Trust & Justice	yes
Candor	Diplomatic	Trust & Justice	yes
Justice	Integrity	Trust & Justice	
Justice	Integrity	Trust & Justice	yes
Law	Integrity	Trust & Justice	
Social justice	Integrity	Trust & Justice	
Truth (Universalism/ Particularism)	Integrity	Trust & Justice	yes
Fairness	Self-sacrifice	Trust & Justice	
Fairness (Institutional Collectivism)	Self-sacrifice	Trust & Justice	
Punishment (Calculus based trust)		Trust & Justice	
Reward (Calculus based trust)		Trust & Justice	

274

Appendix 2 - Hofstede (modified)

	Hofstede Countries	Power Distance	Uncertainty Avoidance	Individualism & Collectivism	Masculinity/Femininity	Long/Short Term Orientation
GLOBE Regions	**Country**	**Index**	**Index**	**Index**	**Index**	**Index**
Middle East	Arab Countries	80	68	38	53	
Latin America	Argentina	49	86	46	56	
Anglo	Australia	36	51	90	61	31
Germanic Europe	Austria	11	70	55	79	3
Latin Europe	Belgium	65	94	75	54	38
Latin America	Brazil	69	76	38	49	65
Anglo	Canada	39	48	80	52	23
Latin America	Chile	63	86	23	28	
Latin America	Colombia	67	80	13	64	
Latin America	Costa Rica	35	86	15	21	
Nordic Europe	Denmark	18	23	74	16	46
Sub-Saharan Africa	East/West Africa	70.5	53	23.5	43.5	20.5
Latin America	Ecuador	78	67	8	63	
Nordic Europe	Finland	33	59	63	26	4
Latin Europe	France	68	86	71	43	39
Germanic Europe	Germany	35	65	67	66	31
Anglo	Great Britain	35	35	89	66	25
Eastern Europe	Greece	60	112	35	57	
Latin America	Guatemala	95	101	6	37	
Confucian Asia	Hong Kong	68	29	25	57	96
Southern Asia	India	77	40	48	56	61
Southern Asia	Indonesia	78	48	14	46	
Southern Asia	Iran	58	59	41	43	
Anglo	Ireland	28	35	70	68	43
Latin Europe	Israel	13	81	54	47	
Latin Europe	Italy	50	75	76	70	34
Latin America	Jamaica	45	13	39	68	
Confucian Asia	Japan	54	92	46	95	80
Confucian Asia	Korea (South)	60	85	18	39	75
Southern Asia	Malaysia	104	36	26	50	
Latin America	Mexico	81	82	30	69	
Germanic Europe	Netherlands	38	53	80	14	44
Anglo	New Zealand	22	49	79	58	30
Nordic Europe	Norway	31	50	69	8	44
Southern Asia	Pakistan	55	70	14	50	0
Latin America	Panama	95	86	11	44	
Latin America	Peru	64	87	16	42	
Southern Asia	Philippines	94	44	32	64	19
Latin Europe	Portugal	63	104	27	31	30
Latin America	Salvador	66	94	19	40	
Confucian Asia	Singapore	74	8	20	48	48
Anglo	South Africa	49	49	65	63	
Latin Europe	Spain	57	86	51	42	19
Nordic Europe	Sweden	31	29	71	5	33
Germanic Europe	Switzerland	34	58	68	70	40
Confucian Asia	Taiwan	58	69	17	45	87
Southern Asia	Thailand	64	64	20	34	56
Middle East	Turkey	66	85	37	45	
Anglo	United States	40	46	91	62	29
Latin America	Uruguay	61	100	36	38	
Latin America	Venezuela	81	76	12	73	
Eastern Europe	Yugoslavia	76	88	27	21	
	Max	**104.00**	**112.00**	**91.00**	**95.00**	**96.00**
	Min	**11.00**	**8.00**	**6.00**	**5.00**	**0.00**
	Averages	**56.57**	**65.69**	**43.43**	**48.84**	**40.50**

Appendix 3 – GLOBE Culture I (modified)

		CLT Leadership Dimensions (GLOBE)							
		Uncertainty Avoidance		Power Distance		Institutional Collectivism		Societal In-Group Collectivism	
Culture Cluster	Country	Practice	Values	Practice	Values	Practice	Values	Practice	Values
Eastern Europe	Albania	4.57	5.37	4.62	3.52	4.54	4.44	5.74	5.22
	Georgia	3.50	5.24	5.22	2.84	4.03	3.83	6.19	5.66
	Greece	3.39	5.09	5.40	2.39	3.25	5.40	5.27	5.46
	Hungary	3.12	4.66	5.56	2.49	3.53	4.50	5.25	5.54
	Kazakhstan	3.66	4.42	5.31	3.15	4.29	4.04	5.26	5.44
	Poland	3.62	4.71	5.10	3.12	4.53	4.22	5.52	5.74
	Russia	2.88	5.07	5.52	2.62	4.50	3.89	5.63	5.79
	Slovenia	3.78	4.99	5.33	2.57	4.13	4.38	5.43	5.71
Latin America	Argentina	3.65	4.66	5.64	2.33	3.66	5.32	5.51	6.15
	Bolivia	3.35	4.70	4.51	3.41	4.04	5.10	5.47	6.00
	Brazil	3.60	4.99	5.33	2.35	3.83	5.62	5.18	5.15
	Colombia	3.57	4.98	5.56	2.04	3.81	5.38	5.73	6.25
	Costa Rica	3.82	4.58	4.74	2.58	3.93	5.18	5.32	6.08
	Ecuador	3.68	5.16	5.60	2.30	3.90	5.41	5.81	6.17
	El Salvador	3.62	5.32	5.68	2.68	3.71	5.65	5.35	6.52
	Guatemala	3.30	4.88	5.60	2.35	3.70	5.23	5.63	6.14
	Mexico	4.18	5.26	5.22	2.85	4.06	4.92	5.71	5.95
	Venezuela	3.44	5.26	5.40	2.29	3.96	5.39	5.53	6.17
Latin Europe	France	4.43	4.26	5.28	2.76	3.93	4.86	4.37	5.42
	Israel	4.01	4.38	4.73	2.72	4.46	4.27	4.70	5.75
	Italy	3.79	4.47	5.43	2.47	3.68	5.13	4.94	5.72
	Portugal	3.91	4.43	5.44	2.38	3.92	5.30	5.51	5.94
	Spain	3.97	4.76	5.52	2.26	3.85	5.20	5.45	5.79
	Switzerland	5.37	3.16	4.90	2.44	4.06	4.69	3.97	4.94
Confucian Asia	China	4.94	5.28	5.04	3.10	4.77	4.56	5.80	5.09
	Hong Kong	4.32	4.63	4.96	3.24	4.13	4.43	5.32	5.11
	Japan	4.07	4.33	5.11	2.86	5.19	3.99	4.63	5.26
	Korea, South	3.55	4.67	5.61	2.55	5.20	3.90	5.54	5.41
	Singapore	5.31	4.22	4.99	3.04	4.90	4.55	5.64	5.50
	Taiwan	4.34	5.31	5.18	3.09	4.59	5.15	5.59	5.45
Nordic Europe	Denmark	5.22	3.82	3.89	2.76	4.80	4.19	3.53	5.50
	Finland	5.02	3.85	4.89	2.19	4.63	4.11	4.07	5.42
	Sweden	5.32	3.60	4.85	2.70	5.22	3.94	3.66	6.04
Anglo	Australia	4.39	3.98	4.74	2.78	4.29	4.40	4.17	5.75
	Canada	4.58	3.75	4.82	2.70	4.38	4.17	4.26	5.97
	Ireland	4.30	4.02	5.15	2.71	4.63	4.59	5.14	5.74
	New Zealand	4.75	4.10	4.89	3.53	4.81	4.20	3.67	6.21
	South Africa	4.09	4.79	4.11	2.64	4.62	4.38	4.50	5.91
	United Kingdom	4.15	4.00	4.88	2.85	4.20	4.17	4.25	5.77
	United States	4.65	4.11	5.15	2.80	4.27	4.31	4.08	5.55
Sub-Saharan Africa	Namibia	4.20	5.13	5.29	2.86	4.13	4.38	4.52	6.07
	Nigeria	4.29	5.60	5.80	2.69	4.14	5.03	5.55	5.48
	South Africa	4.59	4.67	5.16	3.65	4.39	4.30	5.09	4.99
	Zambia	4.10	4.67	5.31	2.43	4.61	4.74	5.84	5.77
	Zimbabwe	4.15	4.73	5.67	2.67	4.12	4.87	5.57	5.85
Southern Asia	India	4.15	4.73	5.47	2.64	4.38	4.71	5.92	5.32
	Indonesia	4.17	5.23	5.18	2.69	4.54	5.18	5.68	5.67
	Iran	3.67	5.36	5.43	2.80	3.88	5.54	6.03	5.86
	Malaysia	4.78	4.88	5.17	2.97	4.61	4.87	5.51	5.85
	Philippines	3.89	5.14	5.44	2.72	4.65	4.78	6.36	6.18
	Thailand	3.93	5.61	5.63	2.86	4.03	5.10	5.70	5.76
Germanic Europe	Austria	5.16	3.66	4.95	2.44	4.30	4.73	4.85	5.27
	Germany East	5.16	3.94	5.54	2.54	3.79	4.82	4.02	5.22
	Germany West	5.22	3.32	5.25	2.69	3.56	4.68	4.52	5.18
	Netherlands	4.70	3.24	4.11	2.45	4.46	4.55	3.70	5.17
	Switzerland	4.98	3.83	4.86	2.80	4.22	4.31	3.85	5.35
Middle East	Egypt	4.06	5.36	4.92	3.24	4.50	4.85	5.64	5.56
	Kuwait	4.21	4.77	5.12	3.17	4.49	5.15	5.80	5.43
	Morocco	3.65	5.32	5.80	3.11	3.87	5.00	5.87	5.68
	Qatar	3.99	4.82	4.73	3.23	4.50	5.13	4.71	5.60
	Turkey	3.63	4.67	5.57	2.41	4.03	5.26	5.88	5.77
	Max	5.37	5.61	5.80	3.65	5.22	5.65	6.36	6.52
	Min	2.88	3.16	3.89	2.04	3.25	3.83	3.53	4.94
	Averages	4.16	4.62	5.17	2.75	4.25	4.73	5.13	5.66
	Std Deviation	0.604412	0.60543	0.407897	0.34883	0.42382	0.48968	0.73003	0.3542
	Mean	4.10	4.70	5.22	2.70	4.22	4.73	5.43	5.71

Appendix 4 - GLOBE Culture II (modified)

		CLT Leadership Dimensions (GLOBE)								
		Gender Egalitarianism		Assertiveness		Future Orientation		Performance Orientation		Humane Orientation	
Culture Cluster	Country	Practice	Values	Practice	Values	Practice	Values	Practice	Values	Practice	Values
Eastern Europe	Albania	3.71	4.19	4.89	4.41	3.86	5.42	4.81	5.63	4.64	5.34
	Georgia	3.55	3.78	4.18	4.35	3.41	5.55	3.88	5.69	4.18	5.60
	Greece	3.48	4.89	4.58	2.96	3.40	5.19	3.20	5.81	3.34	5.23
	Hungary	4.08	4.63	4.79	3.35	3.21	5.70	3.43	5.96	3.35	5.48
	Kazakhstan	3.84	4.75	4.46	3.84	3.57	5.05	3.57	5.41	3.99	5.62
	Poland	4.02	4.52	4.06	3.90	3.11	5.20	3.89	6.12	3.61	5.30
	Russia	4.07	4.18	3.68	2.83	2.88	5.48	3.39	5.54	3.94	5.59
	Slovenia	3.96	4.83	4.00	4.59	3.59	5.42	3.66	6.41	3.79	5.25
Latin America	Argentina	3.49	4.98	4.22	3.25	3.08	5.78	3.65	6.35	3.99	5.58
	Bolivia	3.55	4.75	3.79	3.73	3.61	5.63	3.61	6.05	4.05	5.07
	Brazil	3.31	4.99	4.20	2.91	3.81	5.69	4.04	6.13	3.66	5.68
	Colombia	3.67	5.00	4.20	3.43	3.27	5.68	3.94	6.42	3.72	5.61
	Costa Rica	3.56	4.64	3.75	4.05	3.60	5.20	4.12	5.90	4.39	4.99
	Ecuador	3.07	4.59	4.09	3.65	3.74	5.94	4.20	6.32	4.65	5.26
	El Salvador	3.16	4.66	4.62	3.62	3.80	5.98	3.72	6.58	3.71	5.46
	Guatemala	3.02	4.53	3.89	3.64	3.24	5.91	3.81	6.14	3.89	5.26
	Mexico	3.64	4.73	4.45	3.79	3.87	5.86	4.10	6.16	3.98	5.10
	Venezuela	3.62	4.82	4.33	3.33	3.35	5.79	3.32	6.35	4.25	5.31
Latin Europe	France	3.64	4.40	4.13	3.38	3.48	4.96	4.11	5.65	3.40	5.67
	Israel	3.19	4.71	4.23	3.76	3.85	5.25	4.08	5.75	4.10	5.62
	Italy	3.24	4.88	4.07	3.82	3.25	5.91	3.58	6.07	3.63	5.58
	Portugal	3.66	5.13	3.65	3.58	3.71	5.43	3.60	6.40	3.91	5.31
	Spain	3.01	4.82	4.42	4.00	3.51	5.63	4.01	5.80	3.32	5.69
	Switzerland	2.97	4.92	4.51	3.21	4.73	4.80	4.94	5.82	3.60	5.54
Confucian Asia	China	3.05	3.68	3.76	5.44	3.75	4.73	4.45	5.67	4.36	5.32
	Hong Kong	3.47	4.35	4.67	4.81	4.03	5.50	4.80	5.64	3.90	5.32
	Japan	3.19	4.33	3.59	5.56	4.29	5.25	4.22	5.17	4.30	5.41
	Korea, South	2.50	4.22	4.40	3.75	3.97	5.69	4.55	5.25	3.81	5.60
	Singapore	3.70	4.51	4.17	4.41	5.07	5.51	4.90	5.72	3.49	5.79
	Taiwan	3.18	4.06	3.92	3.28	3.96	5.20	4.56	5.74	4.11	5.26
Nordic Europe	Denmark	3.93	5.08	3.80	3.39	4.44	4.33	4.22	5.61	4.44	5.45
	Finland	3.35	4.24	3.81	3.68	4.24	5.07	3.81	6.11	3.96	5.81
	Sweden	3.84	1.15	3.38	3.61	4.39	4.89	3.72	5.80	4.10	5.65
Anglo	Australia	3.40	5.02	4.28	3.81	4.09	5.15	4.36	5.89	4.28	5.58
	Canada	3.70	5.11	4.05	4.15	4.44	5.35	4.49	6.15	4.49	5.64
	Ireland	3.21	5.14	3.92	3.99	3.98	5.22	4.36	5.98	4.96	5.47
	New Zealand	3.22	4.23	3.42	3.54	3.47	5.54	4.72	5.90	4.32	4.40
	South Africa	3.66	4.26	4.36	3.82	4.64	5.66	4.66	6.23	3.49	5.65
	United Kingdom	3.34	5.06	4.55	4.32	4.15	5.31	4.08	5.90	4.17	5.53
	United States	3.67	5.17	4.15	3.70	4.28	5.06	4.49	6.14	3.72	5.43
Sub-Saharan Africa	Namibia	3.88	4.25	3.91	3.91	3.49	6.12	3.67		3.96	5.40
	Nigeria	3.01	4.24	4.79	3.23	4.09	6.04	3.92	6.27	4.10	6.09
	South Africa d	3.27	4.60	4.60	3.69	4.13	5.20	4.11	4.92	4.34	5.07
	Zambia	2.86	4.31	4.07	4.38	3.62	5.90	4.16	6.40	5.23	5.53
	Zimbabwe	3.04	4.46	4.06	4.60	3.77	6.07	4.24	6.45	4.45	5.19
Southern Asia	India	2.90	4.51	3.73	4.76	4.19	5.60	4.25	6.05	4.57	5.28
	Indonesia	3.26	3.89	3.86	4.72	3.86	5.70	4.41	5.73	4.69	5.16
	Iran	2.99	3.75	4.04	4.99	3.70	5.84	4.58	6.08	4.23	5.61
	Malaysia	3.51	3.78	3.87	4.81	4.58	5.89	4.34	6.04	4.87	5.51
	Philippines	3.64	4.58	4.01	5.14	4.15	5.93	4.47	6.31	5.12	5.36
	Thailand	3.35	4.16	3.64	3.48	3.43	6.20	3.93	5.74	4.81	5.01
Germanic Europe	Austria	3.09	4.83	4.62	2.81	4.46	5.11	4.44	6.10	3.72	5.76
	Germany East	3.10	4.89	4.73	3.23	3.95	5.23	4.25	6.09	3.40	5.46
	Germany West	3.06	4.90	4.55	3.09	4.27	4.85	4.09	6.01	3.18	5.44
	Netherlands	3.50	4.99	4.32	3.02	4.61	5.07	4.32	5.49	3.86	5.20
	Switzerland	3.42	4.69	3.47	3.78	4.27	4.79	4.25	5.98	3.93	5.62
Middle East	Egypt	2.81	3.18	3.91	3.28	3.86	5.80	4.27	5.90	4.73	5.17
	Kuwait	2.58	3.45	3.63	3.76	3.26	5.74	3.95	6.03	4.52	5.06
	Morocco	2.84	3.74	4.52	3.44	3.26	5.85	3.99	5.76	4.19	5.51
	Qatar	3.63	3.38	4.11	3.80	3.78	5.92	3.45	5.96	4.42	5.30
	Turkey	2.89	4.50	4.53	2.66	3.74	5.83	3.83	5.39	3.94	5.52
	Max	4.08	5.17	4.89	5.56	5.07	6.20	4.94	6.58	5.23	6.09
	Min	2.50	1.15	3.38	2.66	2.88	4.33	3.20	4.92	3.18	4.40
	Averages										
	Std Deviation	0.368488	0.63796	0.371818	0.64635	0.46243	0.40512	0.40886	0.33569	0.46704	0.25805
	Mean	3.35	4.58	4.11	3.75	3.81	5.54	4.11	5.97	4.05	5.46

Appendix 5 - GLOBE Leadership (modified)

		CLT Leadership Dimensions GLOBE					
Culture Cluster	Country	Charismatic - Value-Based	Team Oriented	Participative	Humane Oriented	Autonomous	Self Protective
Eastern Europe	Albania	5.79	5.94	4.50	5.24	3.98	4.62
	Georgia	5.65	5.85	4.88	5.61	4.57	3.89
	Greece	6.01	6.12	5.81	5.16	3.98	3.49
	Hungary	5.91	5.91	5.22	4.73	3.23	3.24
	Kazakhstan	5.54	5.73	5.10	4.26	4.58	3.35
	Poland	5.67	5.98	5.04	4.56	4.34	3.52
	Russia	5.66	5.63	4.67	4.08	4.63	3.69
	Slovenia	5.69	5.91	5.42	4.44	4.28	3.61
Latin America	Argentina	5.98	5.99	5.89	4.70	4.55	3.45
	Bolivia	6.01	6.10	5.29	4.56	3.92	3.83
	Brazil	6.00	6.17	6.06	4.84	2.27	3.49
	Colombia	6.04	6.07	5.51	5.05	3.34	3.37
	Costa Rica	5.95	5.81	5.54	4.99	3.46	3.55
	Ecuador	6.46	6.21	5.51	5.13	3.53	3.62
	El Salvador	6.08	5.95	5.40	4.69	3.47	3.43
	Guatemala	6.00	5.94	5.45	5.00	3.37	3.77
	Mexico	5.66	5.74	4.64	4.72	3.86	3.86
	Venezuela	5.72	5.62	4.88	4.85	3.39	3.81
Latin Europe	France	4.93	5.11	5.90	3.82	3.32	2.81
	Israel	6.23	5.91	4.96	4.68	4.26	3.64
	Italy	5.98	5.87	5.47	4.38	3.62	3.25
	Portugal	5.75	5.92	5.48	4.62	3.19	3.10
	Spain	5.90	5.93	5.11	4.66	3.54	3.38
	Switzerland	5.90	5.62	5.30	4.55	4.02	2.94
Confucian Asia	China	5.56	5.57	5.04	5.19	4.07	3.80
	Hong Kong	5.66	5.58	4.86	4.89	4.38	3.67
	Japan	5.49	5.56	5.07	4.68	3.67	3.60
	Korea, South	5.53	5.52	4.92	4.87	4.21	3.67
	Singapore	5.95	5.76	5.30	5.24	3.87	3.31
	Taiwan	5.58	5.69	4.73	5.35	4.01	4.28
Nordic Europe	Denmark	6.00	5.70	5.80	4.23	3.79	2.81
	Finland	5.94	5.85	5.91	4.30	4.08	2.55
	Sweden	5.84	5.75	5.54	4.73	3.97	2.81
Anglo	Australia	6.09	5.81	5.71	5.10	3.95	3.05
	Canade	6.15	5.84	6.09	5.20	3.65	2.96
	Ireland	6.08	5.81	5.64	5.06	3.95	3.00
	New Zealand	5.87	5.44	5.50	4.78	3.77	3.19
	South Africa	5.99	5.80	5.62	5.33	3.74	3.19
	United Kingdom	6.01	5.71	5.57	4.90	4.00	3.04
	United States	6.12	5.80	5.93	5.21	3.75	3.15
Sub-Saharan Africa	Namibia	5.99	5.81	5.48	5.10	3.77	3.36
	Nigeria	5.76	5.65	5.18	5.49	3.62	3.89
	South Africa	5.16	5.23	5.04	4.79	3.94	3.62
	Zambia	5.92	5.86	5.29	5.27	3.43	3.66
	Zimbabwe	6.11	5.97	5.57	5.18	3.37	3.20
Southern Asia	India	5.85	5.72	4.99	5.26	3.85	3.77
	Indonesia	6.15	5.92	4.60	5.43	4.19	4.12
	Iran	5.81	5.90	4.97	5.75	3.85	4.34
	Malaysia	5.89	5.80	5.12	5.24	4.03	3.49
	Philippines	6.33	6.06	5.40	5.53	3.75	3.32
	Thailand	5.78	5.76	5.29	5.09	4.28	3.91
Germanic Europe	Austria	6.02	5.74	6.00	4.93	4.47	3.07
	Germany East	5.84	5.49	5.88	4.44	4.30	2.96
	Germany West	5.87	5.51	5.70	4.60	4.35	3.32
	Netherlands	5.98	5.75	5.75	4.82	3.53	2.87
	Switzerland	5.93	5.61	5.94	4.76	4.13	2.92
Middle East	Egypt	5.57	5.55	4.69	5.15	4.49	4.21
	Kuwait	5.90	5.89	5.03	5.21	3.39	4.02
	Morocco	4.81	5.15	5.32	4.10	3.34	3.26
	Qatar	4.51	4.74	4.75	4.66	3.38	3.91
	Turkey	5.95	6.01	5.09	4.90	3.83	3.57
	Max	6.46	6.21	6.09	5.75	4.63	4.62
	Min	4.51	4.74	4.50	3.82	2.27	2.55
	Averages	5.83	5.76	5.33	4.89	3.85	3.47
	Societal	5.00	5.00	5.00	5.00	5.00	5.00
	Global	6.00	6.00	6.00	6.00	6.00	6.00

278

Welcome!

There are 45 questions in the first session with multiple parts, and 42 questions in the second session - in the first session you will be providing some general information that will not be necessary in the second session. The majority of the questions are multiple choice type.

After the first session I will analyze the responses, and when you do the second session you will see your initial responses alongside the metrics of the conclusions reached by the panel as a whole. On the second session you will have the opportunity to modify your opinions if you choose to do so after seeing the conclusions reached by the entire panel.

If possible, I suggest you set aside about an hour or so for each session. In this way you can minimize the time required to finish the session, find the tempo to the questions, and enjoy the experience. However if you are multi-tasking, the survey is designed so that you can exit and re-enter without the loss of your previous work, and of course you can change your answers during the session.

Your Culture

Let us begin with some information about you and your background.

1. First, information about where you were born and raised. The question is what culture do you feel most represents your view of yourself. Many people are multi-cultural or were raised "on the road" so pick the region that best fits you (these regions are from the GLOBE survey, which only addressed some countries, not all). If you feel a VERY close connection with more than one culture, please check those that apply.

Eastern Europe (Albania, Georgia, Greece, Hungary, Kazakhstan, Poland, Russia, Slovenia)
 Nordic Europe (Denmark, Finland, Sweden)
Germanic Europe (Austria, Germany East, Germany West, Netherlands, Switzerland)
Latin Europe (France, Israel, Italy, Portugal, Spain)
Latin America (Argentina, Bolivia, Brazil, Colombia, Costa Rica, Ecuador, El Salvador, Guatemala, Mexico, Venezuela)
Confusian Asia (China, Hong Kong, Japan, South Korea, Singapore, Taiwan)
Southern Asia (India, Indonesia, Iran, Malaysia, Philippines, Thailand)
Sub Saharian Africa (Namibia, Nigeria, South Africa, Zambia, Zimbabwe)
Middle East (Egypt, Kuwait, Morocco, Qatar, Turkey)
Anglo (Australia, Canada, Ireland, New Zealand, South Africa, United Kingdom, United States)
Other (please specify)

Next, approximately how many years of experience do you have in each of the following categories.
Number of Years in:
Academia
Business
Government
Non-Profit

Lastly, some information about your experience. Approximately how many years of experience do you have in each of the following regions?

Eastern Europe (Albania, Georgia, Greece, Hungary, Kazakhstan, Poland, Russia, Slovenia)
Nordic Europe (Denmark, Finland, Sweden)
Germanic Europe (Austria, Germany East, Germany West, Netherlands, Switzerland) Latin Europe (France, Israel, Italy, Portugal, Spain)
Latin America (Argentina, Bolivia, Brazil, Colombia, Costa Rica, Ecuador, El Salvador, Guatemala, Mexico, Venezuela)
Confusian Asia (China, Hong Kong, Japan, South Korea, Singapore, Taiwan)

Southern Asia (India, Indonesia, Iran, Malaysia, Philippines, Thailand)
Sub Saharian Africa (Namibia, Nigeria, South Africa, Zambia, Zimbabwe)
Middle East (Egypt, Kuwait, Morocco, Qatar, Turkey)
Anglo (Australia, Canada, Ireland, New Zealand, South Africa, United Kingdom, United States)

Introduction

This survey will test the hypothesis that there are universal leadership attributes that are both required and effective regardless of the culture - culture meaning individual, societal, or corporate. The hypothesis is based upon the concept that while there is infinite diversity on our planet, an effective leader will have the attributes and skills, and, the ability to apply them with compassion to each circumstance. So, whether you are an Indian expat who is leading a team in Japan with a transglobal firm on her first international assignment, or you are a first generation Chinese-American with experience in numerous countries leading a team in Germany in a local company, there are global cross-cultural leadership attributes that will enable one to effectively lead others. The Leader will have to adjust the emphasis and blend of attributes depending upon the people who will follow. The hypothesis includes the definition of leadership as being the "ability to inspire the desire to follow, and to inspire achievement beyond expectations." There are two facets of the Cross-Cultural Leadership study: Leadership skills, and culture. Culture may be individual, family, tribe, society, or corporate. Culture will of course vary with the backgrounds of the individuals like the example on the previous page. On each of the questions you will be asked your opinion the notion that the Leadership characteristics are cultural indifferent. That does not mean that a leader uses the same blend and strength of characteristics, but rather adjusts them to fit the needs of the individual.

NOTE: **The Delphi panel was asked to rate the questions in this section on the basis of**

Strongly Disagree, Disagree, Somewhat Disagree, Neutral, Somewhat Agree, Agree,

Strongly Agree

Trust

The definition of trust used in this study is the "willingness of a party to be vulnerable to the actions of another party based on the expectation that the other will perform a particular action important to the trustor, irrespective of the ability to monitor that other party" (Mayer, Davis et al. 1995). The next group of questions explore the Leadership dimension of Trust, and its attributes.

4. Leadership requires the creation and maintenance of Trust, regardless of culture.

5. Competence
Competence - intellectual, social, emotional, and cultural - is a Leadership attribute regardless of culture
Technical competence is an essential ingredient for trust.
Jugement is an essential ingredient for trust.

6. Care and Concern
Care and Concern are Leadership attributes regardless of culture
Esteem, for oneself and others, is an essential ingredient of trust.
Consideration of Face - respect, honor, and reputation for oneself and others - is an essential ingredient of trust.

7. Character
Character is a Leadership attribute regardless of culture (honesty, faithfulness, integrity, conviction).
Honesty and integrity are essential ingredients of trust.
Duty and loyalty - to society, others, and oneself - are essential ingredients of trust.
Admiration - of others and self - is an essential ingredient of trust.

8. Dependability
Dependability is a Leadership attribute regardless of culture (synonyms - accountability, reliability, consistency, constancy, sincerity, expectation)
Predictability is an essential ingredient for trust.
Making and keeping commitments is an essential ingredient for trust.

9. Fearlessness
Fearlessness is a Leadership attribute regardless of culture (loss of anxiety, hope, comfort, security, reduction of threats viewed by followers)
Confidence is an essential ingredient for trust.
Self-sacrifice is an essential ingredient of trust.

10. Humaneness
Humaneness is a Leadership attribute regardless of culture.
Tolerance - personal, social, cultural, religious, etc. - is an essential ingredient of trust.
Respect - personal, social, cultural, religious, etc. - is an essential ingredient of trust.

11. Integrator
Being an integrator - creating and nurturing group identity - is a Leadership attribute regardless of culture.
Setting and defining goals & objectives is an essential ingredient for trust.   Imbuing cohesiveness is an essential ingredient for trust.

12. If you have any comments or conditions to amplify your answers on Trust, please enter them here.

Sullivan Principles

In the next question, use the concept of the Sullivan principles when asked about Integrity & Ethics. Sullivan Principles. Universal human rights, operate without unacceptable worker treatment, respect employees' voluntary freedom of association, compensate employees to enable them to meet at least their basic needs, provide a safe and healthy workplace, protect human health and the environment, promote sustainable development, promote fair competition, neither pay nor accept bribes, improve the quality of life where business is done, provide training and opportunities for workers from disadvantaged backgrounds, promote the application of these principles, and be transparent in our implementation of these principles and demonstrate publicly our commitment to them.

13. Integrity and Ethics Sullivan Principles
Integrity and ethics are Leadership attributes regardless of culture. Demonstrating moral & ethical values are essential ingredients for trust. Having Ethical perspective - recognizing that there are many different ways of seeing integrity and ethics - is essential ingredients for trust.

14. Truth & Justice
Truth and justice are Leadership attributes regardless of culture.
Fairness is an essential ingredient for trust.
Candor is essential ingredients for trust.

Empathy

Empathy, or compassion, is described by his holiness the Dalai Lama: "I believe that at the most fundamental level our nature is compassionate, and that cooperation, not conflict, lies at the heart of the basic principles that govern our human existence." The definition of empathy for this survey (Mullavey-O'Brien 1997) is defined as "the ability to put oneself in another's place, to know others' experiences from their perspective, and to communicate this understanding to them in a way that is meaningful, while at the same time recognizing that the source of one's experience lies in the other." The next group of questions explores the attributes of Empathy.

15. Leadership requires the creation and maintenance of empathy, regardless of culture.

16. Cultural Intelligence
Cultural Intelligence is a Leadership attribute regardless of culture (synonyms insight, understanding, vicarious emotions, connection)
Metaphors, storytelling, and a knowledge of the culture - history, geography, politics, music, art, etc. -in which one works are essential ingredients of Cultural Intelligence.
Knowledge of cultural etiquette, customs, and traditions are essential ingredients for Cultural Intelligence.

17. Humaneness
Humaneness is a Leadership attribute regardless of culture (affection, esteem, rapport, sensitivity)
Compassion is an essential ingredient of Humaneness.
Respect and consideration are essential ingredients of Humaneness.

18. Servant Leadership
Servant Leadership - the concept that to lead one must serve others - is a Leadership attribute regardless of culture.
Self-Sacrifice and extending and giving of oneself are essential ingredients of Servant Leadership.
Empowerment of people is an essential ingredient of Servant Leadership.

19. If you have any comments or conditions to amplify your answers on Empathy, please enter them here.

Transformation

The definition of Transformation for this study is "the ability to inspire achievement beyond expectations." (Similar to (Bass, 1985)). A Transformational Leader will inspire people to risk making changes, and this section will explore the attributes of transformational Leadership.

20. Transformational Leadership is a characteristic of Leadership, regardless of culture.

21. Inspiration
Inspiration is a Leadership attribute regardless of culture (synonyms/characteristics - arouser, confidence builder, encouraging, intellectual stimulation, self-effacing, self-sacrificial, sincere)
Setting high expectations and motivating people are essential ingredients of Inspiration.
Mentoring and coaching are essential ingredients of Inspiration.

22. Charisma
Charisma is a Leadership attribute regardless of culture (synonyms/characteristics - unique, willful, warm, allure, personal appeal, magnetism)
Being decisive and dynamic are essential ingredients of Charisma.
Uniqueness is an essential ingredient of Charisma.

23. Risk Change
Inspiring people to risk change is a Leadership attribute regardless of culture.
Inspiring the desire to change the status quo, restructure ideas, beliefs, structures, etc. are essential in risking change.
Imbuing a feeling of security to take risks is an essential ingredient in risking change.

24. Vision
Having a Vision and the ability to share it are Leadership attributes regardless of culture.
Demonstrating foresight and predicting the future are essential in demonstrating Vision.
Communicating goals and objectives are essential ingredients in demonstrating Vision.

25. If you have any comments or conditions to amplify your answers on Transformation, please enter them here.

Power

According to Napoleon "power trumps everything." This section will explore the dimension of power in Leadership, and its attributes.

26. Power is a characteristic of Leadership, regardless of culture.

27. Knowledge Power
Knowledge Power - technical, cultural, emotional, and organizational, etc. - is a Leadership attribute regardless of culture.
Sharing of knowledge is essential to Knowledge Power.
Being a teacher, mentor, and coach are essential to Knowledge Power.

28. Position Power
Position power (the title you have) is a Leadership characteristic regardless of culture
Legitimate power is a required Leadership attribute.
Political power is a required Leadership attribute.

29. Power Distance
The Power Distance - "the extent to which the less powerful members of organizations and institutions accept, and expect, power is distributed unequally" - of the culture must be considered by a Leader.
The locus of power (organizational and cultural) must be considered by a leader.
Communitarianism (sense of community or family) is an essential consideration for a leader.

30. Referent Power
Referent Power - power given to a leader willingly by a follower (respect) - is a Leadership attribute regardless of culture.
Bravery and confidence are essential Leadership attributes.
Warmth toward and service to others are essential Leadership attributes.

31. Reward & Punishment Power
Reward & Punishment Power are necessary for Leadership regardless of culture.
Coercive power is an essential Leadership attribute.
Reward and Punishment power are essential Leadership attributes.

32. If you have any comments or conditions to amplify your answers on Power, please enter them here.

Communication

As a mentor of mine once said, you cannot listen when your mouth is open. The next questions explore the Leadership dimension of Communications, and its attributes.

33. Effective Communication is a characteristic of Leadership, regardless of culture.

34. Adaptability
Adaptability is a Leadership attribute regardless of culture.
Facilitating mutual understanding is an essential Leadership attribute.
Communicating meaning effectively, and encouraging communications, are essential Leadership attributes.

35. Competence
Competence in communications is a Leadership attribute regardless of culture.
Cultural fluency is an essential Leadership attribute.
Both high & low context communications skills -subtle versus explicit - are essential Leadership attributes.
Active listening - turning off one's cultural filters - is an essential Leadership attribute.

36. Creativity (looking for ways to get the truth across)
Creativity in communications is a Leadership attribute regardless of culture.

Effective story telling is an essential Leadership attribute.
The effective use of metaphor and symbolism are essential Leadership attributes.

37. Patience
Patience in communications is a Leadership attribute regardless of culture.
Creating time to make communications clear is an essential Leadership attribute.
Repetition in communications is a required Leadership attribute.

38. Sensitivity
Sensitivity in communications is a Leadership attribute regardless of culture.
Facework - creating and saving face of oneself, society, and others - in communications is an essential Leadership attribute.

39. Wisdom
Wisdom in communications is a Leadership attribute regardless of culture.
Accurate interpretation of communications is an essential Leadership attribute.
Cultural communications knowledge is a required Leadership attribute.

40. Conflict Management
The ability to effectively manage conflict is an Leadership attribute regardless of culture.
Knowledge of the people and issues is an essential Leadership attribute.
Effective listening skills is an essential Leadership attribute.
Time to prepare and assess the issues is an essential Leadership attribute.

41. If you have any comments or conditions to amplify your answers on Communication, please enter them here.

Culture

The next group of questions will explore the connections between the leadership dimensions that you have already considered, to culture. The cultural dimensions are taken from the GLOBE survey (House, Hanges et al. (2004)). The survey included 17,000 managers from 951 organizations that functioned in 62 societies, and took 10 years to complete. In the survey the respondents were asked to answer questions based on how things actually were in their lives, and how things should be. For our purposes, please consider how things actually are from your experience. The hypothesis is that the dimensions of Leadership (trust, empathy, transformation, power, and communications) are universal regardless of culture. An experienced leader will know that she/he must apply these dimensions in different degrees depending upon the culture(s) involved. The following questions explore the idea of how important each Leadership dimension is to each of the GLOBE cultural dimensions that will be described. One such GLOBE dimension, Uncertainty Avoidance, means the extent that members of a culture (society, group, corporation, etc.) "seek orderliness, consistency, structure, formalized procedures, and laws to cover situations in their daily life." Clearly different cultures view this in different ways. If you are a leader with a team that includes a Singaporean and a Russian, the Russian is more likely to be interested in few rules and the Singaporean perhaps demanding of strict rules. So the question is how important are the Leadership dimensions in balancing the acceptance or rejection of rules. The questions that are posed in this next section ask your opinion on how important the leadership dimensions are in balancing, normalizing, centering, etc. the needs of any culture regardless of where those needs are located on the GLOBE scale.

NOTE: The Delphi panel was asked to rate the questions in this section on the basis of Very Weak, Weak, Somewhat Weak, Neutral, Somewhat Strong, Strong, Very Strong

42. Uncertainty Avoidance means the extent that members of a culture "seek orderliness, consistency, structure, formalized procedures, and laws to cover situations in their daily life." For example the GLOBE survey found that Russia & Hungary ranked low (were less rule based), and that Switzerland and Singapore were at the other extreme.

Rate each of the dimensions of leadership below on how strong you see the connection between it and the concept of Uncertainty Avoidance.

Trust (Care & Concern, Character, Competence, Dependability, Fearlessness, Integrator, Integrity & Ethics, Truth & Justice)
Empathy (Cultural Intelligence, Humaneness, Servant Leadership)
Transformation (Charisma, Vision, Inspiration, Risk Change)
Power (Knowledge, Position, Power Distance, Reward/Punishment, Referent)
Communication (Wisdom, Competence, Sensitivity, Adaptability, Creativity, Patience)

43. If you have any comments or conditions to amplify your answers on Uncertainty Avoidance, please enter them here.

44. Power Distance means the degree that members of a culture accept and endorse authority, power differences, and status privileges." For example the GLOBE survey found that Denmark & South Africa ranked low (were less accepting of authority for example), and that Morocco & Nigeria were at the other extreme.

Rate each of the dimensions of leadership below on how strong you see the connection between it and the concept of Power Distance.

Trust (Care & Concern, Character, Competence, Dependability, Fearlessness, Integrator, Integrity & Ethics, Truth & Justice)
Empathy (Cultural Intelligence, Humaneness, Servant Leadership)
Transformation (Charisma, Vision, Inspiration, Risk Change)
Power (Knowledge, Position, Power Distance, Reward/Punishment, Referent)
Communication (Wisdom, Competence, Sensitivity, Adaptability, Creativity, Patience)

45. If you have any comments or conditions to amplify your answers on Power Distance, please enter them here.

46. Institutional Collectivism means the degree that a culture emphasizes group loyalty at the expense of individual goals, whether the economic system emphasizes group goals, whether acceptance by other members is important, and whether individualism is valued more highly that group cohesiveness. For example the GLOBE survey found that Greece & West Germany ranked low (were more individualistic), and that Korea & Japan were at the other extreme.

Rate each of the dimensions of leadership below on how strong you see the connection between it and the concept of Institutional Collectivism.

Trust (Care & Concern, Character, Competence, Dependability, Fearlessness, Integrator, Integrity & Ethics, Truth & Justice)
Empathy (Cultural Intelligence, Humaneness, Servant Leadership)
Transformation (Charisma, Vision, Inspiration, Risk Change)
Power (Knowledge, Position, Power Distance, Reward/Punishment, Referent)
Communication (Wisdom, Competence, Sensitivity, Adaptability, Creativity, Patience)

47. If you have any comments or conditions to amplify your answers on Institutional Collectivism, please enter them here.

48. Group Collectivism means the degree means the degree that a culture expresses "pride, loyalty and the interdependence of their families." For example the GLOBE survey found that the Netherlands & New Zealand ranked low (were least group oriented), and that India & Georgia were at the other extreme.

Rate each of the dimensions of leadership below on how strong you see the connection between it and the concept of Group Collectivism.

Trust (Care & Concern, Character, Competence, Dependability, Fearlessness, Integrator, Integrity & Ethics, Truth & Justice)
Empathy (Cultural Intelligence, Humaneness, Servant Leadership)
Transformation (Charisma, Vision, Inspiration, Risk Change)
Power (Knowledge, Position, Power Distance, Reward/Punishment, Referent)
Communication (Wisdom, Competence, Sensitivity, Adaptability, Creativity, Patience)

49. If you have any comments or conditions to amplify your answers on Group Collectivism, please enter them here.

50. Gender Egalitarianism means the degree that a culture promotes gender equality. For example the GLOBE survey found that Kuwait & Egypt ranked low (less equality), and that Poland & Slovenia were at the other extreme.

Rate each of the dimensions of leadership below on how strong you see the connection between it and the concept of Gender Egalitarianism.

Trust (Care & Concern, Character, Competence, Dependability, Fearlessness, Integrator, Integrity & Ethics, Truth & Justice)
Empathy (Cultural Intelligence, Humaneness, Servant Leadership)
Transformation (Charisma, Vision, Inspiration, Risk Change)
Power (Knowledge, Position, Power Distance, Reward/Punishment, Referent)
Communication (Wisdom, Competence, Sensitivity, Adaptability, Creativity, Patience)

51. If you have any comments or conditions to amplify your answers on Gender Egalitarianism, please enter them here.

52. Assertiveness means the degree that a culture encourages assertive, aggressive and tough social relationships. For example the GLOBE survey found that Japan & Thailand ranked low (were less assertive), and that East Germany & Albania were at the other extreme.

Rate each of the dimensions of leadership below on how strong you see the connection between it and the concept of Assertiveness.

Trust (Care & Concern, Character, Competence, Dependability, Fearlessness, Integrator, Integrity & Ethics, Truth & Justice)
Empathy (Cultural Intelligence, Humaneness, Servant Leadership)
Transformation (Charisma, Vision, Inspiration, Risk Change)
Power (Knowledge, Position, Power Distance, Reward/Punishment, Referent)
Communication (Wisdom, Competence, Sensitivity, Adaptability, Creativity, Patience)

53. If you have any comments or conditions to amplify your answers on Assertiveness, please enter them here.

54. Future Orientation deals with the issue of how cultures see time - past, present, and future. It means the degree to which a culture "believes that their current actions will influence their future, focus on investment in their future, believe that they have a future that matters, believe in planning for developing their future, and look far into the future for aasessing the effects of their current actions." For example the GLOBE survey found that Russia & Argentina ranked low (were more present oriented), and that Switzerland & Singapore were at the other extreme.

Rate each of the dimensions of leadership below on how strong you see the connection between it and the concept of Future Orientation.

Trust (Care & Concern, Character, Competence, Dependability, Fearlessness, Integrator, Integrity & Ethics, Truth & Justice)
Empathy (Cultural Intelligence, Humaneness, Servant Leadership)
Transformation (Charisma, Vision, Inspiration, Risk Change)
Power (Knowledge, Position, Power Distance, Reward/Punishment, Referent)
Communication (Wisdom, Competence, Sensitivity, Adaptability, Creativity, Patience)

55. If you have any comments or conditions to amplify your answers on Future Orientation, please enter them here.

56. Performance Orientation means the degree to which a culture rewards innovation, high standards, and performance improvement. For example the GLOBE survey found that Greece & Venezuela ranked low (were less concerned with performance), and that Hong Kong & Singapore were at the other extreme.

Rate each of the dimensions of leadership below on how strong you see the connection between it and the concept of Performance Orientation.

Trust (Care & Concern, Character, Competence, Dependability, Fearlessness, Integrator, Integrity & Ethics, Truth & Justice)
Empathy (Cultural Intelligence, Humaneness, Servant Leadership)
Transformation (Charisma, Vision, Inspiration, Risk Change)
Power (Knowledge, Position, Power Distance, Reward/Punishment, Referent)
Communication (Wisdom, Competence, Sensitivity, Adaptability, Creativity, Patience)

57. If you have any comments or conditions to amplify your answers on Performance Orientation, please enter them here.

58. Humane Orientation means the degree "to which an organization or society encourages and rewards individuals for being fair, altruistic, friendly, generous, caring, and kind to others." For example the GLOBE survey found that West Germany & Spain ranked low (did not encourage fairness for example), and that Ireland & the Phillipines were at the other extreme.

Rate each of the dimensions of leadership below on how strong you see the connection between it and the concept of Humane Orientation.

Trust (Care & Concern, Character, Competence, Dependability, Fearlessness, Integrator, Integrity & Ethics, Truth & Justice)
Empathy (Cultural Intelligence, Humaneness, Servant Leadership)
Transformation (Charisma, Vision, Inspiration, Risk Change)
Power (Knowledge, Position, Power Distance, Reward/Punishment, Referent)
Communication (Wisdom, Competence, Sensitivity, Adaptability, Creativity, Patience)

59. If you have any comments or conditions to amplify your answers on Humane Orientation, please enter them here.

11. Finished
Thank you very much for completing the survey!

You will now be directed to my webpage so that you can contact me with any questions or problems. Just click on the Email Me link in the right hand navigation bar.

Appendix 7 – Cross Reference

GLOBE Cultural Variables vs Other Authors

Author	Description	Uncertainty Avoidance	Power Distance	Institutional Collectivism	In Group Collectivism	Gender Egalitarianism	Assertiveness	Future Orientation	Performance Orientation	Humane Orientation
Hofstede	Power-Distance		0.61 CVC							
Hofstede	Individualism-Collectivism			0.15 CVC	-0.82 CVC					
Hofstede	Masculinity-Feminity					-0.16 CVC	0.42 CVC			
Hofstede	Uncertainty Avoidance	0.32 CVC								
Hofstede	Long Term Orientation (face)							yes - no eval	yes	
Trompenaars	Universalism-Particularism									
Trompenaars	Individualism-Communitarianism			yes	yes					
Trompenaars	Neutral-Emotional				yes		yes			
Trompenaars	Specific-Diffuse	yes		yes	yes				yes	
Trompenaars	Achievement-Ascription			yes	yes				yes	
Trompenaars	Communications			yes	yes					
Hall	Fast-Slow Messages (medium)			yes	yes				yes	
Hall	High-Low Context			yes	yes				yes	
Hall	Space (physical)									
Hall	Time							yes		
Hall	Fast-Slow Information		yes	yes	yes			yes		
Hall	Action Chains		yes	yes	yes					
Hall	Interfacing		yes							
Hall	Right Responses			yes	yes					
Sagiv	Egalitarianism					yes				
Sagiv	Harmony							yes		yes
Sagiv	Embeddedness				yes					
Sagiv	Heirarchy		yes							
Sagiv	Mastery								yes	yes
Sagiv	Affective Autonomy									yes
Sagiv	Intellectual Atonomy						yes			yes
Schwartz	Embeddedness	0.74 CVC		0.14 CVC	0.15 CVC					
Schwartz	Intellectual Autonomy	-0.61 CVC		-0.13 CVC	-0.14 CVC					
Schwartz	Heirarchy		0.33 CVC							
Schwartz	Egalitarianism					0.65 CVC	-0.44 CVC			
Schwartz	Mastery								0.12 CVC	
Inglehart		0.47 CVC	0.41 CVC	0.54 CVC	0.60 CVC	0.43 CVC	0.42 CVC	0.58 CVC	0.47 CVC	0.40 CVC

NOTE: CVC = Convergent Validity Coefficient

Appendix 8 - Training for Company Representatives

Accenture
Agilent
American Express
Assured Solution
Atlantic LNG Trinidad
Atlas Methanol Company
Bank of America
Bank of Oklahoma
Batelle
Baxter Healthcare
Baycare Hospital
Baylor College of Medicine
Best Buy
BG Trinidad & Tobago
Cabina Gulf Oil (Chevron)
Centra Software
Circuit City
Cisco Systems
City of St. Petersburg
Claude A. Benjamin Jr. & Associates
Columbia House Company
Convergys Computing
Cornerstone Controls
Department of Defense
DeVry University
Duke Medical Center
Duke University Health Systems
Eckerd
Entergy
ETSD
Florida Department of Transportation
Florida Department of Juvenile Justice
Florida Power & Light
General Electric
Guardian Holding Ltd.
Honda
Honey Baked Ham
Honeywell
Infotech Caribbean Ltd.
International Project Management
Invensys
Jabil
Jacobs
JP Morgan Chase
Legion of Christ
Lincoln Financial
Lockheed Martin
Memorial Hospital
Ministry of National Security Trinidad & Tobago
Mohegan Sun
Morton Plant
National Gas Company of Trinidad & Tobago

National Security Agency
Nielsen
Nortel
Northrup Grumman
Northwest Airlines
Nova Engineering
Oxy Petroleum
PBS&J
Pemex
Petroleum Company of Trinidad & Tobago
Pfizer
Pinellas County
Pomeroy IT Solutions
Portable Works Ltd.
Power Generation Company of Trinidad & Tobago
Progress Energy
Publix
RA Jones
Raymond James
Raytheon
RBTT Bank Ltd.
Sams Club
SBC Communications
Schlumberger Information Systems
Shell Oil
Smiths Aerospace
Sprint
SSAI
St. Petersburg College
Stock Building Supply
Telecom Network
The Home Depot
Titan Corp
TS Trinidad & Tobago
University of the West Indies
University of South Florida
US Air Force
US Army
US Army Afghanistan
US Army Corps of Engineers
US Coast Guard
US Postal Service
Venture Production Trinidad Ltd.
Verison
Veterans Administration
Vistakon
Wachovia
Walmart
Water and Sewer Authority of Trinidad
WCI Communities
Wells Fargo
Worley Parsons

Appendix 9 - Papers

- *It's About, Time* – Paper for PMI New Zealand
- *Global Project Management Communication Challenges & Guidelines* – Paper for PMI USA
- *Global Education for Project Management* – Paper for IPMA, Moscow
- *Global Construction Project Management: A Model for Virtual Teams* – CIB Lisbon
- *Communities of Practice for the International Construction Industry* – CIB Lisbon
- *Conflict Management, Negotiation, and Effective Communication: Essential Skills for Project Managers* – AIPM Australia
- *Communities of Practice* – RMIT University
- *Knowledge Environment* – RMIT University
- *Project Stakeholder Management* – RMIT University
- *Project Management Leadership* – RMIT University
- *Cross Cultural Leadership Research Preparation* – RMIT University
- *Global Education, Affordable Excellence* – Technology, Colleges & Community (Web conference)
- *Nurturing A Knowledge Environment for International Construction Organisations Through Communities of Practice* – Co-authored. Construction Innovation Journal on Information and Knowledge Management in Construction
- *Cross-Cultural Conflict Management* – RMIT University
- *Cultural Knowledge Transfer Using Metaphors* – RMIT University
- *Virtual Teams* – Keynote Presentation for PMISCC conference in Trinidad
- *Frameworks For Knowledge Management Initiatives In The Field Of Project Management Using Metaphor for Improved Visibility* – Co-authored. Paper for CIB Dubai Conference
- *Cross-Cultural Leadership in Construction* – Paper for CIB Dubai Conference
- *Risk & Opportunity Management in Projects* – Co-authored. Paper for CIB Dubai Conference
- *Conflict Management, Negotiation, and Effective Communication: Essential Skills for Project Managers* – Co-authored. Australian Institute of Project Management
- *Metaphor, Poetry, Storytelling, & Cross-Cultural Leadership* – Management Decision

www.ingramcontent.com/pod-product-compliance
Lightning Source LLC
Chambersburg PA
CBHW051224050326
40689CB00007B/799